GRASSROOTS ORGANIZATIONS

Second Edition

GRASSROOTS ORGANIZATIONS

A Resource Book for Directors, Staff, and
Volunteers of Small, Community-Based
Nonprofit Agencies

Second Edition

Robert L. Clifton

University of Colorado at Denver

Alan M. Dahms

Metropolitan State College

WAVELAND

PRESS, INC.

Prospect Heights, Illinois

For information about this book, write or call:

Waveland Press, Inc.
P.O. Box 400
Prospect Heights, Illinois 60070
(708) 634-0081

$10⁰⁰ 1/16/96

THE PEOPLE, YES

The people, yes, the people,
Until the people are taken care of one way
or another,
Until the people are solved somehow for the
day and hour,
Until then one hears "Yes but the people
what about the people?"
Sometimes as though the people is a child to
be pleased or fed
Or again a hoodlum you have to be tough with
And seldom as though the people is a caldron
and a reservoir
Of the human reserves that shape history.

The people is the grand canyon of humanity
and many many miles across.
The people is pandora's box, humpty dumpty,
a clock of doom and an avalanche when
it turns loose.
    —Carl Sandburg

About the Authors

Robert L. Clifton, Ed.D. is the Director for the Division of Extended Studies at the University of Colorado at Denver. His energies in this position are directed primarily on developing a weekend "Citizens College" that will recognize previously learned competencies of working adults in a curriculum focused on local and national issues. Dr. Clifton was responsible for developing the first undergraduate program in Colorado specifically designed to prepare graduates for administrative positions in small, nonprofit organizations. He has served as an administrator of a small community as well as the chief executive officer of a large metropolitan county.

Alan M. Dahms, Ph.D. is a licensed clinical psychologist in private practice and a faculty member at Metropolitan State College of Denver. He has authored more than two dozen articles in the professional literature and has written or co-written several textbooks in the area of psychology including *Thriving: Beyond Adjustment* and *Emotional Intimacy: Overlooked Requirement for Survival*. Most recently he served as writer and senior producer of *Patients as Educators: Videocases in Abnormal Psychology*. Dr. Dahms is active as a consultant and finds especially fascinating the dynamics of healthful functioning, key elements of effective coping behaviors, and the effectiveness of helping relationships.

Contents

Contents

Preface

Queen Victoria called upon the subjects of Great Britain to put their faith in the Categorical Imperative, the belief that each person has a predisposition to treat others as they would like to be treated.

The Social Darwinists believe that people who are less fortunate than others deserve their fate regardless of the circumstances which may account for their situation.

President George Bush called for a renewed personal involvement in caring for the needs of others through his metaphor of "a thousand points of light."

Conservative William F. Buckley and the liberal senator from Massachusetts, Ted Kennedy, both believe the time has come when the nation should either require or at least offer the 60 million students across the country an opportunity to help meet the human and social needs of our nation.

These four observations tend to summarize the juxtapositions of naivete, cynicism, idealism, and practicality which, in various combinations, have historically represented our response toward the so-called "have nots" of each generation. The question now is which one of the four positions will most influence the role to be played by the tens of thousands of "grassroots organizations" whose function it is to respond to the needs of others.

These grassroots programs and agencies have existed in our society from its beginning. Indeed, the forty-one founders of the Mayflower compact could easily be described as volunteers of the first small, community-based, nonprofit agency in the New World when, as they came ashore, they pledged to work for a just and equal way of life. The genius of democracy in America initiated by those forty-one founders is revealed in the enormous capacity of the American people to improve their adverse conditions through voluntary associations.

From those earliest beginnings, however, we have gained many insights. We have learned, for example, that it may not be reasonable or prudent to wait passively for large governmental programs or agencies to respond either effectively or with dispatch to unmet social needs. Similarly, it is naive to depend exclusively upon the benevolence of society's most affluent members to adequately address those same needs.

In our efforts to organize, write, and edit this book, we have come to believe that the most comprehensive response to those needs will be accomplished through the myriad of services provided by small, nonprofit, grassroots organizations empowered by average citizens serving in a voluntary capacity—a direct, historical linkage, we might add, to those forty-one founders of the Mayflower Compact.

The purpose of this book is to help the managers, staffs, and volunteers of these agencies better understand the unique culture of their organizations. We would quickly point out, however, that *Grassroots Organizations* is not a "how-to" book. Rather, it should be viewed as a work in progress—a catalyst to provoke a more intensive search for awareness and knowledge in order to make these organizations even more effective.

We use the metaphor of the juggler throughout the book because we are continually amazed by the sophisticated balancing act required of the directors of these grassroots organizations. Simultaneously, they must identify needs, recruit and manage volunteers, communicate to various publics, obtain necessary funding, reward and inspire their staffs, continually prove their effectiveness, maintain their energy levels, and do it all with very limited staff and financial resources. We believe the successful directors of these small programs run the most cost-effective human-service efforts in the nation. The explanation for this is simple—in order to survive, they must!

We first attempted to address the administrative needs of these small, nonprofit organizations in *Grassroots Administration*, published in 1980. In that original publication, we were pretentious enough to assume on our own what topics should be included. In this edition, however, the topics were selected after listening carefully to agency directors and staff members. The material that emerged was then further refined through focus groups comprising practitioners, students, academics, and recipients of the services provided by these small agencies.

Included within each chapter are comments made by directors who have gained significant recognition for the success and effectiveness of their programs or agencies. These insights were helpful to us as editors in making sure we were keeping on the right track. We hope they will also serve as a "reality check" for the readers.

We believe this book will be an important resource for students enrolled in the growing number of programs designed to prepare them for professional positions in the human-service field. We also believe the material will be valuable to the countless volunteers who commit time, energy, and *talent* to a limitless array of service clubs, religious groups, neighborhood associations, and other programs serving special-need populations.

Chapter 1 provides a historical context as well as a future challenge for meeting the complex social and human needs of our society. This chapter also gives definition to what often appears to be a rather amorphous relationship and structure in small, community-based, nonprofit agencies and programs.

In chapter 2 we emphasize the importance of anticipating and, therefore, controlling the changing conditions and environment of the future. Chapter 3 helps the reader more fully appreciate the truly unique culture within which these grassroots organizations must operate. Chapters 4 through 12 and the appendices are descriptions of each of the many balls managers and staff must learn to juggle and keep properly spaced in the air at the same time.

As we have already noted, this book provides a framework, a beginning, and we encourage the reader to use the annotated bibliography and the list of recommended reading at the end of the book as an excellent source for further information and research.

The parentage for a book like this is broad and involves many people. Our own personal and professional interests in grassroots organizations have been expressed in many settings, including academic and applied research, professional consultation, and on-the-line work with many of these small, nonprofit agencies and programs.

Of course, we owe much to the individual contributors. Our criteria for the selection of those we asked to prepare material for inclusion were fairly basic. They are all recognized authorities on the subjects they were asked to develop and, especially, they understand the unique nature of grassroots organizations. In this context, we owe a special note of thanks to the several contributors who are affiliated with the Center for the Improvement of Public Management, University of Colorado at Denver.

We would like to thank Laurie Prossnitz, our editor; Neil Rowe, publisher of Waveland Press; and the many anonymous reviewers whose positive critiques were of great help to us.

A special thanks to Barbara Conn who was completing her graduate work in Public Administration and was primarily responsible for developing the material in the annotated bibliography.

We also want to acknowledge the special contribution of Mavis Knopp, Associate Director, Community Service Development Program for Metropolitan State College at Denver, and the agency directors she interviewed for the "From the Directors" sections that accompany each chapter.

Finally, thank you Heather Clifton and Pollard Dahms for once again nurturing and supporting us through another intense research and writing project.

Robert L. Clifton
Alan M. Dahms

Introduction

Just as society must juggle the varied needs of its citizens, it must also balance the contributions of the private, public, and nonprofit sectors in meeting those needs. The two articles reproduced here skillfully articulate the vital role that nonprofits have played in the past and will play in the future. Peter F. Drucker, an eminent authority on for-profit business management skills as well as a co-founder of the Peter F. Drucker Foundation for Non Profit Management, views grassroots organizations as America's first line of attack on its social problems. Because nonprofits have succeeded where government has failed, Drucker urges a strengthening of the nonprofit sector through better management, results-oriented fundraising, and a change in the attitude of government and government bureaucracies.

Surely another means of strengthening nonprofits is by harnessing the energy and idealism of the 60 million students across the country. The article by Senator Edward M. Kennedy of Massachusetts lauds the enactment of the National and Community Service Act of 1990 and the opportunities it will provide for service learning programs for students from kindergarten to college. Senator Kennedy points out the enormous benefits that will accrue to society, in terms of both those who are helped and those given the opportunity to provide help.

It Profits Us
to Strengthen Nonprofits

Peter F. Drucker

America needs a new social priority: to triple the productivity of the nonprofits and to double the share of gross personal income—now just below 3%—they collect as donations. Otherwise the country faces, only a few years out, social polarization.

Federal, state and local governments will have to retrench sharply, no matter who is in office. Moreover, government has proved incompetent at solving social problems. Virtually every success we have scored has been achieved by nonprofits.

The great advances in health and longevity have been sponsored, directed and in large part financed by such nonprofits as the American Heart Association and the American Mental Health Association. Whatever results there are in the rehabilitation of addicts we owe to such nonprofits as Alcoholics Anonymous, the Salvation Army and the Samaritans. The schools in which inner-city minority children learn the most are parochial schools and those sponsored by some Urban League chapters. The first group to provide food and shelter to the Kurds fleeing from Saddam last spring was an American nonprofit, the International Rescue Committee.

Double Rehabilitation

Many of the most heartening successes are being scored by small, local organizations. One example: The tiny Judson Center in Royal Oak, Mich.—an industrial suburb of Detroit—gets black women and their families off welfare while simultaneously getting severely handicapped children out of institutions and back into society.

Judson trains carefully picked welfare mothers to raise in their homes, for a modest salary, two or three crippled or emotionally disturbed kids. The rehabilitation rate for the welfare mothers is close to 100%, with many of them in five years or so moving into employment as rehabilitation workers. The rehabilitation rate for the children, who otherwise would be condemned to lifetime institutional confinement, is about 50%; and every one of these kids had been given up as hopeless.

The nonprofits spend far less for results than governments spend for failures. The cost per pupil in the New York Archdiocese's parochial schools—70% of whose students stay in school, stay off the streets and graduate with high literacy and salable skills—is about half that in New York City's failing public schools.

Two-thirds of the first-offenders paroled in Florida into the custody of the Salvation Army are "permanently" rehabilitated— they are not indicted for another crime for at least six years. Were they to go to prison, two-thirds would become habitual criminals. Yet a prisoner costs at least twice as much per year as a parolee in the custody of the Salvation Army.

The Judson Center saves the state of Michigan $100,000 a year for each welfare mother and her charges—one-third in welfare costs and two-thirds in the costs of keeping the children in institutions.

Though the majority of the students in private colleges and universities get some sort of financial aid, their parents still pay more than do the parents of students in state universities and colleges. But the state-university student's education actually *costs* a good deal more than (in some states twice as much as) that of the student in a private nonprofit institution—with the difference paid by the taxpayer.

The nonprofits have the potential to become America's social sector—equal in importance to the public sector of government and the private sector of business. The delivery system is already in place: There are now some 900,000 nonprofits, the great majority close to the problems of their communities. And about 30,000 of them came into being in 1990 (the latest year for which figures are available)—practically all dedicated to local action on one problem: tutoring minority children; furnishing ombudsmen for patients in the local hospital; helping immigrants through government red tape.

Where 20 years ago the American middle class thought it had done its social duty by writing a check, it increasingly commits itself to active doing as well. According to the best available statistics, there are now some 90 million Americans—one out of every two adults—working as "volunteers" in nonprofits for three hours a week on average; the nonprofits have become America's largest "employer."

Increasingly these volunteers do not look upon their work as charity; they see it as a parallel career to their paid jobs and insist on being trained, on being held accountable for results and performance, and on career opportunities for advancement to professional and managerial—though still unpaid—positions in the nonprofit. Above all, they see in volunteer work access to achievement, to effectiveness, to self-fulfillment, indeed to meaningful citizenship. And for this reason there is more demand for well-structured volunteer jobs than there are positions to fill.

Some observers (such as Brian O'Connell, head of Independent Sector, the national association of the large nonprofits) believe that, within 10 years, two-thirds of American adults—120 million—will want to work as nonprofit volunteers for five hours a week each, which would mean a doubling of the man- and woman-power available for nonprofit work.

And the nonprofits are becoming highly innovative. When some friends and I founded the Peter F. Drucker Foundation for Non Profit Management a year ago, we planned as our first public event a $25,000 award for the best innovation that would "create a significant new dimension of non profit performance." We hoped to receive 40 applications. We received 809—and most were deserving of a prize.

The actual award went to the Judson Center, but the big nonprofits are as innovative as the small fry in many cases. With several billion dollars in revenue, Family Service America—headquartered in Milwaukee—has become bigger than a good many Fortune 500 companies; it now is probably the biggest American nonprofit next to the Red Cross. It has achieved its phenomenal growth in part through contracting with large employers such as General Motors to help employee families with such problems as addiction or the emotional disorders of adolescent children.

For the nonprofits' potential to become reality, three things are needed. First, the average nonprofit must manage itself as well as the best-managed ones do. The majority still believe that good intentions and a pure heart are all that are needed. They do not yet see themselves as accountable for performance and results. And far too many splinter their efforts or waste them on non-problems and on activities that would be done better—and more cheaply—by a business.

Second, nonprofits have to learn how to raise money. The American public has not become less generous—there is little evidence of the "compassion fatigue" nonprofit people talk about. In fact, giving has been going up quite sharply these past few years—from 2.5% of personal income to 2.9%. Unfortunately, a great many nonprofits still believe that the way to get money is to hawk *needs*. But the American public gives for *results*. It no longer gives to "charity"; it "buys in." Of the charitable appeals most of us get in the mail every week, usually just one talks of results—the one that gets our check.

The nonprofits will have to get the additional money they need primarily from individuals—as they always have. Even if there is government money—mainly via vouchers, I expect—and money from companies, they can supply only a fraction of what is needed.

Finally, we need a change in the attitude of government and government bureaucracies. President Bush has spoken glowingly of the importance of the nonprofits as the "thousand points of light." If he really believes this, he should propose allowing taxpayers to deduct $1.10 for each dollar they give to nonprofits as a cash donation. This would solve the nonprofits' money problems at once. It also could cut government deficits in the not-so-very-long run— for a well-managed nonprofit gets at least twice the bang out of each buck that a government agency does. Some of the voucher programs already enacted cut public school budgets, since some of the district's per-pupil spending moves with the child into the private sector.

Instead of such a policy, however, we have the IRS making one move after the other to penalize and to curtail donations to nonprofits—and the tax collectors of the big states are all doing the same. Each of these moves is presented as "closing a tax loophole"; in fact, none has yielded a penny of additional revenue and none is likely to do so.

First Line of Attack

The real motivation for such actions is the bureaucracy's hostility to the nonprofits—not too different from the bureaucracy's hostility to markets and private enterprise in the former Communist countries. The success of the nonprofits undermines the bureaucracy's power and denies its ideology. Worse, the bureaucracy cannot admit that the nonprofits succeed where governments fail. What is needed, therefore, is a public policy that establishes the nonprofits as the country's first line of attack on its social problems.

In my 1969 book "The Age of Discontinuity" I first proposed "privatization," only to have every reviewer tell me that it would never happen. Now, of course, privatization is widely seen as the cure for modern economies mismanaged by socialist bureaucracies. We now need to learn that "nonprofitization" may for modern societies be the way out of mismanagement by welfare bureaucracies.

National Service and Education for Citizenship

Edward M. Kennedy

Service to others—to the community and the nation—is an idea as old as 1776. It was the spirit of the first national frontier and of President Kennedy's New Frontier. Throughout history, Americans have served the nation in times of crisis—in war, depression, or natural disaster. In quieter times, they have served their communities, helping a neighbor in need or a stranger in trouble.

The famous observer of early America, Alexis De Tocqueville, wrote that "an enlightened self-love continually leads Americans to help one another and disposes them freely to give part of their time and wealth for the good of the state." He noted that, in the United States, individualism is balanced by a strong commitment to the public well-being.

The uniquely American crisis of De Tocqueville's century, the Civil War, also saw the creation of the Red Cross, which brought nurses to the battlefields to comfort and minister to the wounded and dying. Later in that century, settlement houses—neighborhood centers that provided social services—began to emerge.

During the Great Depression, President Franklin Roosevelt created the Civilian Conservation Corps, through which thousands of unemployed young Americans found work and a new sense of purpose. In his inaugural address in 1961, President Kennedy appealed to this tradition by urging all Americans to ask what they could do for their country. The legacies of his Administration—the Peace Corps, VISTA (Volunteers in Service to America), and countless local projects across the nation—continue. Each year, millions of Americans serve their communities, their country, and the underdeveloped nations of the world.

Democracy means more than the freedom to pursue our own self-interest. It also means the responsibility to participate in the life of the community and the nation—the responsibility to give something back to America in return for all it has given us. This commitment to public service has been the hallmark of the best of the American experience. Yet there are disturbing signs that we have lost sight of that principle in recent years, and we need to find it again in the 1990s.

The world's oldest democracy now ranks last in the world in voter participation—down 20% since 1960. Even more disturbing, the youngest voters are those least likely to cast their ballots on Election Day. Americans who do not vote are also less likely to engage in other aspects of civic life. It is not surprising that the failure to respond to the census questionnaire correlates closely with the failure to exercise the right to vote.

To their credit, many young people are asking for more ways to get involved. Indeed, where service opportunities are available, young Americans have set an example by directing their energies to meet the challenges before them.

Most teenagers who donate their time and caring to their communities do so through their schools or churches, often because a teacher, a friend, or a parent suggests that they join in. According to a recent poll, 90% of 14-to 17-year-olds who had been asked to volunteer did so. We do not have to compel young people to become involved in community service. All we have to do is ask—and provide the opportunity.

That is the purpose of what may be the most important legislation enacted by the 101st Congress: the National and Community Service Act of 1990. This act will fund programs enabling students from kindergarten through college to serve their communities and enabling older Americans to volunteer as well. It will expand the nation's full-time and summer youth corps programs, which bring young people together to work to meet environmental and human service needs. And it will fund innovative, state-sponsored programs that offer educational scholarships and other benefits to young adults who make a substantial commitment to community service. The legislation provides federal appropriations of $62 million in fiscal year 1991, $95.5 million in fiscal year 1992, and $105 million in fiscal year 1993 to support these activities.

While the new act will increase opportunities for Americans of all ages, its most important outcome may well be its impact on young citizens in the earliest grades. About a third of the funds are targeted on programs for students, and schools across the country will have an incentive to involve students in community service. By teaching young children to help others, we will also be encouraging the values that will keep America strong for the next generation.

By learning that they can make a difference in the lives of others, students discover their power to control their own lives. Service programs are particularly effective in helping to motivate disadvantaged young people. For example, when at-risk students tutor younger children, the tutors themselves consistently show improved academic achievement.

Once exposed to the needs of the community and the

responsibility of helping others, young people will have an increased sense of community involvement and a more realistic view of the value of their own learning. This effect was movingly articulated by a sixth-grade volunteer speaking at a Senate hearing on national service: "There are some times when even just to see the homeless people lets you down about your city. But I've never come to the point where I say it's just so bad that I don't feel that I can help. I feel that you just have to keep on trying, no matter how hard it is." It is not surprising that the majority of young volunteers continue to serve after their initial experience or that most volunteers decide to increase their time commitment.

Service-learning is a time-tested educational tool that traces its lineage back to John Dewey. It helps students understand the relevance of their coursework and enables them to test their classroom work against the reality of the world around them. Service-learning should be a central component of current efforts to reform education. There are few better ways to inspire a child's interest in science than by allowing him or her to analyze and clean up a polluted stream. There are few better ways to help a student understand grammar than by having him or her tutor a recent immigrant learning to speak and write English.

Service projects involving groups of students allow young persons to learn to work together and develop leadership roles. In addition, they offer opportunities for students to analyze problems and propose and execute solutions. When students are put in positions of responsibility, they are counted on to show up on time and ready to work and to see a project through to completion. They learn the consequences of letting down those they intended to help. These "life skills" are important for later success.

Ultimately, these benefits add up to young Americans who are better prepared to be citizens. They will be better educated and more confident, and they will have valuable experience in meeting the needs of their communities.

We know the serious domestic challenges waiting to be met: 23 million Americans are illiterate; more than half of all adolescents use drugs before age 18; the number of homeless families doubled over the last decade; we have failed to protect our environment adequately. The challenges are many, and volunteer efforts are no substitute for effective action by the public and private sectors. But it would be a mistake to waste the talents of 60 million students across the country. It is time to harness their energy and idealism by offering them opportunities to serve. In doing so, we will be helping to guarantee the continued vitality of our democracy in the years ahead.

Chapter

1

The Juggling Act
Robert Clifton and Alan Dahms

> If a man gets the idea of any social improvement whatsoever, a school, a hospital, a road, he does not think of turning to the authorities. He announces his plan, offers to carry it out, calls for the strength of other individuals to aid his efforts, and fights hand to hand against each obstacle.
> —Alexis de Tocqueville

> Currently, we are overwhelmed with increased needs and what appears to be an inability to solve them. I question this inability because I think America is capable of rearranging priorities to meet a basic standard of living.
> —Kip Tiernan (founded Rosie's Place in 1974. It was the first women's drop-in center and emergency shelter in the country. It continues to exist without government or state funds).

Robert Clifton, Ed.D. is Director of the Division of Extended Studies at the University of Colorado at Denver. He has served as a municipal administrator and as chief executive officer of a large metropolitan county. Alan Dahms, Ph.D. is a licensed clinical psychologist and a faculty member at Metropolitan State College of Denver. His writings include *Emotional Intimacy: Overlooked Requirement for Survival* and *Thriving: Beyond Adjustment.*

Introduction

The metaphor of a juggler is an apt comparison when referring to the multiple tasks which must be carefully balanced by the directors and staffs of small, community-based, nonprofit agencies. The same metaphor also characterizes an even larger and more difficult balancing act—that performed by our nation trying to meet the varied human needs of its citizens.

When the balls of the juggler are all appropriately sequenced and moving in perpetual motion, it becomes the quintessential display of movement and balance, seemingly done with very little effort. But when that flow is disrupted ever so slightly, we quickly realize how truly fragile is the relationship between the juggler and the objects being tossed in the air. And when the balance totally disintegrates, the balls falling without grace, the juggler reaching to save whatever is possible, the scene is disturbing and even pathetic. Nevertheless, as members of the audience, we commiserate with the failure and encourage the juggler to try again.

As a nation, we openly admit to the need of much improvement in order to adequately meet the basic human needs of each person in our society. Still, over the course of our history we have crafted a complex interplay of diverse forces working toward the "common good." Yet with all of our faults or failures as a nation, this unique interplay of forces all pointed in a common direction may represent our highest quality as a free, democratic society. We know that the balance is far from perfect and, indeed, it appears at times to totally disintegrate. But, hopefully, we will never become discouraged from picking up the fallen balls and continuing to try to make it all work.

The Past

The Categorical Imperative

Classic thought, from the Chinese to the teachings of Hinduism to the ancient Egyptian codes, expressed concern for the less fortunate and at least offered an implied obligation for each nation to find some way to meet the basic human needs of the members of its society. Curti (1973) points out that the term "philanthropy" first entered the English language in the seventeenth century as a translation from Greek and Latin perhaps best rendered as love (*philia*) of humankind (*anthropos*).

One dominant theme emerges as we look at all the major historical periods. There always appears to be great debate as to the relative roles of the secular or political authorities, the religious institutions, and the volunteer units (individual or organized) in addressing society's needs. In medieval Western Europe, for example, as military/political power gave way to the emerging dominance of the Roman Catholic church, care of the less fortunate

From the Directors

Career changes brought me to the Womens Funding Alliance, which represents ten organizations raising funds in the work place. As I reflect carefully, though, I seem to be doing what I have done for some time. As a professional educator I learned the importance of communication. As a paid staff member for a Seattle City Councilperson, I learned the skills needed in politics. The similarities between politics and successfully administering nonprofits are startling. Analogous are the following requirements: constant hustle, educating others about your cause, continuing efforts in the face of uncertain outcomes, being "on task" both in and out of the office (in both work and personal life), competitors, the fine line between job and personal commitments.

*In politics, the election results tell you how you did. Such markers are harder to come by in nonprofits, for your work is **never** finished even for a moment.*

Our issues are controversial. We're not simply selling cookies; we discuss difficult social issues such as rape, domestic violence, and sexual harassment. These are issues society does not address easily nor does government support programs that offer solutions.

In grassroots organizations, you become an expert before you want to be. After a few months, people turn to you for advice. The energy required makes grassroots, nonprofit work a young person's game—if not in actual years, at least in terms of energy levels!

—Karen Campbell, Executive Director
Womens Funding Alliance (Seattle)

(which represented the great bulk of the population) usually fell by default to the members of small, but very committed religious orders. The members of these groups were dedicated to helping alleviate the massive human tragedies that could be found all around them. The combined indifference of the feudal landlords and the higher authorities of the church lay behind what little efforts were exerted to help those at the bottom of the socioeconomic ladder.

As the rise of individualism occurred during the Renaissance period of the sixteenth century, a certain faith in the goodness of the individual began to manifest itself. It was believed that people, by their very nature, were naturally inclined to treat others as they would want to be treated themselves. This belief became known as the *categorical imperative*. As we now review this period of history, it is hard to believe how important this cultural value was when we consider the common absence of its application.

Nevertheless, it was believed that the categorical imperative was the very thread which held the fabric of society together. It was thought that without it, chaos and anarchy would surely prevail. Further, during the Victorian period of the 1800s, it was considered by many to be the moral imperative that allowed for the very existence of the British Empire itself. A common table prayer at the time went as follows:

> We thank thee God for this food.
> We thank thee God for this prayer.
> And we thank thee God above all for the categorical imperative.

Democracy in America

The notion of the categorical imperative, however, took on a very different meaning as it traveled from England to the New World. The forty-one founders of the Mayflower Compact who came ashore and pledged to work for a just and equal way of life based on mutual benefit gave a new and pragmatic application to the categorical imperative. Those founders could appropriately be described as America's first voluntary, small, nonprofit, organization. From that point forward, one of the most distinguishing characteristics of the American culture has been our tendency to band together in volunteer groups or associations in order to address individual or societal needs.

This characteristic was particularly noted early in our history by the French statesman, Alexis de Tocqueville. Sent by the French government in 1831 to examine prisons and penitentiaries in

America, Tocqueville's classic, two-volume *Democracy in America* was first published shortly after his return to France. His organized observations resulted in the first comprehensive examination of the political and social institutions of our fledgling nation. In virtually every college sociology or political science class, his observations are still used to better understand the American character both in its historical past and its current condition.

At the time Tocqueville explored America, our nation and the socioeconomic classes within it were being remolded as the preliminary stages of industrialization were taking place. It was within this changing environment that Tocqueville made his most insightful observation of the American character. He was fascinated by the tendency of Americans to form voluntary associations, completely apart from the officialdom of government, in order to address the problems of the society.

> If a man gets the idea of any social improvement whatsoever, a school, a hospital, a road, he does not think of turning to the authorities. He announces his plan, offers to carry it out, calls for the strength of other individuals to aid his efforts, and fights hand to hand against each obstacle. I admit that in fact he often is less successful than the authorities would have been in his place, but in the total, the general result of all these individual strivings amounts to much more than any administration could undertake; and moreover the influence of such a state of affairs on the moral and political character of a people, would more than make up for all the inadequacies if there were any (1981:39).

Tocqueville saw this voluntary association as uniquely American and very influential for promoting the democratic flavor of the country. He further wrote:

> Americans combine to give fêtes [lavish often outdoor entertainment; a large elaborate party], found seminaries, build churches, distribute books, and send missionaries to the antipodes [diametrically opposite parts of the earth]. Hospitals, prisons, and schools take shape in that way. Finally, if they want to proclaim a truth or propagate some feeling by the encouragement of a great example, they form an association. In every case, at the head of any new undertaking, where in France you would find the government or in England some territorial magnate, in the United States you are sure to find an association (1969:513).

Noblesse Oblige Versus Rugged Individualism

During Queen Victoria's day, there was great faith, at least among the privileged, that the duty of *noblesse oblige* (nobility obligates), imposed on the more fortunate by the categorical imperative, would somehow alleviate the needs of the downtrodden and less fortunate. Yet, in the Dickensonian world of industrial England, that expectation rarely was realized.

Nor was the humanitarian benefit from the upper class any more apparent and certainly not any more efficacious in the United States during the same period. Indeed, at the turn of the twentieth century, it was widely accepted in this country that one's bootstraps and a good grip to pull on them were all that was needed to succeed. Those who failed were commonly seen as deserving their fate in some perverse misapplication of social Darwinism.

Government Intervention

The Great Depression of the late 1920s and early 1930s, however, made it obvious to all but the most arrogant that it makes no difference how hard one grips the bootstrap if there are no boots. Rugged individualism, laissez faire, social Darwinism, noblesse oblige—by whatever name—it was clear that the socioeconomic fabric of the country was falling apart.

The so-called less fortunate had suddenly moved from being a subservient and largely hidden minority to a very visible and angry majority. To even begin to meet their most basic needs required bold, new directions. So, a new ball was placed in motion. For the first time in our history, massive government intervention became part of the delicate juggling act of social responsibility. Thus was launched Franklin Roosevelt's New Deal, with its Work Projects Administration, Social Security, Tennessee Valley Authority, Civilian Conservation Corps, and many other publicly funded enterprises and relief efforts.

At first, government was reluctantly accepted as an undesirable but necessary bridge between the "haves" and the "have nots." But as the Depression slowly turned into recovery and, finally, into post-war prosperity, government's supporting role was not only accepted but became expected for the "truly down and out." The problem was that the "truly down and out" had somewhat unobtrusively grown in definition and in size to gigantic proportions. The "temporary" government programs evolved into inertia-laden bureaucracies inadequate in their operation as well as purpose to meet the needs of this sizable population.

The Sixties

By the time of the so-called social reawakening of the 1960s, it was clear that massive, centralized government programs could not meet the myriad socioeconomic needs of the residents of individual neighborhoods and communities across the nation. Whether the needs were really new and different or simply the surfacing of long, submerged concerns, people were falling through the cracks of the established support systems by the millions.

Both domestic and foreign government policies were being challenged by increasingly large numbers of individuals and coalitions of groups. Inspired by the nostalgic ring of the New Deal, the political response to this cacophony of protest was a series of national calls for action. Beginning with John F. Kennedy's "New Frontier," the metamorphosis of national responsibility continued through Lyndon Johnson's "War on Poverty" and Richard Nixon's "New Federalism."

Each administration tried to craft the necessary "balance" between the obvious social needs of the country, the historic belief in the Puritan work ethic, and the growing disenchantment with what some called "giveaway" programs. Each response gave rise to its own parade of governmental agencies known by such titles and acronyms as Peace Corps, Vista, Job Corps and, in every community across the nation, the Community Action Program (CAP)—the local political and physical center for the distribution of the federal largess by whatever name.

The End of the Federal Largess

By the time Ronald Reagan began his presidency, these national calls for action and the federal largess necessary to carry out such missions had waned considerably. For all but the most sanguine, the stark reality of how far the priorities of the country had changed was the end of the Nixon-created program known as "revenue sharing."

This program, supported by both conservatives and liberals, in small jurisdictions as well as large ones, returned to local communities massive amounts of federal tax dollars with minimal strings attached. It was the revenue sharing program which had largely supported the hundreds of thousands of small, community-based, nonprofit agencies that sprang up during the 1960s to meet the particular needs of special groups throughout the country.

The Present

The New Paradigm

Thomas Kuhn (1970), a philosopher of science, made the observation that new frames of reference, or *new paradigms* (from the Greek *paradeigma*: example, model, pattern), are not accepted gracefully by older, more established points of view. For example, the early Greek view of the earth being at the center of the universe was so strongly supported by the church authorities that for centuries to even suggest something different was considered blasphemous. During the Renaissance period, however, this position gradually changed to our present heliocentric view with the sun at the center of our solar system.

The old view (paradigm) disappeared very slowly even though the new view was being defined by the likes of Copernicus, Galileo, and Kepler. The difficulty in this process is to somehow anticipate the new pattern or paradigm while still being regulated by the rules and principles of the old one. Clearly, the emerging paradigm of how we are to effectively meet our social and human needs will threaten the old views of how things should be done.

The volatile period of the 1960s provided us with new, albeit painful, insights as to how to meet the broad array of human and social needs of the nation. The new paradigm already taking shape has clearly abandoned the simple "quick fix" to society's most difficult problems. While the new pattern may not yet be fully developed, it is obvious that it will be far more complex than anything we have experienced before.

We now know that it is not enough to depend on the *noblesse oblige* of the philanthropist living in the big white house on the hill. Nor is it enough to rely on the *noblesse oblige* of our elected representatives in the vicinity of the big white house in Washington or in their respective state capitols.

In ways similar to the reawakening in the 1960s, we also know that neither massive government intervention nor good intentions alone are enough to provide for every citizen the minimal opportunity for a better life. At the very least, real and lasting solutions will require the positive and delicate balance of the private, public, nonprofit, and educational sectors of our society integrated into a comprehensive common effort. We must find a way for these sectors to work together to maximize the benefit of our scarce resources in order to meet the needs of such diverse groups as teenagers with babies, older persons in isolation, latchkey kids in suburbia, adults learning to read, victims of incest, people in substandard housing, victims of domestic violence, addicts of all kinds, the homeless, victims of AIDS, and many, many more.

The thread needed to join the public, private, and educational sectors will be supplied by the seemingly amorphous network of tens of thousands of small, community-based, nonprofit agencies and programs across the nation. It cannot be described precisely how this network will create a new balance and source of energy and commitment. At the very least, we know that this new paradigm will be multifaceted, uncertain, confusing, and without operating manuals. Moreover, it will often appear necessary to violate the "First Law of Wing Walking" well known to barnstorming pilots: "Never let go of what you've got until you've got hold of something else."

What Are Small, Community-Based, Nonprofit Agencies?

"Small" and "community-based" are important aspects of the agencies and programs discussed in this book. These are also the words that distinguish such agencies from other nonprofits that are much larger in both function and operating budget.

Community-based agencies are those whose mission is primarily focused to meet a specific social or human-service need within a given community. The need may very likely be of national concern as well and, in fact, the agency may be part of a national association or organization. The difference is that the small, nonprofit agency within a community is focusing on a particular problem within the demographic context of its immediate environment.

These agencies are smaller than the more institutionalized nonprofit entities in terms of their operating budgets and the concomitant number of staff members. Nevertheless, these grassroots organizations have proven to be far more effective in achieving their missions than their larger counterparts. Essentially, there are three basic reasons for this.

First, the staffs and directors of these smaller organizations have indicated a much greater willingness to take risks. While this characteristic does not guarantee success, it certainly affords them a better opportunity to stay ahead of changes taking place which could have a significant impact on their ability to effectively deliver services.

Second, the *extremely* limited financial sources usually available to these types of nonprofit agencies simply demand that they operate on a very cost-effective ratio of expenses versus income. While larger agencies and programs must operate under limited funding restraints as well, it is usually easier for them to bridge shortfalls, secure additional revenues, or even lay off personnel without totally decimating the entire program. Generally, none of these options are available to grassroots organizations.

Finally, these agencies prove to be more effective for the simple reason that their size affords them the "opportunity" to operate on a more personal level with their respective clients and with the community itself. No matter how humanistic and caring a larger organization may appear in its advertisements, it will inevitably get caught up to some degree with conventional bureaucratic inertia.

Who Runs These Agencies?

While it can be misleading to overgeneralize, the typical staff of a small, community-based, nonprofit organization consists of a director, an assistant director or project coordinator, a secretary (often part-time), and the all-important volunteer support system. It is the volunteers who are frequently called upon to perform the highly specialized functions that would normally be the responsibility of the regular staff of larger organizations. Depending on an agency's finances, of course, specific support staff can range from being totally volunteer, to a combination of such classifications as college interns, part-timers, shared-timers, consultants, and so on.

The directors of these organizations, of necessity, must possess a wide range of administrative abilities. Their responsibilities include writing grant requests, working with the board of directors, supervising staff, developing public relations, managing volunteers, being fiscally accountable, and being politically aware.

Because there are few academic programs specifically designed to prepare individuals for these administrative positions, most directors and senior staff gain their competence through on-the-job training. If they have earned college degrees, they very likely majored in one of the social sciences—psychology, social work, sociology, or political science. These are the disciplines that traditionally have been most concerned with human needs and social issues.

Although the graduates of these academic disciplines may have a strong desire to alleviate human suffering and resolve social problems, they frequently lack the specific skills and knowledge needed to be effective administrators. Because their agencies normally cannot afford the individualized expertise required for the various staff support functions, the directors of these agencies must somehow learn to do it all. It is a demanding task requiring a broad array of administrative skills, such as the ability to prepare budgets, develop funding proposals, evaluate programs, manage public relations, write reports, develop strategic plans, determine goals and objectives, and, at the same time, provide leadership and vision for the organization. If such managers and directors are not experts themselves at each of these functions, they must at least know enough to ensure that each is being done correctly. The following job advertisement, which appeared in a major newspaper, is an indication of the current situation:

> *Coordinator for Community Services.* Must have B.A. degree in Social Work, Psychology, Sociology, Political Science or related field. Experience desired in writing funding proposals, community organizing, program assessment, use of computers, public relations, and volunteer management.

Obviously, the knowledge and experience requirements asked for in the advertisement are generally not provided in the academic disciplines that are noted.

It is our judgment, therefore, that it is far more demanding to be an effective administrator in one of these small, nonprofit agencies than to be the director of some large organizational entity that can afford to hire certified professionals for all of the many support staff roles. Near the outset of each chapter in this book, we have excerpted comments from agency directors whom we found to be outstanding examples of this administrative excellence.

How Are Such Agencies Funded?

The operating funds for grassroots agencies are usually derived from a variety of sources including individual contributions, federal or state grants, private foundation or corporation grants, and special fund-raising events. In a nonscientific survey conducted in 1978, we examined one hundred agencies in Colorado that met our criteria of being community-based. Nearly half had operating budgets of $100,000 or less. Fourteen agencies had budgets of less than $25,000. In a similar survey of 98 agencies conducted in 1988 by the Denver Technical Assistance Center, fifty-nine of the agencies contacted had operating budgets of $500,000 or less and none had budgets of less than $25,000. Clearly, even the cost of operating a small, "storefront," nonprofit organization has escalated considerably.

Another interesting comparison that can be made from the information obtained from the two surveys is the difference in the reliance on federal and state sources of funding. As one might expect, there has been a noticeable decrease in the proportional amount of government funding, particularly federal, for these agencies over the past several years.

In the course of our inquiry about the operating budgets, we made a somewhat unrelated discovery about the total number of grassroots agencies. When we first examined this subject in 1978, it was estimated that there were nearly 4,000 nonprofit agencies in the state of Colorado alone. United Way and other organizations now put that number for Colorado in excess of 10,000. Nationally, the number is approaching one million. Over 30,000 came into existence in 1990 alone. Perhaps the most interesting aspect of this observation is that this growth has taken place in spite of (or maybe on account of) a significant decrease in governmental financial support.

Although our sampling in both surveys was anecdotal and in no way exhaustive even within the state of Colorado, we believe the information suggests interesting insights into the current and future administration and operation of these types of agencies and programs.

What Services Do They Provide?

The services provided by small nonprofits are nearly as varied as the organizations themselves. Allowing for much overlap, most of the services fall into five broad categories: referral, education, job placement, advocacy, and outreach.

Referral.   These services are particularly valuable for those people in need of help who are intimidated by the larger, more bureaucratic systems established for this same purpose. Some referral type agencies, such as women's resource centers, are prepared to help almost anyone who has a problem, while others deal with the needs of a very specific clientele. Sometimes, in these latter agencies, the individual staff members may be former clients themselves.

Education.   This category includes a wide range of services including job training, development of consumer skills, remedial learning, alternative schools, special training for the physically or mentally disabled, and adult literacy or "right to read" programs.

Job placement.   Helping clients find employment is a good example of a service that requires the combination of all the categories—referral, education or training, outreach, and advocacy.

Advocacy.   Advocacy-type agencies strive to make the general public aware of the services they provide and, at the same time, to demonstrate the need for those services. Often the community-based agency or program may be affiliated with a large national organization such as the American Civil Liberties Union, the National Association of Neighborhoods, or the Children's Defense Fund.

Outreach.   These programs are extremely varied. Some are what might be called "quality of life supplements." Agencies in this category may be responsible for acquiring materials and labor for the renovation of old houses, for providing temporary lodging, or for acquiring food staples.

Outreach programs may also provide one-to-one helping relationships such as Big Brothers or Sisters and Partners. Through the personal relationships established in these programs, clients come to realize that someone cares enough to invest time and emotional effort to help them. Needless to say, these small, community-based agencies are excellent at providing this type of service.

Of course, counseling is a classic form of outreach provided by these agencies. Both short-term and long-term counseling can be found along with various "substance-abuse" programs. Another interesting example of outreach is a "brokering" service for other small nonprofits. In this activity, an agency will assist other programs and agencies with specific staff support or technical expertise.

An important function of all of these agencies is basic research and data collection. Prospective funders and legislative decision makers respond best to requests for money when presented with accurate and comprehensive information about the extent of existing needs and the important factors that influence solutions.

Who Are the Clients of These Agencies?

There are countless less fortunate individuals in our society who are statistically described in hundreds of different ways. These include such disparate groups as the elderly, teenagers "on the run," family members coping with violence or abuse, veterans, the homeless, and so on. It is difficult to determine the exact number of individuals being served by the thousands of small, community-based, nonprofit agencies and programs across the country. An individual, for example, who is referred to a specific agency by another agency becomes a statistic in the records of both.

Whoever they are, these individuals are already social casualties. For whatever reasons, they have been unable to access or, in some cases, even locate the "established" governmental systems that are theoretically designed to help them. Among this group are those who desperately need inexpensive, effective, and immediately accessible help and support. This is what grassroots organizations can do better than any other structure in our society.

How Are These Agencies Initiated and Developed?

An agency or program often begins with nothing more than a creative response to a problem. Someone might say, "If only we could find a way to help." Soon thereafter, some ad hoc planning sessions may take place, volunteers are recruited, necessary start-up funds are obtained, and a new program or even an agency may be on its way.

Unfortunately, getting through the steps just described is the easy part. The euphoria of the new idea and the first wave of volunteer enthusiasm will meet its first real test when significant financial and extended volunteer commitments are required.

Of course, we hope this book will serve as a guide and "reality check" for those wishing to transfer their new idea from an idealistic vision into practical implementation. In many ways, creating a small, nonprofit program or agency is similar to starting a small business in the private sector: it requires good advance planning, initial funding, a marketing strategy, and especially hard-working, dedicated individuals who understand the seemingly impossible task of finding ways to effectively meet identified human needs with very limited resources and support.

A very defined cycle seems to exist with regard to the birth, life, and sometimes, death of these organizations. During the initial phase, an idea is conceived, a mission is determined, start-up money is obtained, volunteers are recruited, and the delivery of services begins. In the intermediate stage, the programs are modified to better meet the actual needs and to overcome the unforeseen problems. In the final stage, the agency either becomes an established entity, is absorbed into a large agency, or it dies. If an agency or program can "make it" for five years, it is a good indication that it has a real chance at survival.

The Future

The 1990 National and Community Service Act, passed in the closing days of the 101st Congress, was intended, according to

Senate Majority Leader George Mitchell (D-Maine), "to establish a new social contract that defines not only what our country will do for our citizens but what our citizens will do for our country." These words, reminiscent of John F. Kennedy's 1961 inaugural address, hailed the act that created a Commission on National and Community Service. The purpose of the commission is to assist up to four regional clearinghouses in giving support to public and private nonprofit agencies experienced in managing volunteer support programs. Initial hopes were that the act would encourage many young, dedicated volunteers to help in a variety of human-service settings.

Earlier, President George Bush had invoked his own metaphor for small, community-based, nonprofit programs in his 1988 speech accepting the Republican nomination in New Orleans. He likened America to "a brilliant diversity spread like stars, like a thousand points of light in a broad and peaceful sky." Later, at his inauguration, he linked the imagery of the points of light to volunteer service. The Office of National Service's head, C. Gregg Petersmeyer, asserted in 1991 that by the end of Bush's first term more than one thousand points of light would have been honored by the White House.

Leave aside for a moment the degree to which that commitment was fulfilled. More important is the fact the call for increased volunteer efforts is now coming from all points on the political spectrum. William F. Buckley, in a book being well received by both liberals and conservatives, issues a national call to action in *Gratitude: Reflections on What We Owe to Our Country* (1990). Buckley believes it is time to implement a program that would induce, if not require, a one-year period of national service from all people upon reaching the age of 18. Such service would be in addition to or in place of military service and directly related to volunteer service in the nonprofit sector. Targeted activities would run the gamut of help-giving concerns, from aging to zero population growth.

Buckley points out that although an immense amount of money has been spent by federal agencies since the federal poverty programs were first initiated under Lyndon Johnson, many such projects are now in disarray. At the same time the problems of unemployment, drug use, illegitimacy, inner-city crime, homelessness, and illiteracy are rising at faster rates than ever before. He proposes several models for such a program:

1. *School Based*—Unpaid hours would be donated by high school seniors before they were eligible to graduate.

2. *Draft Based*—An alternative to military service.
3. *Voluntary*—Essentially what we currently have.
4. *Universal Service*—One year of civil or military service.
5. *"Buckley Model"*—One year of service required before enrolling in a college or university.

Joining the conservative Buckley in this call for a national service program is his otherwise longtime political adversary, Senator Edward M. Kennedy. The senior senator from Massachusetts is also calling for special attention to the 1990 National and Community Service Act. Both men believe that such a national service requirement would benefit individuals and society in equal measure.

That belief is strongly supported by many others across the political spectrum and especially by educators. Many of the nation's high schools are already implementing community-service requirements for their students. Colleges and universities are beginning to develop their own requirements in this area.

A task force of the American Psychological Association (McGovern et al., 1991), for example, has recommended that all psychology majors complete a laboratory in interpersonal skills and group process and that this be integrated whenever possible into an actual community-service project. The task force goes on to suggest that a volunteer experience should be an integral part of every student's undergraduate education. Other academic disciplines are beginning to develop similar programs or are at least considering the value and impact of such curriculum changes.

As noted in the National and Community Service Act, student volunteer work could result in some specific monetary benefits such as direct financial support or student loan forgiveness, both of which have proven to be very powerful incentives for young people in their pursuit of higher education. Financial rewards can also be a very positive stimulant to other groups as well. In Denver, for example, senior citizens can earn up to $250 in property tax credits by doing volunteer work in the Denver Public Schools. Each volunteer must spend at least one hundred hours helping out in the schools by November 1 of the calendar tax year. The variety of tasks undertaken include tutoring, being a classroom aide, working in school libraries, or befriending young learners.

In a profound way, these calls for individual contributions to society may reflect a softening of the extreme cult of the rugged individual that has tended to polarize people along some artificial measurement of success and failure in life. In order to fuel the spirit of capitalism, it was considered necessary to manifest the work ethic. This position, however, has contributed to a cultural ambivalence toward those in need (Ho 1985). "After all, is it not their own fault they are in such circumstances?" In this sense, we Westerners may find valuable lessons in the Confucian-based emphasis on societal cooperation considered necessary to meet the collective needs of the people.

It is too early to say what President Clinton will do during his administration to help meet the increasing social and human needs of Americans. We can, however, hope that the words of his election night victory statement are manifested in the development of *real* programs during his time in office: "This was more than a victory of a party . . . it was a victory for the people who feel left out and left behind and want to do better."

Summary

The fact that you are reading this book indicates that you are interested in finding more effective ways to meet the basic human needs of our nation. If you have decided to personally commit yourself to this task, be forewarned that it will not be an easy venture. Your reward, however, will be a sense of personal worth and satisfaction in knowing that you are part of a process that can benefit individual lives.

The last few years of the twentieth century have witnessed an exciting and unprecedented opportunity for a renewed commitment to the basic principles of democracy—equity, fairness, justice. The calls for these democratic values are being heard from Eastern Europe, the former Soviet Union, mainland China, South Africa, and other nations all over the world.

At the same time, however, similar calls are also being heard from within our own nation. Americans have an unprecedented opportunity to make a renewed commitment to these fundamental principles. Tocqueville's observations, written more than 160 years ago, provide us with an excellent script. Tocqueville wrote that what he most admired of this fledgling nation, experimenting on a grand scale with democracy, was the "average citizen" and the "small-group leader." He made the profound observation that the "voluntary associations" created by these people can serve as a vital check to the *abuses of power* which are always a threat in a democratic society.

There is an active role for each of us to play as "average citizens." But in order to play these roles effectively—to become "small-group leaders"—we need to acquire more skills, we need to continue as learners, we need to find new ways to adapt to changing conditions, and *we need to act on our commitments*!

Continuing Concerns

1. What specific evidence from current events can you cite that demonstrates *noblesse oblige* activities: that is, the efforts of the more fortunate to help others in need?

2. In your opinion, what is the emerging balance among grassroots organizations, government efforts, and private sector programs in meeting societal needs?

3. What political developments are occurring at national, state, and local levels that will help both society in general and grassroots agencies in particular master the juggling act?

4. What local efforts can you identify that encourage creative grassroots organizations to be developed and supported?

Chapter

2

Toward the Year 2000
Robert Clifton

Be realistic: Attempt the impossible!
—Graffiti written on the walls of the Sorbonne during the student riots in the late 1960s, noted by Mortimer Adler

The word impossible *is a very strong word. When you say, "Impossible!" you ought to say, "relative to my present state of ignorance, it's impossible."*
—Mortimer Adler

Introduction

Toward the year 2000! The historic sweep of the second hand at
11:59 P.M. on December 31, 1999 will represent a great deal more
than simply rolling over three zeros after a two as if we were playing
some cosmic slot machine. That numerical moment will
simultaneously mark the ending and the beginning of a year, a
decade, a century, and a millennium. In addition to all this, that
moment will represent a significant turning point in a critical era
of our history—an era which has, in fact, *already begun*.

Futurist Alvin Tofler has written three insightful volumes that
cover this critical era, beginning in the mid-1950s and extending
to the year 2025. It is a span of time that he refers to as the "hinge
of history." By the time we reach the year 2000, we probably will
have already gained a pretty good insight as to whether we have
adequately prepared ourselves for this historic moment or whether,
as Tofler suggests, "we will find ourselves in the middle of an abrupt
collision with the future being experienced by people totally
unprepared for it."

In his first publication, *Future Shock* (1971), Tofler attempted to
prepare us for the *process* of change. In his second book, *The Third
Wave* (1980), he concentrates on the possible *directions* in which
these processes are taking us. The final volume of this trilogy,
Powershift (1990), focuses on the *control* of changes still to come—
who will shape and direct them, and how.

The Phenomenon of Change

While all three publications cover the same time period, Tofler
writes that "each of the three books uses a different lens with which
to probe beneath the surface of reality . . . ." In each of the books,
however, the central subject is the same—*change*. And for those
wishing to stay ahead of the "change curve," they too must probe
beneath the surface of reality or, perhaps, what *appears* to be
reality. The future success and relevance of any nonprofit program
or agency will depend on the capacity of its director, its staff, and
others to deal with the phenomenon of change—to anticipate
change, to manage change and, at times, to bring about change.
But, how do we do this?

The acceleration of change we are experiencing in the world is
almost beyond one's comprehension. Some analysts say that the

sum total of our knowledge base is already being doubled every eight years. Others argue that the doubling process may be occurring closer to every three or four years. No one disputes the fact that, by any definition, it is at least exponential in its expansion.

In *American Renaissance: Our Life At the Turn of the 21st Century* (1989), authors Marvin Cetron and Owen Davies write, "No matter how old you are in the year 2000, profound *change* will have been written into your life. Do not think for one minute that *change* is not on its way." By whatever measurement, that vast reservoir of knowledge collected over the past five thousand years of recorded history will be nearly imperceptible in its direct impact

From the Directors

I am very fortunate, for I love getting up in the morning and coming to work. Nothing could be more rewarding to me than having social change as my life's work. Others do volunteer/social change work on their own time after finishing their "jobs." My work gives me a chance to express all my interests and commitments; no discontinuity exists.

I am fortunate also in that my graduate degree from Bryn Mawr Graduate School of Social Work and Social Research prepared me in areas including administration, supervision, and planning. The training was invaluable. I believe schools of social work need to prepare more professionals to join our ranks.

Grassroots organizations are forced to spend disproportionate amounts of time on fund-raising, not because of our lack of skills in gaining support, but because of the failure of government at federal, state, and local levels to provide for the social service needs of people and communities. The impact of this failure can't be overrated. We grassroots organization folks need to join hands across the nation by using effective political action to demand the proper levels of governmental support for social needs. How tragic it is when, instead of joining hands in mutual support, we fight among ourselves in a feeding frenzy for dwindling available resources.

—Nancy Langen Steketee, Director
  Center for Responsible Funding (Philadelphia)

fifty years from now. Every nonprofit manager must ponder that fact and what it means to him or her professionally within his or her respective agency or program and perhaps, even more fundamentally, what it means in terms of the day-to-day functioning simply as a human being.

The Bridge Between Optimism and Pessimism

Optimists like John Naisbitt and Peter Drucker call upon us to take advantage of these shifting and unknown winds. Such people admonish us to simply change our perceptions and to view the partially filled glass as half full rather than half empty. Naisbitt refers to the approaching end of the twentieth century as a time between eras. He says, "We are neither here nor there." But he also calls it "a great and yeasty time, filled with opportunity, if we can learn to make uncertainty our friend" (Naisbitt and Aburdene 1990).

No small challenge, of course, as it is that very uncertainty that sometimes seems to paralyze us into inaction. We are much more comfortable when our "truths" are clearly defined and irrevocable. We want our lives and our world to be orderly and predictable and we are disturbed and even angry when they are not. Instead of preparing for that unknown path which lies ahead, it seems so much easier to put it out of mind entirely or at least to worry about it tomorrow.

Those who chastise us for this attitude of indifference are labeled as pessimists or, worse yet, purveyors of doom. The former chief executive of Colorado, Dick Lamm, must now live with his national sobriquet of "Governor Gloom" for his horrific projections of the future described in his book, *Megatraumas* (1985). What is lost in translation, however, whether it is from the dark side of the so-called pessimists or the sanguine view of the optimists, is that we have it within our capacity to largely determine our future for better or for worse. But to do so, we must begin to take action now!

In Rushworth Kidder's book, *An Agenda for the 21st Century*, he interviews twenty-two of the world's great individuals—artists, scientists, political leaders, philosophers—asking each one this fundamental question: What are the major issues that will face humanity in the twenty-first century? Although all of those who were interviewed expressed varying degrees of concern over such common topics as the threat of nuclear war, the population crisis, the destruction of our environment, and the inadequacies of our educational systems, overall, they were generally optimistic in their outlook. They all agreed, however, that such optimism is conditioned by the urgency with which we begin "to alert humanity, to awaken thought, to focus on the central issues" (Kidder 1987).

The Importance of Being Proactive

The question then arises as to what the central issues are and in what manner and to what extent such issues should become the focus of the nonprofit community as well as the rest of the nation. Should the nonprofit sector concentrate its energies on the proclaimed "war on drugs" with former President Bush's promised commitment of $7.5 billion? Or should this vital service sector of our economy somehow join in the recovery process of the scandalous savings and loan debacle which in 1991 dollars was estimated to cost $350 billion or more?

Should the national focus be the immediate battle against the known tragic legacies of alcohol abuse or the less defined but potentially more devastating erosion of the ozone layer? Should we worry about the foreclosure of family farms throughout the country or the greenhouse effect? Should we pay more attention to solid waste or budgetary waste?

As overwhelming as this phenomena of change may seem, it is not at all impossible to cultivate a *proactive* approach in which future events can be planned for and even managed, as opposed to the more prevailing *reactive* response to change. Ironically, the word "proactive" still cannot be found in most dictionaries. Nonetheless, common usage of the word suggests that it is the act of taking the initiative. The root derivations, however, give us a more substantive meaning. Literally, it means taking charge—*being responsible for your actions*. On the other hand, "reactive" suggests just the opposite. We sometimes call this reactive stance "crisis management"—a definition all too familiar in many organizations.

The Paradigm Effect

In order to better prepare ourselves for the unknown events of the future, we first need to have an understanding of *paradigms* and a phenomenon which might be called "the paradigm effect." As used in the context of this discussion on the future, paradigms are simply models or patterns of the various cultures in which we work and live. Such paradigms establish boundaries, provide regulations, determine values and, in short, shape how we think and act. The interrelationship and behavior of your own family are determined by the norms established for that paradigm.

Paradigms also determine the "sanctioned" rules for success—what is right and what is wrong, and what is acceptable and what is not. Further, it is also important to note that the paradigm within which your family operates may not necessarily be consistent with the cultural paradigm of your neighborhood, your place of work, your community, the nation, and even the world.

The properties of a particular paradigm may appear to change as viewed from different perspectives. The essence of Tofler's *The Third Wave*, for example, suggests that the entire history of the world can be viewed from the vantage point of three significant historic periods or paradigms. To do this, however, observers need to distance themselves far enough in time and space so that the world is viewed as one single entity as opposed to the myriad political, geographical, and historical pieces through which we normally see ourselves. In this context, Tofler describes our history—past, present and future—in terms of three giant global waves. Each "wave" or period fits within a large encompassing paradigm which establishes the underlying rules and norms determining behavior.

The first of his metaphorical waves he defines as the agricultural period, which lasted for nearly 10,000 years. Tofler writes that the second wave began less than 200 years ago with the onset of the industrial revolution and that we are just now entering the third of these global paradigms. It is during the second period or wave that Tofler offers us an interesting lesson into the intricacies of understanding the nature of paradigms.

President George Bush, following the United States victory of "Desert Storm" in the Persian Gulf war, talked about "a new world order"—in effect, a new world paradigm. Such a new order, however, was predicated on the assumption that for the past 75 years or so of Tofler's second wave the world has been engaged in some dichotomous struggle between the communists and the capitalists.

Tofler, on the other hand, would argue that if we can distance ourselves far enough from the passions of this period, there is an incredible sameness about these two economic-political-social systems. This is particularly true when we examine the rise of the bureaucracies and the movement toward the specialization of labor and their attendant impacts on the rest of society.

In other words, there is a tendency to describe this past century as a war between two highly different and contradictory paradigms from which the one called capitalism has now emerged the victor and will, therefore, provide us with "a new world order." The danger of that kind of assessment is that it may very well keep one from recognizing the signals (subtle and otherwise) that are already providing us with insights as to what may be the *real* shape and scope of our emerging, global, paradigm.

Paradigm Paralysis

On a more personal level, the lesson to be learned from the larger global example is that we have a natural tendency to filter information and data, both past and present, to fit our own *preconceived notions* of the way we want things to be. When anticipating the future, when preparing for unknown changes, this kind of myopia and subjectivity can be disastrous.

A classic example of such linear thinking is described by the noted "futurist" Joel Barker in his excellent videotape on paradigms. Barker describes a situation in the watchmaking industry to which most people can personally relate. In 1968, the Swiss controlled 65 percent of the world's market in the purchase of watches and 85 percent of the world's profit in this area. Within ten years, however, they were below 10 percent in both areas. What happened was that a major paradigm shift in this industry had occurred—it was called "the quartz movement."

The real irony of this example is that the quartz movement was, in fact, invented by the Swiss themselves in 1967. But they were so confident that no one would buy a watch with no bearings, not even a mainspring, that they didn't even patent their invention. However, two visionary companies did—Texas Instruments and Seiko of Japan—and a major paradigm shift in the watch industry took place.

What took place among the Swiss watchmakers is an example of *paradigm paralysis* and it is essentially brought about by limited imagination or seeing only what one wants to see coupled with a lack of openness to new ideas.

What If?

You may have seen a television commercial by Hewlett-Packard where a young executive is driving somewhere in the middle of a barren, open space and the frown on his face suggests that he is deep in thought. He passes what appears to be a sort of last-chance, broken-down, one-pump filling station. Suddenly, he stomps on the brakes, makes a U-turn, squeals into the station and asks the grizzled old attendant if he has a telephone he can use. The scene then shifts to a Madison Avenue boardroom with the young man saying to an obviously important senior executive, "You know that project we were talking about? Well, I was thinking, *what if . . .*", and the voice trails off.

"What if?" is exactly the question we need to be asking ourselves if we want to avoid paradigm paralysis and to effectively anticipate new paradigm shifts. It is easy to be impressed by the visionary thinking suggested in the commercial and how that same thought process is so important for each of us to cultivate in our own lives.

There is a rather interesting sidebar, however, to the Hewlett-Packard commercial. Many years ago, a young employee actually went to some managers at Hewlett-Packard and said, in effect, "What if?" Even then, HP was one of the giants in the newly developing computer industry. The young employee was a low-level technician working for the company helping to design calculators but was finding the work increasingly boring. So, he went to HP's research and development department and said, "What if?" to a new idea about a radically different use of computers with which he had been experimenting.

The people in research and development, however, quickly rejected his "far out" idea. After all, he was only a minor technician. *He didn't even have an academic degree.* The young man's name was Steve Wozniak and the "what if?" idea was the personal home computer that the world now knows as Apple!

While we can applaud the visionary, risk-taking implication in the Hewlett-Packard commercial, one wonders if the Steve Wozniak vignette had anything to do with the inspiration for that TV advertisement. For the integrity of the commercial (and the company), we can hope it did.

To avoid paradigm paralysis, as well as to anticipate impending paradigm shifts, you have to recognize the boundaries of your current environment and then extend yourself beyond those limits. The people who help create new paradigms are those who can look beyond the center of things and on to the fringes—to the outer edges.

Past Successes No Longer Count

It should also be noted that when a major paradigm shift does occur, past successes mean virtually nothing. It is very easy to see this when considering the historical accomplishments of what were once great civilizations, empires, or nation-states and then to view these same entities following a major paradigm shift, The examples of paradigm paralysis and the inability to anticipate paradigm shifts have occurred throughout history. They range from the decline of the ancient civilization of Mesopotamia to the more recent repudiation of the international structure and dictates of communism.

A paradigm shift that occurs in the culture of your organization's service area can have the same potential impact as that which took place with the decline of the world's great civilizations. Namely, when a paradigm shift occurs, *everyone* goes back to square one. Past successes and achievements of your own organization no longer count. What does count is how well you have anticipated the paradigm shift and whether you can take advantage of the new, emerging norms and rules that will determine the future success of your organization.

Anticipating Paradigm Shifts

The question, of course, is how you can avoid becoming a victim of paradigm paralysis and, at the same time, cultivate those characteristics that will help you anticipate impending paradigm shifts. Both of these aspects of "change" are, in a sense, one in the same—one leads to the other and vice versa.

Fortunately, there are several things *you can do* in order to better anticipate impending paradigm shifts, to manage the changes which have already occurred through paradigm shifts, and to be a part of bringing about paradigm shifts in the future. While these characteristics are easy to intellectualize, they require a conscious commitment to actually put into practice and become a natural part of your own behavioral makeup. Like most areas of self-improvement, the easy part is knowing what to do; the hard part is doing it.

Openness

To start with, it is absolutely essential that you develop a sense of openness. To advocate this characteristic is not to simply suggest that you should become some sort of intellectual vacuum for everything new and different. Openness does require, however, an elimination of prejudices and a careful scrutiny of biases that can sometimes serve as the genesis of ultimate prejudicial behavior. Further, openness does not require an automatic rejection of everything considered truth spelled with a capital "T." But at the same time, it does suggest the cultivation of a healthy and positive skepticism toward all absolutes.

Adaptability

Closely associated with openness is adaptability. The essence of adaptability in this context is to convert apparent adversity into opportunity. Recently, in Denver, a former state legislator who is an African-American announced he was going to run for mayor of that city. Initial polls not only indicated that he couldn't win but that he very likely would not even be considered a major candidate. Early polls put him a distant third and sometimes fourth behind the acknowledged front-runners. To add to his problems, significant financial contributions were virtually nonexistent and even before the primary took place he was unable to buy either TV or radio spots. Further, he did not possess the "charisma" of the front-runner or the old-line connections of the next nearest challenger.

What he did, however, was to turn these negatives into advantages. He began to literally walk the city, eventually traversing more than 300 miles! Each night he stayed in a different home representing every socioeconomic class in the city. Suddenly, he no longer needed paid commercials; his cause was picked up by the press and he started getting more *free* publicity than all the other candidates combined. The average person understood the kind of adversities he was enduring—he was perceived as "one of them."

Capturing 33 percent of the primary vote, he barely edged out one of the front-runners who came in third. But, by the time the general election took place one month later, it wasn't even close and Wellington Webb became the first black mayor to be elected in a major city in this nation without a large black population.

Innovation

In the "brave new world" of change, one must also be an innovator. By this we do not mean blind adventurousness, but rather, a calculated development of new ideas. Innovation requires using both the right side and the left side of the brain, In *Innovation and Entrepreneurship* (1985), Drucker talks about the only thing that he believes successful innovators have in common. He states that "they are *not* 'risk-takers.' They try to define the risks they have to take and to minimize them as much as possible." He goes on to say, "They are successful to the extent to which they systematically analyze the sources of innovative opportunity, then pinpoint the opportunity and exploit it." Drucker adds that innovators "are not 'risk-focused,' they are 'opportunity-focused'" (Drucker 1985).

Perspective

The key to these behavioral changes is perspective. In an absolute quantitative sense, there is no difference whether the glass is half full or half empty. In an attitudinal and perceptual sense, however, the difference is profound. One of the best examples of the power of perception can be found in improvisational comedy. The very essence of this art form is to take the obvious and perceive it differently. To do this, of course, requires the nurturing and development of one's creative and imaginative faculties. Change can certainly be destabilizing and there is a natural fear of the unknown. But, if one continually views all change as threatening and to be avoided at all costs, if the *perception* of anything different is always negative, it will be nearly impossible to become "opportunity-focused."

Faith

There is another characteristic that is very important to cultivate if you are to become a change agent for your organization and in your life. It is the development of a certain faith in other people. If you have had any kind of managerial experience, you have undoubtedly been "burned" by some situation in which you relied on another person. Our normal reactive response to this is to adopt the classic "cover your rear" mentality.

A faith in other people does not necessarily advocate some sort of humanistic philosophy that all people are basically good. Nor does it imply any religious context. What it means, however, is that sometimes it is simply not going to be possible to seize "the opportunity" if you are looking for a guarantee that every person will behave exactly as you expect. As already stated by Drucker, visionary leaders minimize their risks. Nevertheless, there are times when you must act on the basic belief and trust in another human being.

During the harvest season a few years ago, there was a picture in the newspaper of a parade of giant harvest combines making their way to the wheat farms in eastern Colorado. The story below the picture told of the unique trust these dry land wheat farmers and combine operators had with each other. For the most part, the arrangement to harvest the wheat is made at the end of each preceding season and the agreement is often completed with nothing more than a handshake and a casual "see ya next year." Given the enormous financial ramifications of this arrangement combined with the legalistic world in which we now live, this act of simple, basic, faith and trust is rare indeed.

Trend Tracking

Combined with everything else just discussed you have to stay aware of impending changes and, for the most part, this will require disciplining yourself for approximately an hour each day in *what* you read and *how* you read it. By doing this, you can begin to anticipate paradigm shifts by becoming aware of the major trends that are already shaping your future. To do this, you must develop some sort of system to identify and track these potential trends. One of the best such systems to assist you in this regard is described in a book called *Trend Tracking* (1990) by Gerald Celente. You need to read the book (see the bibliography at the end of this text), but briefly summarized the system recommended by Celente contains the following elements.

Selecting Fields.   These are simply the broad topics or areas for classifying information that you want to track, i.e., education, health, family, environment, and so on.

Developing Categories.   Special categories can then be determined within each of the broader fields. The specific categories will tend to develop naturally due to your own professional or personal interest within each field. Celente cautions you, however, not to "ignore trends that look as if they won't affect you. If they're really trends, they will affect you. . . ."

Setting Up Files.   As you develop your categories, set up corresponding files. This does not have to be an elaborate computer system. A desk drawer with hanging folders or those expanding accordion folders work especially well. You simply want something that is easy to store the articles you have read.

Reading Newspapers and Journals.   Celente recommends the daily reading of at least three specific papers. *The New York Times* or its equivalent (i.e., *Washington Post*, *Christian Science Monitor*, *Atlanta Constitution*) should be one of the papers you read daily.

The second paper he suggests is *USA TODAY*. When you read Celente's book, you will discover that the format of *USA TODAY* is especially adaptable to his system. Of course, it is important to also read your local papers as well.

In addition to these three types of newspapers, Celente recommends certain trade or professional journals and also newsletters such as the *Kiplinger Report* or Naisbitt's *Trend Setting*. The key to trend tracking, according to Celente, is the integration of data from many fields of information. Relying on polling, economic forecasting, or political prognosticating alone will likely result in spurious indicators of future trends. Celente's "globalnomics" system, however, is less of an analytic tool and more of a management system that will help you tie together seemingly unrelated fields.

When reading the papers using the globalnomics approach you specifically look for those articles or stories that should be clipped and placed in one of your category files. Celente's criteria for this is to ask the question: "Does it have social, economic, and political significance? If not, skip it."

If the article or story meets the social, economic, and political significance criteria, write the date and the abbreviated initials of the paper above the article along with the category in which it best fits. Then clip it out and file it. The purchase of two specific tools can aid you in using this system. When you read the paper have a "clip-it" handy (can be purchased at any place selling office supplies) and always read the paper with a felt-tip pen in hand. Highlighting key sentences, names, dates, and so on can save you time later when reviewing the information you have collected in your files.

Seeing Trends.   The key to the system outlined by Celente "is making connections between seemingly unrelated fields." A trend according to Celente "is a definite, predictable direction or sequence of events. It follows logically, even inescapably, from causes that usually span a number of fields or disciplines."

It is important to distinguish between a one-time event and a trend. A trend may be developing when you can take several events and begin to tie them together with the test of whether these seemingly unrelated events have social, economic, and political significance.

A classic example of the use of this formula can be seen in the many "separate events" of ethnocentrism taking place all over the world. We read about the calls for separate identity taking place within countries ranging from Canada to the Russian Republics.

But does any one of these events suggest a trend? Celente says you can decide this by asking two questions. "What caused it? What likely effects will it have?" And, he would add, does the "apparent trend have social, economic, and political significance?"

Perhaps to emphasize the point more dramatically, if this call for ethnic separatism is a real trend, could the same thing also take place here in the United States? A number of significant individuals have not only suggested that it could but say that there are early signs that it is already happening.

This summary description of Celente's system of trend tracking should, in no way, substitute for the reading of his book. Not only must you interpret his system for yourself, but the system you eventually develop must work for you.

Summary

In various ways, every author referred to in this chapter emphasizes that the responsibility for change lies within each of us. On the final page of *The Third Wave*, Tofler writes, "We must begin with ourselves, teaching ourselves not to close our minds prematurely to the novel, the surprising, the seemingly radical. This means fighting off the idea-assassins who rush forward to kill any new suggestion on grounds of its impracticality, while defending whatever now exists as practical, no matter how absurd, oppressive, or unworkable it may be" (Tofler 1980).

The importance of attitude change in positively anticipating the future is well illustrated by Stephen Covey in *The 7 Habits of Highly Effective People* (1989). It is fitting that this chapter closes with four related thoughts from his book:

> What matters most is how we *respond* to what we experience in life.

> Difficult circumstances often create paradigm shifts, whole new frames of reference by which people see the world and themselves and others in it, and what life is asking of them. Their larger perspective reflects the attitudinal values that lift and inspire us all.

> Taking initiative does not mean being pushy, obnoxious, or aggressive. It does mean recognizing our responsibility to make things happen.

> Whenever someone in our family, even one of the younger children, takes an irresponsible position and waits for someone else to make things happen or provide a solution, we tell them,

"Use your R and I!" (resourcefulness and initiative). In fact, often before we can say it, they answer their own complaints, "I know—use my R and I!" (Covey 1989).

Of course, there will be many who will tell you that such approaches are idealistic and that your creative vision of "what if?" is simply impossible. When this happens, try to recall the Adler quote given at the beginning of this chapter: "The word *impossible* is a very strong word. When you say, 'Impossible!' you ought to say, 'relative to my present state of ignorance, it's impossible.'"

Finally, to those who say it can't be done, please get out of the way *of those who are doing it*!

Continuing Concerns

1. What are three behavioral changes you might make in order to avoid falling victim to paradigm paralysis?
2. Design a simple yet effective process that might be used to encourage openness and innovation in both policy and programming in a grassroots organization.
3. How might you encourage yourself and others in a grassroots organization to use your "R and I"?
4. Describe what you consider to be a trend that may signal a new service-delivery paradigm is replacing an old one in meeting human needs in your local area.

Chapter

3

The "Culture" of the Nonprofit Organization

Wendy S. Green

> . . . there is a possibility—underemphasized in leadership research—that the only thing of real importance that leaders do is to create and manage culture . . .
> — E. Schein

Wendy S. Green, MPA, is a former Director for the Western Institute for Police Administration. She currently manages the decision-making process in controversial programs for an environmental consulting firm.

Introduction

Organizations often use charts and diagrams of what they "do" to explain themselves to outsiders. Unfortunately, such schematic explanations of the formal structure generally offer very little insight into what really makes them tick. This chapter will focus on a relatively new concept—organizational culture—which can provide valuable information about an organization that cannot be gleaned in the more traditional ways. Examination of an organization's culture can tell us quite a bit about what is really valued by its people and what really goes on inside it.

An organization's culture can have a tremendous impact on its ability (or inability) to achieve its goals! Strong, healthy cultures can be created and managed to maximize the use of an organization's limited resources in pursuit of its mission. Conversely, weak or dysfunctional cultures can greatly hinder an organization's ability to operate, resulting in wasted resources, demoralized staff, and an inability to achieve its goals. This chapter will provide an introduction to the concept of organizational culture and will discuss tools that can be used to examine, diagnose, and manage the culture of your nonprofit organization.

What Is Culture?

When we hear the word "culture," we often think of the visible characteristics of groups of people which distinguish them from other groups. We think of the lilting sound of Peruvian flutes, of Scottish plaid kilts, colorful African tribal art, and intricate Chinese paper-cuts. Curiously, the culture of a defined group can be practically invisible to its members, yet clearly distinguishable to outsiders looking in. Indeed, we often do not realize the uniqueness of our own cultural practices until outsiders point them out to us or until we observe others with very different ways of doing things.

We learn about our cultures within the context of our families, neighborhoods, organizational affiliations, and places of worship. In addition to learning such cultural traits as what to wear, eat, and celebrate, we also learn the meaning of birth and life, how to honor the dead, and how we should relate to each other. In sum, culture is a collection of behaviors and of interpretations that hold together social units.

Applying Cultural Concepts to Organizations

Like all other social units, all organizations (big and small) have cultures. *Organizational culture* can be defined as the patterns of values and assumptions that affect how people interpret events and how they behave relative to those events. The theory surrounding organizational culture is based on a series of assumptions about the nature of organizations:

1. What is most important about any event is *not* what happened but *what it means*.

2. The meaning of an event is determined not simply by what happened but by the ways people *interpret what happened*. In fact, the same event may have very different meanings for different individuals.

From the Directors

The mission of the Exchange is basically to connect children who are waiting to be adopted with people who want to adopt them.

Once we were in place, our biggest challenge was to not grow too fast. After our first big telethon, we had people standing in the hallway the next day. I couldn't believe it. We quickly learned the importance of long-range planning and it has been a critical part of our program strategy ever since.

Sometimes a director can be so important in the early developmental stages of a program or an agency that the people begin to identify the successes only with that person. But leadership is also knowing when to let go. It's so important that the staff, the board, and the volunteers are given the opportunity to become truly vested with the dream.

—Dr. Dixie Davis, Executive Director
  Rocky Mountain Adoption Exchange (Denver)

3. Much of what happens within organizations is ambiguous or uncertain. It is, therefore, difficult or impossible to know what happened, why it happened, or what will happen next.
4. Such ambiguity and uncertainty make rational approaches to analysis, problem solving, and decision making very difficult.
5. When faced with uncertainty and ambiguity, *humans create symbolic ways to interpret what is happening* in order to reduce ambiguity, resolve confusion, increase predictability, and provide direction. Even when the events remain illogical, random, fluid, or meaningless, the created realities (which comprise the culture) make them seem otherwise.
6. Because events do not have intrinsic meanings in and of themselves, such meanings are *created and learned* within a social context. Many organizational events are more important for what they express than for what they produce (Bolman and Deal 1991).

As a result, the people within an organization develop a series of symbolic understandings that comprise the organization's culture. Newcomers to an organization may find it difficult or even impossible to sort out the ambiguity which surrounds much of organizational life until they develop an understanding of the shared cultural interpretations. The culture of an organization enables people to interpret events more easily, resulting in behavior that is more rational and predictable.

Work groups within a single agency can also develop their own subcultures, resulting in multilayered cultures all within one organization. Likewise, an organization's culture may reflect its developmental stage. For example, young organizations often have very fluid cultures as the individuals in them are still coming to consensus about how to interpret events. Organizations that have been around longer generally have more entrenched cultures that can be resistant to change. Even developed cultures may experience profound changes under new leadership or following a period of major reorganization.

It has been said that "culture is to the organization what personality is to the individual—a hidden, yet unifying theme that provides meaning, direction, and mobilization" (Kilman et al. 1985). Culture, therefore, will likely guide and inspire individual behavior much more effectively than formal rules and regulations, structured authority, and prescribed rationality. In effect, *it is the organizational culture that provides the energy that motivates and provides direction to people within organizations*!

Components of Organizational Culture

Organizational culture is more easily understood when divided into three levels. Level One is composed of the visible artifacts of the culture. (The term "artifacts" has been borrowed by those discussing organizational culture from cultural anthropologists. Artifacts are the creations that are the products of social units.) Level Two is comprised of the organization's values. Level Three is composed of basic underlying assumptions. The next three sections of this chapter will take a closer look at each of these levels.

Level One: Artifacts

The artifacts of an organization's culture are the creations (activities, behaviors, events) which comprise the most visible level of that culture. Outsiders can often see this level of an organization's culture quite clearly, while those inside the organization may be less aware of their own cultural artifacts. However, outsiders are unlikely to be able to understand what the artifacts really mean. Level One cultural artifacts include the following.

Heroes.   These are the central figures within the organization's culture. In small nonprofits, a hero is likely to be the founder of the organization. However, a hero can also be that person who sets the standards of service within the organization, or perhaps someone who is well known for expert handling of the press or organizational critics.

Priests.   These individuals act as caretakers for the organization's rites, rituals, and ceremonies. They take responsibility for and assume a central role in performing prescribed activities. They ensure that there are no deviations from standard practices such as recognition of staff and others, proper acknowledgment of political and financial support, and continuity to special events like staff retreats or promotions.

Storytellers.   The individuals within an organization who retell the myths and repeat the shared history of the organization are known as storytellers. They are frequently the experts on the "way things are done around here" and can tell you how current practices came to be and offer justifications as to why those particular practices are superior to other ways of doing things. The individuals who act as storytellers may act in the roles of priest and hero as well, particularly in small or new organizations.

Myths.   These are the traditional and legendary stories that convey the past history of the organization. Such stories may be factual or they may be embellished versions of history. For example, one nonprofit organization shows newcomers a video about the founding of the organization that glorifies the dedication of the founder and the importance of the mission for the organization. Cultural heroes often play a central role in the myths of an organization and the myths are usually perpetuated by the storytellers.

Uniforms and Language.   Such artifacts can play an important role in defining membership in the culture. Uniforms may be as simple as clothing of a special color, as subtle as norms about casual or business attire, or as official and identifiable as complete uniforms. More importantly, they serve to identify who belongs to the group. Similarly, slogans, acronyms, jargon, and special meanings for words enable members to communicate in ways that can only be completely understood by insiders. Both uniforms and language provide group cohesion and a sense of belonging to something special and unique.

Celebrations and Ceremonies.   These are the special, even sacred rites and observances that follow prescribed forms. They can include such activities as the indoctrination of new employees, annual picnics, and retirement parties. For example, one small nonprofit organization celebrates completion of each year's budget preparation with a potluck dinner at the home of a board member.

Rites.   Rites are the more mundane, yet prescribed, occurrences that occur with some regularity. They generally conform to set patterns of *ritualistic behavior*. They may take the form of everyday coffee breaks, weekly staff meetings, or periodic in-service training programs. Rites also include ritualized management practices and responses to events.

Behavioral Norms and Standards.   Also included as Level One cultural artifacts are behavioral norms and standards. Examination of norms and standards for performance can provide valuable insight into what is valued by the organization. Norms and standards can be very resistant to change, even when explicit policy statements are made to the contrary.

Other cultural artifacts include humor (what the individuals within an organization find to be funny), communication patterns, the distribution of power, and standardized ways for handling problems and conflicts. One final aspect focuses on who gets ahead in the organization (and who doesn't) and how such achievers are rewarded (or conversely, how misfits are punished).

Level Two: Values

The second level of culture includes the values that are shared by members of the culture. Such values come to be shared by the members of an organization as they collectively deal with organizational problems. As Schein explains:

> Someone in the group, usually the founder, has convictions about the nature of reality and how to deal with it, and will propose a solution based upon those convictions. That individual may regard the proposed solution as a belief or principle based on facts, but the group cannot feel that same degree of conviction until it has collectively shared in successful problem solution (1987:390).

When a suggested solution to an organizational problem works and the group experiences a shared sense of success, the group will likely adopt it as a value. When the value continues to provide the group with effective solutions to their problems, the stated value begins a process of what is called by the academics "cognitive transformation." If the application of the value continues to be effective, it then becomes a Level Three basic underlying assumption for the organization. However, the solution must continue to work in order for the transformation to ultimately become complete. If the solution does not work reliably, it may still continue to function as a value, but at the second level of the organization's culture.

Whether or not a value becomes a Level Three assumption is not a reflection on how important it is to the leader or founder. Indeed, Schein argued, some organizational values remain conscious and explicitly stated because they provide normative or moral aspirations for the group. Such Level Two values may continue to provide guidance for individuals in dealing with new, uncontrollable, or ambiguous situations affecting the organization. In this way, Level Two values can also help predict or explain group or individual behavior.

Values that have not proven dependable or useful during shared learning experiences may become what Argyris and Schön (1974) called "espoused values," which predict only what people will say, but not what they will do. The result is behavior that is inconsistent with the stated values of the organization. Needless to say, such inconsistencies may hinder an organization's ability to effectively fulfill its mission and goals.

Level Three: Basic Underlying Assumptions

According to Schein, the testing of an organization's value against reality (observing if the solution continues to work in a variety of circumstances) is necessary for a value to become a basic underlying assumption. When solutions to problems work reliably and repeatedly, they then come to be taken for granted by the organization (Schein 1987:391).

Once a value has become a basic underlying assumption, there is usually very little variation within the group in the way the concept is viewed. The assumptions may be about the nature of the organization and its services or the nature of its relationship to the people outside the organization. The basic underlying assumptions, therefore, comprise the group's shared perception of reality at the unconscious level.

Such assumptions can have a tremendous impact on the organization. For example, if an underlying assumption holds that staff will not do anything unless they are specifically asked to, the management philosophy will be quite different than if it is believed that people will make their greatest contribution in an environment of minimal oversight and direction. Likewise, basic underlying assumptions can impact on how organizations treat their clientele. For example, an organization that operates on an assumption that homeless people are helpless will treat its clients quite differently than an organization that assumes its clients can learn to help themselves.

Basic underlying assumptions can be difficult to isolate and identify because they are frequently so universally accepted that their existence may not even be acknowledged by individuals within the organization. Schein asserts that good detective work and commitment are required for identifying underlying assumptions, not because "people are reluctant to surface their assumptions, but because they are so taken for granted. Yet when we do surface them, the cultural pattern suddenly clarifies and we begin to feel we really understand what is going on and why" (Schein 1987:393). Interviews with staff may prove illuminating in identifying the basic underlying assumptions.

Examining Your Organization's Culture

Examination of one's own culture can be quite difficult as proximity colors our ability to see our own organizations. Outside consultants, however, have a different problem in that they may need help deciphering the meaning of specific cultural components. This section offers suggestions to insiders who hope to examine an organization's culture.

   In order to identify the cultural components within your own nonprofit organization, consider the following questions:

1. First, consider the artifacts that express your organization's culture.

   a. *Heroes, priests, and storytellers*: Who do you look up to as your heroes? Who conducts your special ceremonies? Who repeats your stories to your newcomers?

   b. *Myths, history, and tradition*: How is the past expressed in the present? How do you teach your traditions to your new hires?

   c. *Language and appearance*: How do you communicate with each other? What words have special meanings for you? How do you appear, to yourselves and to outsiders?

   d. *Celebrations, ceremonies, rites, and rituals*: What activities do you do repeatedly? What do you celebrate? How do you behave when you attend your ceremonial events?

   e. *Norms and standards*: What are the "shoulds" and "oughts" that tell you how to behave? How do newcomers learn what is expected of them?

   f. *Punishments and rewards*: Who gets ahead in your organization (achievers) and what is it that they do right? Who is not successful (misfits) and what have they done wrong? How do you reward your achievers and punish your misfits?

2. Look a little deeper at the cultural artifacts of your organization. What do your artifacts *mean* and what values do they express? Do these reflect what is of *real* importance in your organization? Do you have values that serve only normative purposes? Do you have espoused values that are not predictive of actual behavior? Why aren't such espoused values consistent with actual behavior?

3. What basic underlying assumptions comprise the shared perception of reality for your organization? Such assumptions might focus on the nature of the organization, how it delivers its services, and the nature of the organization's relationship with its physical and social environment. What does your organization assume about how people act, what they care about, what they believe in, and what they need?

As was mentioned earlier, it can be very difficult to "see" the culture of your own organization. You may find it helpful to ask board members, clients, volunteers, staff, and other professionals who work with your organization for help in answering those questions.

Diagnosing Organizational Cultures

After examining your culture, how can you determine whether it is healthy or not? This section will provide some guidance for diagnosing cultures, identifying healthy aspects, and finding potential problems. Examination of the existing culture is likely to reveal some strong or healthy aspects as well as other characteristics which are less beneficial to the effective operation of the agency.

Oftentimes an insider can get meaningful information about the health of a culture *if* that person can remain objective. Deal and Kennedy, in their excellent book, *Corporate Cultures: The Rites and Rituals of Corporate Life*, assert that in order to be an observer of your own culture, "you must avoid making value judgments about what is important and what is not. Just observe what is — not what you think should be — and remember that the patterns are subtle" (1982:134).

Deal and Kennedy outline the following steps for diagnosing organizational cultures. Although they focus on the private corporate world, the guidelines can be equally helpful for small, non-profit organizations as well.

1. Study your physical setting. The setting that an organization provides for its employees says a lot about how the organization feels about its people. Be particularly concerned if you find that different classes of employees face physical settings of different qualities.
2. Read promotional brochures and other literature put out by your organization to see what it says about you to outsiders.
3. Look at how your organization treats outsiders, particularly clients and strangers. How does the reception area "feel"?
4. Interview people who work or volunteer for the organization. Ask questions about their perceptions of the history of the organization, why it is successful or important, what kind of people work for it, and what it feels like to work for the organization.

5. Find out how other staff and volunteers spend their time. People tend to spend more time on those activities they feel are most important. Comparing what people say they do with how they really spend their time can provide insight into whether a culture is cohesive or fragmented (1982:129-33).

Other questions Deal and Kennedy recommend asking are: Does the culture reward the "correct" values—according to the espoused values of the organization? How long do people stay with the organization, and why do they leave? What is being discussed or written about the organization? And finally, what passes through the cultural network (or informal lines of communication)? What stories and anecdotes get repeated, and what do they mean? (Deal and Kennedy 1982:133-35)

Healthy Versus Dysfunctional Cultures

An organization's culture should, at the very least, not contradict fulfillment of the organization's mission. Ideally, it should nurture the organization, support the organizational mission and goals, and allow it to make the most of its resources. Once you have examined your organization's culture, how can you determine if it is healthy?

Components of healthy cultures include widely-shared philosophies and a perception that people (including staff, clients, and volunteers) are the organization's greatest asset. Also important is a widespread endorsement of the cultural heroes, rituals, and ceremonies that support the organization's mission.

Conversely, problems to watch for include a lack of clear values related to how best to do the job, contradictory values, heroes that are destructive or disruptive, and rituals that are disorganized or contradictory to the goals and mission of the organization (Deal and Kennedy 1982:135-36).

Other, even more important cultural problems to watch for include:

1. An *inward focus* that ignores the "real" world. Particularly dysfunctional cultures emphasize such things as pleasing the boss, the board of directors, or coworkers instead of customers or clients.
2. A *short-term focus* that highlights the present but fails to consider strategic goals and long-term organizational survival.

3. *Morale problems*, especially chronic problems, can be indicated by pervasive unhappiness and rapid or unnecessary turnover.
4. *Fragmentation or inconsistency* of the culture within an organization might indicate that the organization is at odds with itself. All parts of a healthy organization should share not just artifacts, but also values and underlying assumptions. It may take careful analysis, however, to determine if differences within an organization are healthy or threatening to the organization (Deal and Kennedy 1982:136-39).

Managing the Existing Culture of Your Organization

A primary task of leadership involves the management of culture. As might be guessed, the first step in managing culture is to examine and diagnose the culture as it currently exists. The next step involves discussing and conceptualizing of a healthier or more effective culture, within the realm of what is actually possible. Obviously, the focus should be on reinforcing the favorable components while doing what is possible to minimize any negative cultural components or impacts of the culture.

An example of how positive aspects of the culture can be reinforced might involve looking at how valued employees are rewarded. In small nonprofit organizations people are rarely well paid. If the organization already has a periodic awards ceremony that recognizes people for their contributions, make sure that the event is *very special* by ensuring that the staff who receive recognition feel genuinely rewarded for their efforts. Such efforts can help valued individuals feel appreciated even when resources are not available for more tangible rewards.

Likewise, negative sides of the culture can be minimized over time once they have been identified and strategies have been developed and implemented to alter their impact. For example, rearranging offices may cut down on communication between two individuals who have a negative influence on each other. Similarly, training programs can focus on changing behaviors that contradict organizational values by teaching or reinforcing more appropriate behaviors.

In order to minimize the impacts of staff turnover on the existing culture, hiring practices should incorporate two-way communication about the more important values within the organization's culture. Care must be taken during interviews to learn if prospective employees or volunteers can understand, appreciate, and support that culture. As a result, the manager or leader can at least avoid hiring people who espouse values that are inconsistent with the organization's culture. More comprehensive training, designed to help new employees understand the organization's culture, should be a part of the orientation program for all new employees and volunteers.

It is crucial when developing a strategy for managing culture to examine each of the stated values of the organization and determine if they have been truly incorporated into the operational value system of the organization. If you really do feel that new, creative ideas are important to the survival of the organization, but staff have learned that their ideas are rarely heard, a serious look should be given at how this *espoused* value can be converted into a true value or even an underlying assumption. Alternatively, in-service training can be designed to reinforce the organization's values and underlying assumptions and might prove useful if older employees don't have a clear understanding of the existing culture.

Remember that positive values are learned within organizations when solutions to organizational problems work reliably and successfully over a period of time. It may be that there are obstacles hindering the effective solution of a problem even when people are responding as positively as possible. The bottom line is that in order for people to learn new behaviors, or to change old behaviors, each person must feel that he or she has a vested interest in making such a change. That vested interest can be as tangible as money or as intrinsic and simple as satisfaction.

As a director or leader, you should become an expert on the existing culture of your organization. Focus on how you really want it to be, and work towards achieving that vision. Also, in seeking to better manage your organization's culture, consider the following questions: What can *you* do to support the healthy cultural aspects? And what can *you* do to minimize the negative impacts of the existing culture?

Making Significant Changes in the Organizational Culture

It is important to point out that most writers in the field of organizational culture are very hesitant to make suggestions as to how managers or directors can make deliberate attempts to bring about large-scale changes in an agency's culture. That hesitancy is better understood after returning to the definition of organizational culture given earlier: the patterns of values and assumptions that affect how people interpret events and how they behave relative to those events. Large-scale change to the organizational culture must therefore affect the values and basic underlying assumptions that are shared by its members. Unfortunately, when a leader attempts to change the shared meaning within the organization, it may prove very difficult to control the process and to predict what new assumptions will be adopted to replace the old ones. As Schein says, "The desire to change culture may become tantamount to destroying the group and creating a new one, which will build or evolve a new one" (1987:383).

Deal and Kennedy share Schein's view. They suggest that deliberate, large-scale change should be considered only in four circumstances that might be faced by small, nonprofit organizations: 1) when the organization's environment is undergoing fundamental changes, 2) when the organization faces stiff competition for its goods or services from other providers, 3) when the organizations's performance is mediocre, or worse, or 4) when the organization is growing rapidly (1982:161). The important thing to note is that all four situations result from a significant change in the "fit" between the organization and its environment. *Short of one or more of these circumstances being present, large-scale organizational change should not be attempted.*

If it has been determined that change is in fact needed, Deal and Kennedy offer the following suggestions:

1. Allow sufficient time for the changes to happen naturally.
2. Position an existing cultural hero in charge of the change process.
3. Develop rituals that measure and celebrate progress during the change process.
4. Provide relevant training to support new, desired behaviors.
5. Use existing peer groups to influence acceptance of the suggested changes.
6. Create an environment of security. Change is frightening to individuals. Maintain the status quo in as many areas as possible.
7. Convey two-way trust in all communication related to the changes to be undertaken.
8. Take advantage of the declining fit with the environment (1982:164-69, 175-76).

Remember that change is only necessary and recommended when the fit between the organization and its environment poses a significant threat to the organization. Make sure that all individuals acknowledge the threat and support the strategies for change that have been chosen to counteract it.

Summary

Schein concluded that the effective management of organizational culture is the essence of leadership within the organization:

> [O]ne of the most decisive functions of leadership may well be the creation, the management, and . . . the destruction of culture. Culture and leadership, when one examines them closely, are two sides of the same coin, and neither can really be understood by itself. In fact, there is a possibility — underemphasized in leadership research — that the only thing of real importance that leaders do is to create and manage culture . . . (1987:381).

The study of your organization's culture can be fascinating. However, the potential for misinterpretation and the threat of botched change should leave you with a healthy respect for existing cultures. Further reading is recommended before any major changes are attempted (see Annotated Bibliography at the end of this book).

Continuing Concerns

1. Propose a specific process by which members of your grassroots organization can become more aware of possible differences between their espoused values and actual behavior; between theory and practice.
2. Analyze print or electronic media statements describing a selected organization in terms of artifacts: Heroes, Priests, Storytellers, Myths, Uniforms and Language, Celebrations and Ceremonies, Rites, and Behavioral Norms.
3. Why is it that effective leaders need to be experts on their organizations's culture and that, even if they are, attempts to orchestrate changes in that culture are fraught with difficulty?

Chapter

4

The Operational Life Cycle

Cheryl Simrell King

> . . . In another moment down went Alice after it, never once considering how in the world she was to get out again. The rabbit-hole went straight on like a tunnel for some way, and then dipped suddenly down, so suddenly that Alice had not a moment to think about stopping herself before she found herself falling down a very deep well. Either the well was very deep, or she fell very slowly, for she had plenty of time as she went down to look about her, and to wonder what was going to happen next.
>
> —Lewis Carroll, *Alice in Wonderland*

Cheryl Simrell King, Ph.D., has extensive experience in strategic planning and program evaluation. Currently a faculty member in the Graduate Program in Public Administration at The Evergreen State College, she has worked as researcher and as a consultant to public as well as private, nonprofit agencies.

Introduction

Running a small, community-based nonprofit organization can be very much like Alice's fall down the deep well if you do not know where you are going. Without plans and objectives, one can have plenty of time to look around while falling and to wonder what will happen next. Without long-range plans, you may find yourself at the bottom of the well, forced to drink from small bottles to make the organization larger or smaller, depending on the needs of your clients and stakeholders. Planning, setting objectives, and evaluating your program relevant to its objectives can keep you from falling without any clue as to where you are going.

Preparing and implementing strategic plans that are needs-based, client-conscious, and that lead to goals and objectives will help ensure that you have done what is necessary to plan for the future of the organization. Evaluating the effectiveness of your organization will allow you to determine what works and what doesn't, thus affording you an opportunity to modify your plans and objectives. Today, most programs will not be funded without some evaluation process built into the initial plans.

In the past, program evaluation has been a mystifying concept—conjuring up images of complicated scientific studies. Yet, program evaluation can be performed by a trained agency director with the assistance (if needed) of an outside consultant. Output from the evaluation can be transferred back into the planning process and can be shared with funding sources to demonstrate the need for continued program funding. Neither planning, objective setting, nor evaluation should be done in the absence of the others. This chapter addresses these three areas and illustrates how each complements the others.

The Need for a Strategic Plan

To borrow a frequently repeated phrase from Lewis Carroll's *Alice in Wonderland*, "If you don't know where you are going, any road will get you there." Strategic planning allows organizations to determine where they would like to be in the near and long-term future and to choose the right roads for getting there.

Perhaps you are asking yourself, "Is a strategic planning process really different from a regular planning process? Am I not involved in planning every time I plan to hire a new person or plan to relocate my office staff?" In order to run your organization smoothly, you *do* need to plan your resource needs, staffing, client services and fund-raisers. In fact, this type of planning goes on virtually every day. This everyday planning is planning at the *operational* level. In other words, operational planning deals with the day-to-day operation of your organization. Without operational planning, your organization would not survive. *Strategic* planning, on the other hand, focuses on the global level: on the mission of your organization, the goals and objectives of the organization, and the action plans to ensure that the goals and objectives will be accomplished.

Recently, a nonprofit organization approached a university-based consulting group to ask for advice regarding fund-raising and development. The nonprofit was a small operation that focused on providing opportunities for recovering mental health patients that would help them succeed in the world outside of the institution. The organization was funded by a modest, three-year federal grant and was in its second year of operation. Realizing that federal funds might not be renewed at the current level, the director was interested in uncovering other funding sources to ensure that the organization could continue.

From the Directors

We are an umbrella agency, a federation of 24 nonprofit social change organizations representing an alternative to the United Way, with growth of 25 percent to 35 percent each year. We have gone from nothing to raising over $300,000 through workplace campaigns last autumn alone. What a juggling act trying to balance a small staff that is being drained of energy in the midst of furious activity! I need to constantly remind myself and my colleagues, "It's working." "Workplaces are expanding their campaigns." "The activity is paying off." "Monies are flowing to organizations working for social and economic justice."

—Deb Furry, Executive Director
Community Works (Boston)

In the initial interview it was revealed that the organization did not have a strategic plan. It had a general goal of funding a certain number of start-up operations a year, but had no idea of what the future held, what the overall organizational mission was, and what action plans would be needed to accomplish its goals. The only thing that was known was the fact that they did not want the organization to go belly-up.

Any credible funder will ask for detailed strategic plans before they make a decision to invest or give money to an organization. Investors and funders want to know where the organization is going, how it plans to get there, and what criteria it will use to measure its success. In order to ensure that their money is used wisely and that the expected results will be achieved, they want a blueprint of what the organization is going to do. This blueprint is the strategic plan.

In the private sector, banks and other lending institutions ask for detailed business plans from any start-up company requesting funds or seed-money. Included in a business plan are the mission and goals of the new company, the strategies that will be employed to achieve these goals, and the elements that will be used to measure success (these are usually profitability measures over a five- to ten-year time frame). Organizations in the public or not-for-profit sector also must develop business plans in the form of strategic plans. These plans drive the daily operations of the organization and, equally important, ensure that the organization continually keeps focused on its mission and purpose.

The consultants involved with the organization described earlier recommended that the agency develop an overall strategic plan *before* concentrating on a fund-raising plan. The strategic plan would naturally lead to a developmental plan indicating which foundations and populations to target and what fund-raising activities to pursue. The strategic plan would also include time-frames within which the development activities must be accomplished. In short, the strategic plan would tell the organization which road to take to arrive at its desired goals. Organizations with strategic plans *do* know where they are going and, therefore, can choose the best route for getting there.

Who Should Be Involved in the Initial Strategic Planning Session?

A word of advice about the initial strategic planning session. Having too many people initially involved in the development of the strategic plan can be difficult and time consuming. At the same time, however, involving your board, key employees, and other selected stakeholders early in the planning process may help ensure acceptance of the plan by these people. Although this will require more time invested up front, the time will be more than made up during implementation if all stakeholders are positioned to be behind the plan and, therefore, not sabotaging the efforts.

It is also helpful to hold your initial planning session in a retreat format if at all possible. This will allow the people involved to be removed from the normal distractions of the workplace or the workday. Strategic planning sessions are best done on the weekend in a setting outside of the city or town where you live. Of course, if such sessions can be held during the work week, there is an added inducement. However, this may not be possible due to cost. Either way, this change in setting often relaxes participants and allows them to think more creatively than they would in an office conference room.

A final word of advice. This initial step will go more smoothly if you have a third party facilitate your strategic planning session. This third party could be a professional facilitator or simply an uninvolved person from the outside who is trained in the strategic planning process. The facilitator's role is to ensure that the participants stay on-task and that the agreed upon ground rules are adhered to throughout the process.

The Elements of a Strategic Planning Process Defined

Essentially a strategic plan involves scanning the organization's environment, developing a vision or mission statement, defining strategic goal areas, setting strategic objectives, outlining action plans to achieve the goals, and evaluating the action plans. The output of the evaluation then feeds back into the planning process as illustrated in Figure 4.1.

Conducting an Environmental Scan

The environmental scan is your opportunity to get input from all key stakeholders, clients, and other interested parties. It is the research or information-gathering part of the strategic planning process. The environmental scan is the first step in a strategic planning process and should be done *before* the initial planning session takes place.

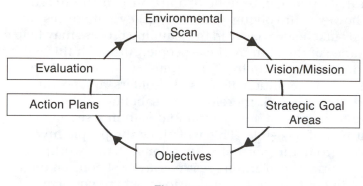

Figure 4.1
Strategic Planning Process

The goal of the environmental scan is to define the current strengths and weaknesses of the organization, to suggest what should be changed or modified, to suggest the broad topic areas upon which the organization should focus, and to identify the opportunities and/or threats inherent in the future. This analysis is called a SWOT analysis—strengths, weaknesses, opportunities and threats. As much as possible, personal interviews should be conducted with all key stakeholders using the SWOT model. Results should then be compiled and presented to the strategic planning team at the beginning of the initial strategic planning session.

The first step in the environmental scan is to define the people who are important to the success of your organization, i.e., those people who have a "stake" in the future of the organization. Primarily, you are looking for individuals other than the organization's staff. Such people would include key stakeholders, clients, and other interested parties.

Key Stakeholders.   Stakeholders are defined as those people who have an interest in your organization, have a "stake" in the organization's future, and who could exert influence upon your future (either positive or negative). Some stakeholders may be considered friends to your organization, but not all will be. It is crucial that you get input from key stakeholders because of their *potential influence* upon your organization. The environmental scan allows them to be part of the strategic planning process, which will help ensure their acceptance later when the plan is implemented. Examples of stakeholders include, but are not limited to: funders, political leaders, constituents, and directors of other organizations related to your mission. Your board of directors may also be included in this group but should be included with discretion. Sometimes board members, as well as staff, will have difficulty "seeing the forest because of the trees." You want to ensure candor and objectivity as much as possible in implementing your environmental scan.

Clients. Clients are any group of people who are impacted or affected by your organization. In your agency, the clients may be the people directly being served as well as other organizations that assist your agency in serving these people (referral organizations, other service organizations, etc.). The important thing is to be sure that you include all of your client groups, direct or indirect, in the environmental scan.

Other Interested Parties. There may be other individuals or organizations who are interested in the future of your organization or may be able to provide helpful input into your strategic planning process. These individuals or groups may include experts in the field, competing organizations, academicians, or others.

It is sometimes helpful to ask yourself the following questions in identifying stakeholders, clients, and other interested parties:

- Who has the relevant expertise?
- Who will be directly or indirectly crucial to the successful implementation of the plan?
- Who will be affected by the plan?
- Are all possible viewpoints represented?

For example, a comprehensive strategic plan was conducted for a coalition of small communities in a rural resort area. A leadership forum was convened to conduct the strategic planning process. This leadership forum included all of the key business, municipal and county leaders in the five counties involved in the coalition.

The forum identified approximately 50 key stakeholders, clients, and other interested parties to be included in the environmental scan. This is an extremely large number of people to be interviewed; chances are you will have significantly fewer. The list ranged from a prominent rancher to the head of a local Chamber of Commerce, from the local leader of the American Association for Retired Persons to the director of the top day-care provider in one of the counties. In short, the list included all people who should be heard from in the environmental scan, but who would not necessarily be *directly involved* in the actual development of the strategic plan.

Defining the Mission/Vision of the Organization

Perhaps the most difficult part of the strategic planning process is defining the mission/vision of the organization. The mission and/or vision is the overall, global purpose of the organization. In several short sentences, it defines the reason for the organization's existence. It does not define the specific goals that an organization will pursue in order to achieve the mission, nor does it define how an organization will measure its success. It simply defines the general mission or purpose of an organization. And, as would be expected, this statement serves to drive the final development and implementation of the entire strategic plan.

Almost all organizations have a mission. Many times, if an organization has not completed a strategic plan, that mission is considered to be simply understood. When a mission is formalized, however, it provides the foundation for everything that an organization does. It is important that all staff members be able to state, in their own terms, the mission of the organization. When everyone directly involved with the organization can identify with its mission or vision, it becomes a relatively easy process to evaluate individual action and behavior as well as specific program direction and implementation.

Clearly, however, such acceptance of purpose and direction can only be obtained if there is a real opportunity for both the actual development and, most importantly, eventual acceptance of the mission or vision statement by everyone directly related to the organization. This does not mean that everyone can or even should be involved in the initial strategic planning session where the first development of the mission/vision statement takes place. It does mean, however, that final adoption of such a statement should only take place after everyone in the organization has been able to offer input and can cultivate a personal understanding and acceptance.

The actual development of the mission or vision statement should be viewed as an early opportunity to gain a conceptual consensus on the functioning and future directions of the organization. From the comments and information gained from the environmental scan, you will have acquired a great deal of insight into the activities and functions of the organization that must be seriously considered in developing your statement.

What is most important at this point, however, is that current expectations be positively integrated with a long-term vision of ten or twenty years from the present. This is often where it becomes important to use an outside facilitator—someone who can encourage those involved to stretch their imagination in order to anticipate and to help plan and direct future changes. It is common to spend a significant first part of your initial strategic planning session focusing on developing this mission or vision. While it can be a long and, at times, frustrating ordeal, the final product is invaluable in the long run.

For small organizations, this process will no doubt seem both reasonable and plausible to bring about. Some surely will argue, however, that this total empowerment is really not possible in larger and more complex organizations. However, it not only *can* be done in larger organizations, but in some respects, it becomes even more important to the ultimate operational efficacy of the larger entities.

A case that illustrates this point involves Continental Air Lines, which in 1991 made a decision to replace the airline's logo with an entirely new signature, i.e., a new graphic representation of their mission was painted on the tail of every Continental plane. Yet, when pilots, ticket counter employees, flight attendants, red caps, and other employees were randomly and casually asked (by this author) what the new logo was intended to symbolize and how it reflected the mission or vision of the airline, not one could give any certainty as to what meaning the logo was intended to convey or why the old symbol was no longer considered appropriate. The real irony was that nearly everyone *attempted* to come up with some rational explanation for the change and what it meant. Assuming these people were representative of most Continental employees, it makes you wonder how much synergistic energy might have been mobilized if all of the airline's employees had been incorporated into the development of this change, and how they might have better focused and directed their obvious loyalty and commitment to the airline.

Defining Strategic Goals

Strategic goals are statements about those areas on which the organization has determined it must focus in order to fulfill its mission. These are broad, long-term areas under which you will identify specific, short-term objectives (strategic objectives). Keep in mind that while the goals represent general categories of accomplishment, they still must be stated in such a way that it can be determined whether or not they have been successfully achieved.

The group of leaders from the five counties discussed previously identified several key areas on which they needed to focus in order to achieve their mission of creating a cooperative effort between the counties and their respective communities to ensure a prosperous region with a high quality of life for its residents. These key areas

were transportation, cooperative governance, economic development, environmental issues, and quality of life. For each of these
areas, then, a specific goal statement was developed. For example,
in the areas of economic development and environmental issues,
the coalition agreed that a long-range goal common to both areas
was needed. The goal statement was then written to combine the
need for the development or relocation of new businesses in order
to diversify the economic base. As part of the goal, however, they
also noted that these new businesses must be environmentally
friendly and pose no threat to the environment or to the defined
quality of life currently existing in the area. Once a goal statement
is agreed upon, then the specific short-term objectives for how to
achieve that goal can be easily developed.

Setting Strategic Objectives

Strategic objectives "operationalize" the strategic goal areas. The
short-term (twelve to eighteen months) objectives more specifically
define what must be achieved if the broader goal is to be successfully met. Although goals are often referred to as objectives and vice
versa, the terms shouldn't be used interchangeably. You are encouraged to refer to your long-term desired end results as goals and
the more short-range results as objectives. Some will argue that this
is a matter of semantics, but clarity and consistency in this regard
will eliminate confusion, especially among new staff members.

An example of an agency's long-term goal statement might be
as follows: To determine minimum acceptable standards of physical
and emotional health which should be maintained at all times in
the immediate neighborhood. An example of an objective subsumed
under that goal might be as follows: To complete a comprehensive
survey of the neighborhood to determine its assessment of
minimum health needs and the extent to which those needs are
currently being met.

Outlining Action Plans

Action plans are the first place in the strategic plan where you
actually translate the strategic goals and objectives into operational
strategies. The action plans state who will do what, how, where,
and by when in order to achieve the strategic objectives. They state
who will be responsible for achieving each objective, when the
objective is to be achieved, how the objective will be achieved, and
by what means. In other words, the action plans drive the everyday
business operations of your organization.

Program Evaluation

Evaluation is the stage in which you assess the progress being made toward achieving your objectives and your ultimate goals as stated in the strategic plan. An evaluation can be a *static* process; that is, it can be performed at a fixed point in time, or the evaluation can be *dynamic*; that is, it is ongoing and fluid. Both methods should be utilized.

A static evaluation is a planned event or series of events which results in changes to the plan and changes to daily operations. With static evaluations, programs are implemented and, after the program has had time to work, an evaluation is performed to test its effectiveness. If the program is found to be ineffective or is not meeting its goals, changes are implemented and another evaluation is scheduled after the changes have had a chance to work. Change is made only after formal evaluations are performed.

Dynamic or fluid evaluations, on the other hand, are less formal and are a constant feature of the program. Implementers are allowed to informally evaluate the effectiveness of the program and to make needed changes throughout implementation. A benefit of dynamic evaluations is that the program is *organic* or constantly adapting to meet the changing needs of the clients or circumstances. An obvious drawback to this approach is that assessment and needed changes are more instinctively determined. Such instinctive reactions, however, can be valuable and complementary to the more formal evaluative process.

The strategic plan of your organization should be seen as an ongoing, living process that is really never completed. The overall strategic plan should be revisited at least on an annual basis and changes should be made due to such factors as external environmental changes or the results of the evaluation process itself. Indeed, as previously noted in Figure 4.1, the evaluation step becomes, in effect, the first phase of the next environmental scan.

Why Is Evaluation So Important?

One the most readable books on program evaluation is a Hazeldon Foundation Program Management manual called, *Outcome Evaluation: How to Do It* by J. Spicer. It is a very short, highly readable guide for beginners. Although it was first published in 1980, the information is pertinent and applicable today.

Spicer introduces program evaluation and uses the following quote from Patton (1978:28) to define evaluation:

> Evaluation research is the systematic collection of information
> about activities and outcomes of actual programs in order for
> interested persons to make judgments about specific aspects of
> what the program is doing and affecting.

Spicer goes on to explain that the results of program evaluations
are crucial because they serve as significant inputs into management and decision making. As Spicer states, "Everyone is an
evaluator." We all have anecdotal examples of the success of our
programs; we all have an intuitive sense of whether our programs
work. Rare is the director who cannot regale the staff with stories
about successes with some clients and problems with others.
Unfortunately, however, these evaluations often stay at the intuitive
level and do little to assist in program planning and program
administration. Information that results from systematic evaluation
can be used to improve programs, to ensure that clients' needs are
met, and to ensure that the organization is meeting the goals and
objectives of the strategic plan.

Major Types of Program Evaluation

The four major types of program evaluation are listed below. An
evaluation can involve any one of these or any combination.

Formative Evaluations.   These focus on acquiring information
that will be used to develop or improve a program. Programs that
are interested in development or change should use this type of
evaluation. Formative evaluations can be either dynamic or static.

Summative Evaluations.   Such evaluations focus upon making
overall judgments about the program. These evaluations often focus
upon the effectiveness of the program in meeting its goals and
objectives. Summative evaluations are static evaluations in that
they are done after implementation.

Process Evaluations.   Process evaluations focus upon what was
done during the program; that is, how clients were treated, how
many staff members worked in client services areas, and so on.
Process evaluations are interested in how things are done, not the
result.

Outcome Evaluations. Outcome evaluations determine the
effects of the program vis-a-vis the clients. Here the primary
emphasis is on clients and the impact of the program on clients.

Program Research

Program evaluation is essentially a research process designed to test the extent to which your program is accomplishing its stated goals and objectives. Good program evaluation, therefore, means developing good research techniques.

Basic Research

A newcomer to the research process is often intimidated by the "psychobabble" associated with this activity. As a program director or a chief administrative officer, the thought of doing research on your program can be very frightening. The research profession appears to have deliberately made the field untouchable to the layperson. Take heart. It is not as confusing as it looks.

Keep in mind that at any point along the way in your evaluation, you can seek out the services of a consultant to ensure that you are on the right track. Consultants can perform a variety of roles including providing help with the design phase, reviewing questionnaires or other data collection techniques, and assisting you with an analysis of the data collected. If your organization can afford it, it may be best to hire a consultant to perform the evaluation for you. This guarantees your stakeholders that the evaluation is objective and is not biased by insiders directing the research. If you cannot afford to hire a consultant, however, the following steps may help demystify the field a bit and provide you with a place to begin.

Background Research

The background research section of a program evaluation outlines the program being evaluated, lists the reasons for the evaluation, includes a brief review of the literature on other program evaluations in your area, and outlines the specific information objectives of the study. It is in this section that you state what kind of evaluation you are performing (e.g. outcome versus process). You also need to specifically define or operationalize the elements or outcomes of the program that you are going to measure. One of the biggest problems with program evaluation is that it is often difficult to precisely define those elements, or outcomes. The method that you choose for evaluation is determined by the specific outcome and how it is defined.

In a program evaluation of an experiential education program, for example, the biggest problem encountered was how to measure the success of the program. The program goals and objectives were very lofty and esoteric, filled with educational and psychological rhetoric: "treat the participants as individuals," "develop skills for handling new and different situations," and "develop leadership traits." The challenge of that particular evaluation was to find precise ways to measure these rather vague statements. The evaluation team choose an evaluation model that was more experiential-based rather than quantitative-based. In other words, because it was so difficult to measure these goals and objectives, the team choose to use a design that was based upon personal interviews and observation (a qualitative design) rather than a design based upon statistical measures of outcomes (a quantitative design).

Drug and alcohol abuse treatment programs are also examples of programs that have difficult-to-measure outcomes. How do you measure the success of such programs? Do you measure it through a commitment to get off alcohol and other drugs or by long-term compliance with that commitment? How long is long-term? You can see how these measurement issues can be very thorny.

One way to help decide how to measure your variables is to do a *brief review of the literature.* This does not have to be an academically robust review. Nevertheless, it should include an examination of some of the pertinent studies of other programs and program evaluations in your field. You can often obtain evaluations of similar programs from professional associations, federal research groups like the General Accounting Office, or in publications related to your field. A visit to the nearest college or university library may also prove fruitful.

It is also important to clearly state your *information objectives* in your background research effort. Each information objective should state exactly what will be studied in the research and how the research will help make decisions about the program or agency. Spending appropriate time beforehand to ensure that the objectives are clearly stated and linked to a program or planning decision will very likely save you from doing an evaluation that will simply not be useful to your program.

Methodology

Most of us can tackle the information objectives and the literature review with no problems, but find ourselves in a state of panic over exactly how the study should be designed. Do not panic. It is not as complicated as it looks. Remember, if you run into trouble there are always consultants to help.

As mentioned before, there are two basic kinds of research design: qualitative and quantitative.

Qualitative Designs. These are designs that do not produce statistically reliable results. They often rely upon the use of personal interviews, focus groups or observations (qualitative methods have their roots in anthropology) for data collection. Qualitative designs are often used for process evaluations and for evaluations that have difficult-to-measure goals and objectives. The main limitation of qualitative designs is that the results are not statistically valid; that is, the probability of making an incorrect decision from qualitative research is higher than from a quantitative design. What qualitative designs give you is a good snapshot of the complex issues that may be affecting your program. Qualitative designs are also useful as a first step before acquiring information from more robust quantitative designs.

Quantitative Designs. These designs are based upon statistically valid samples and usually involve the measuring of variables in precise, quantitative terms. If at all possible, a decision to continue or stop a program should be made from information and data obtained from a quantitative design. Quantitative methods vary from simple surveys to more sophisticated experimental methods that involve the use of treatment groups (groups that receive an intervention) and control groups (groups that do not receive an intervention). Quantitative designs generally require some statistical analysis of the results.

Whichever design you choose to use, there are some other important factors to consider. One of the key problems with program evaluation is that you can never be *entirely* sure that any success measured in the evaluation is totally due to your program. The only time you can say that a given program has directly brought about a predetermined change is when you can control for the effects of all other factors that may influence that particular change. The only way to truly do this is in an experimental lab. Since most of us cannot run our programs in laboratories (for ethical as well as a host of other reasons), we have to be satisfied with results that *indicate* the goals and objectives of the program are being met, as opposed to results that *prove* that a program is or is not successful.

Quasi-experimental Designs

Fortunately, there are many research designs that allow us to get very close to the point of proof without the requirement of conducting our research in an experimental lab. These designs are called *quasi-experimental* designs. The basic components of quasi-experimental designs are random samples, control groups, pre-tests, and post-tests.

Random Samples.   A sample is a subset, or portion, of the total group you are studying. We use samples in research because it is usually too costly to study an entire population group. If the population is large, a small, but randomly selected sample of the total population will give you information nearly as reliable as if you had questioned every member of the group being studied. The key, however, is to insure that when you select your sample, you must make sure that every person in the population group being studied has an *equal probability* of being included in your sample. The way to get a random sample is to use a table of random numbers (in any basic statistics book) or to use a computer generated program to sample your data. Consult a basic statistics book to find out how large your sample should be relative to the total population of the group being studied.

Control Groups.   In order to test the effectiveness of your program and to control for all other possible explanatory variables, you must compare the results of people who have been through your program with people who have not been through your program. For example, in a drug treatment program the *treatment group* would be those people who have been through the program and the *control group* should be a group of similar people who have not been through the program. If your treatment group shows significant improvement and the control group does not, you can *assume* the change in the treatment group can be attributed to your program.

Pre-tests and Post-tests.   It is important to pre-test your sample *before* treatment and compare the results with the results of tests *after* treatment. This way you can test for differences that can be evidenced as a result of having been in the program. This is why it is so important to have your evaluation carefully planned before you start your program.

Although it is best to use all of these techniques, in the real world it is not always possible. Indeed, many academic evaluations are criticized for the adherence to these principles to the detriment of the evaluation (e.g. the evaluation is not usable because it followed research principles rather than following the needs of the program). The goal is to follow the standards or steps of a quasi-experimental design as much as possible. Every time you omit any one of the steps outlined in your design, you trade off some degree of validity in your final results.

Data Analysis

Depending upon your design, your statistical analysis can be very easy or it can be very complicated. The more complicated your design, the greater the probability that you will need professional help with this stage. Keep in mind, however, that the data acquired from most research projects can be analyzed rather simply. Save the more complicated analyses for the academics.

The two basic kinds of statistical analyses are *descriptive* statistics and *inferential* statistics. Each is discussed below.

Descriptive Statistics.   Such statistics involve describing a data set. Sports statistics and Wall Street statistics are examples of descriptive statistics. RBIs (runs batted in) for baseball players participating in the World Series are an example of descriptive statistics. Their purpose is only to describe what happened in any given situation.

Inferential Statistics.   These are somewhat more complicated than descriptive statistics. National political polls are an example of inferential statistics. With inferential statistics, you are taking data from a sample (who you studied) and inferring the results to the population (all you could have studied). In making an inference, there is bound to be some error.

Statistical tests tell us how much error there is in making our projections or inferences. If you are going to project from a sample to a population, you must necessarily use inferential statistics.

Conclusions/Recommendations

Finally, a program evaluation should take the results of the analysis and make conclusions and recommendations for program changes. When doing this, keep your audience in mind and make sure the presentation of the data can be described or shown in ways that are easily interpreted by any observer. Statistical results are often best presented by using charts, graphs, or other visual techniques.

Summary

In order to know where to go and how to get there, it is crucial that a program have a strategic plan. Part of the strategic plan is an evaluation plan that measures the progress toward achieving the stated goals and objectives. Strategic plans are different from the plans that drive the day-to-day decisions of the organization. Strategic planning and evaluation will help you decide where you want to go, help you choose the right road to get there and will help keep you on the right road. This will go a long way toward ensuring the success of your organization.

In addition to contributing to the long-run health of your organization, a planning and evaluation strategy will make the day-to-day management of your organization easier. If you want your organization to survive and prosper and if you want your organization to be more manageable, then you should pursue an aggressive planning and evaluation strategy. Alice was satisfied with her random adventures. Will you be satisfied with yours?

Continuing Concerns

1. How can concentration on operational-level planning at the expense of strategic-level planning ultimately be self-defeating for an organization?

2. Describe currently existing "dynamic" and "static" program evaluation procedures in a selected small organization.

3. Explain the relative drawbacks and benefits of qualitative (as opposed to quantitative) research methods for complex organizations engaged in service to clients.

4. How are the planning capabilities needed by grassroots managers similar to those of for-profit business managers from the point of view of potential funding sources?

Chapter

5

The People Who Make Up an Organization

Jane Covode

Because demographics are changing, the work force is more diverse, individual goals are becoming more heterogeneous, and therefore organizational leaders face a significant challenge. Managers and human resources professionals must find ways to increase employee satisfaction, commitment, and involvement in organizational life; improve the quality of working life; and increase worker efficiency and productivity.

—Judith R. Gordon, *Human Resource Management*

Jane Covode, MBA, is the former Director for the Colorado Association of Community Center Boards. She is currently serving as a volunteer in a small village in Mexico.

Introduction

Human beings are an organization's greatest resource. In past management literature and practice, human beings were seen as "units" of labor, necessary "inputs" to production which had to be managed efficiently for the corporation to be profitable. This often meant getting the most out of people for the least possible cost. Management has been slow to realize that human beings are like any other resource. We can no more utilize people without thought about replenishment and future development than we can water, land, or oil. This applies as much to nonprofit service organizations as to for-profit businesses and industries. In fact, "burn-out" has become a standard condition in human service organizations. Still, we continually deplete our most valuable resource.

Of all the balls the effective manager must continually juggle, human resources is the most important. Human beings should be developed and nurtured as an organization's richest resource to the extent that they are empowered to exercise choice, and to help the organization achieve its stated purpose. To truly empower people to reach their fullest potential is to maximize human resources to the greatest degree. This chapter will identify the major categories of people who make up a nonprofit organization. The purpose here is to briefly describe each group's role in order to better utilize an organization's most valuable resource—people.

Empowerment

Today we are realizing that it is only through the empowerment of people that an organization can become effective. Having power means being able to choose among alternatives, to influence decision making, and to exercise control over situations. Empowerment must include consumers, board members, volunteers, and paid staff.

Empowerment begins with the consumer of the agency's services. Consumers drive the mission of the organization. Human service organizations exist to support people in meeting needs which they cannot meet themselves. Empowerment of the consumer means that the consumer is involved in identifying those needs and designing effective ways to meet them.

Board members have the designated responsibility for "governing" the organization and are the link between the organization and the public. The board as a body must be able to assure that the organization is carrying out its purpose efficiently and effectively. Given this responsibility, it is imperative that board members also be empowered. The board can delegate authority to paid staff, but it cannot delegate its responsibility and is ultimately accountable for all actions of the organization.

An effective nonprofit organization attracts volunteers in addition to board members who care about its mission and wish to be involved. Empowered volunteers are a potent force for achieving the organizational mission and generating community support.

From the Directors

Our organization started with a challenge. At a retreat twenty-six years ago, we sisters were told to get out into the world and to get our hands dirty. Some of us decided to do a survey in a low income area of our city and discovered that nearly 75 percent of the adults who lived there did not have their high school diploma. So, from nothing more than that, I started what became the Adult Learning Source focusing primarily on promoting adult literacy.

We had a budget of $450 for our first year and, of course, no paid staff. Nevertheless, we attracted 40 students and 16 volunteers. Last year we had nearly 2,500 students. Most importantly, I think we are becoming a national model in family literacy for showing how critical it is to develop the interaction between parent and child when you are dealing with adult literacy.

I think the manner in which we involve our volunteers—their training, the recognition and the value we place upon them—is so important to our success. Another reason for our success is that we never veer from our vision. We don't bend our mission to fit whatever funding might be available at some given time. I believe this has given us great credibility to both our funders and to the people in the community.

—Sister Cecilia Linenbrink, Executive Director
Adult Learning Source (Denver)

Finally, staff must be empowered in order to carry out the work of the organization. Clarifying the relationship and roles of board members, volunteers, and staff is necessary to maximize staff potential.

The elements of empowering people and maximizing their potential are the same whether or not people receive a paycheck. All people need to feel committed to the organization's mission, need to have the knowledge and skills necessary to do their task, and receive encouragement, support and feedback on the job. This applies as much to unpaid board members and to other volunteers as to those employees who are paid.

Consumers

Identifying Needs

If the mission of the human service organization is to support people in meeting needs which they cannot meet themselves, the role of the consumer is to help identify those needs. This approach and the use of the word "consumer" represents a significant departure from past practice in many paternalistic public or nonprofit agencies which traditionally decided what people needed. Such agencies simply developed the services and then delivered them to "clients" without checking whether those services were either needed or wanted. If the mission of the organization is not clearly articulated by the board, volunteers, and paid staff to the community, the organization will not be effective. It is important to remember, however, that while the mission drives the organization, the consumer drives the mission.

How do we know we are meeting consumer needs? It is not as easy as just designing a product and seeing whether consumers buy it. Consumers may not even be directly paying for the service and, in any case, may have little choice in the service that is being offered. In the nonprofit sector, we must take special care to assure we know the consumer "demand." Consumers should be active at every level of the organization: as board members, volunteers, and sometimes even as paid staff. Human service agencies must not only afford opportunities for consumers to be heard but they must also listen to what they have to say.

Feedback Loops

These opportunities to be heard are both formal and informal. For example, consumers should be part of the formal planning process, involved in setting and reviewing the organization's mission statement, in tracking trends (indeed, their actions may *be* the trends of the future), and in designing services. Evaluation of how efficiently and effectively services are provided should also include formal surveys or meetings of consumers as well as informal feedback loops. The idea of a loop is important because consumer feedback should be communicated to all levels of the organization. It is particularly important that the "grassroots" input of the consumer gets beyond the agency's first layer of personnel. Consumer advisory councils to the agency or to particular programs can provide another method of assessing needs, expectations, and satisfaction.

Boards of Directors

General Responsibility

The board of a for-profit or nonprofit corporation *is* the corporation. The board of a for-profit has a responsibility to stockholders to make a profit. The nonprofit board has a responsibility to the public at large to carry out the mission for which the organization was given nonprofit status. Board members of nonprofit corporations cannot be paid. Individual members of a board cannot act on behalf of the whole board although they can be held accountable for their individual actions. In short, boards only exist when they actually meet and formally make decisions and form policies.

The board has both external and internal responsibilities. It has the external public responsibility to keep to its mission and it has the internal management responsibility to implement the mission. The board may delegate the authority to manage the organization to paid staff but it cannot delegate its responsibility. Ultimately, the board is responsible for whatever the organization does.

Legal Responsibility

A board's specific legal responsibilities include adhering to state and federal law and reporting requirements, maintaining the tax exempt status, safeguarding corporate documents (such as articles of incorporation, bylaws, and tax exemption papers) and keeping minutes and financial records. Each member is expected to perform these duties taking "due care" as any responsible person would do in such a position. In other words, board members are expected to attend meetings and know what is going on in the organization but are not expected to have any special skills or knowledge beyond that of an ordinary person. To assure and demonstrate that members are acting responsibly, advice should be sought from professionals when necessary, individual votes should be recorded on important or controversial matters, and members should disclose anything which could represent a conflict of interest.

Policy Responsibility

A board determines the policies that guide an organization in carrying out its mission. Policies generally address *what* the agency will do and *where* it will go rather than *how* it will do things. Determining who the agency serves and what services to offer are in the realm of policy. Policies should be kept to a minimum, be precisely and clearly stated, and be easily obtainable for anyone to read.

Marketing Responsibility

Agencies have many publics with whom exchanges are desired in addition to the direct consumer: indirect consumers (families, friends), media, government, corporations, volunteers, suppliers. When a board looks at all its publics and determines what it wants to get from them and give in return, it is, in effect, developing a marketing strategy or plan. Fund-raising, volunteer development, and public relations strategies all flow from this plan. Board members can and should be critical players in effecting exchanges between the organization and its many publics. They must understand the nature of the exchange, their role, and the role of staff so that the board and staff are not at cross purposes in marketing the organization to its publics.

Maintaining Board Quality

It is one thing to know the role and responsibilities of the board and quite another to undertake them. The responsibility for maximizing the human resources of the board and insuring that the quality of the board is always maintained rests with the *nominating committee* of the board. An effective nominating committee does far more than draft a slate of officers before an election. It is responsible for board member recruitment, training, support, and leadership development. This includes developing job descriptions for board members and officers and developing a plan for recruiting people who have the skills, talents, and community connections the board needs, along with appropriate representation of identified groups in the community. Potential board members should be clear about what is expected from them in terms of time and commitment to the board and what they can expect in return.

New board members must receive orientation to the mission and to the culture of the organization. All board members should have training in board effectiveness and be informed about the issues confronting the agency on an ongoing basis in order to make good decisions. It follows from the above discussion that the nominating committee should be a standing committee and function year round.

Other Committees of the Board

Two other standing committees are necessary to good board functioning: the executive committee and the finance committee. The executive committee, chaired by the president of the board, acts between board meetings (such action must be ratified by the board at its next meeting) and supports the president in planning meetings and framing issues for consideration by the whole board. The finance committee, chaired by the treasurer of the board, reviews financial matters and advises the board in this area. Depending on the size of the board and its plans, other committees may be appointed as necessary to fulfill particular functions (and may be disbanded when finished). The ideal board has active committees carry out the responsibilities of the board. It is through these committees that specific analysis of problems are made and recommendations are brought to the whole board for ultimate decision making.

Volunteers

Communicating the Agency's Mission

Maximizing the full potential of volunteers is one of the most difficult challenges in developing human resources (including board members). At worst, volunteers are viewed as a cheap resource and treated that way. At best, volunteers are treated in the same manner as paid staff.

Volunteer management should be considered a key factor in the effectiveness of any small, nonprofit organization and therefore, it must be developed and nurtured at all times by the board and management. If the board and leadership of an organization are not committed to volunteer involvement, a volunteer program will certainly not be successful. The board must be clear about the relationship of volunteer involvement to the mission of the organization. If volunteers cannot understand how their work promotes the mission of the organization, they will not be committed. Of course, if the mission of the organization is unclear or not reflected in actuality through the work of the organization, volunteers will quickly question their involvement and, indeed, the purpose of the agency itself.

Volunteer Program Management

After approving a plan for a volunteer program, the board must provide necessary resources in the combination of people, dollars, and time to assure its success. This includes assigning direct responsibility for volunteer program management to a specifically designated person. Responsibility for volunteers should not be just another item in the job description of a staff member or board member with other major responsibilities.

The director or manager of the volunteers should report to the executive director or, if a board position, to the president. The responsibilities of the position include identifying the role of volunteers in relation to the mission, writing volunteer job descriptions, developing a marketing plan for recruiting volunteers, and the screening, selection, training, supervision, support, and evaluation of volunteers. If this sounds like a job description for selection and management of paid personnel, it is. The management of volunteers should not be any different from the management of paid staff. In fact, it is a more challenging management responsibility because there is not the basic incentive of a paycheck. A small agency may not be able to afford a full-time paid position for this purpose. Nevertheless, a paid or unpaid person must be given the direct responsibility for the management of the volunteer program. This is essential to the success of any agency.

Volunteer Job Descriptions

Often volunteers are welcomed into an organization before anyone has discussed specifically what it is they are expected to do. This is a surefire way to lose volunteers and create bad will toward the organization. Volunteer job descriptions must outline the title of the job, the responsibilities entailed, qualifications required, training and supervision provided, time requirements and, most importantly, the benefits which will result for the volunteer.

Obviously, in order to do this, everyone in the organization (board and staff) must have a part in discussing what it is volunteers could do for the organization. A primary consideration should be whether volunteers would want to perform particular functions. Sometimes we expect volunteers to do the things no one else wants to do and then wonder why we can't attract any volunteers. Another very important consideration is to determine the amount of board and staff time and the specific resources necessary to enable the volunteers to do the jobs expected. For example, if a volunteer is asked to help get out a mailing, all resources (envelopes, stamps, etc.) needed to do that job should be made available. This also includes specific directions, who to ask for help if needed, and precisely when and how long volunteers are expected to work.

Volunteer Recruitment

With a clear job description and commitment by board and staff, recruitment can begin. This must be done as part of the organization's overall resource development plan. Brochures and general information on the agency should include volunteer opportunities. The resource development plan should also include requests for volunteer support as well as contributions of money or goods.

Specific volunteer markets should be targeted. If an organization has determined that it needs a large number of volunteers for a one-time event such as a weekend house painting that requires little advance training, a broad market can be targeted through flyers distributed in grocery stores or notices in newsletters. This portion of the resource development plan thus becomes a part of the agency's companion marketing plan.

If volunteers must have certain qualifications, or are to be carefully screened and trained, and must commit to an extensive period of time, it may be better to make personal presentations at churches or community organizations where these people are most likely to be found. It should not be forgotten that *people commit to people* so board members and current volunteers are the most successful recruiters.

Interviewing and Selecting Volunteers

The interviewing and selection process is based on the specific job description. Interviewing a prospective volunteer requires a clear agenda and purpose. If the organization is prepared to take anyone who walks in the door then it isn't necessary to fill out applications; to discuss qualifications, commitment, and benefits; or to see if the person is right for the job (or would even like the job). However, if the organization has larger expectations for its volunteers and wants to be sure a particular person can do the job and will gain satisfaction from it, the interview becomes a very important step. As incongruous as it may appear, an agency should be prepared to turn down a potential volunteer. In most cases, of course, a volunteer may not be right for one job or activity but may be very appropriate for something else. Obviously, the agency won't know this if they have not planned ahead in their volunteer program.

The interview should be a conversation with the purpose of determining if the potential volunteer is right for the job, motivated to do it, and able to make the commitment it requires. It is an opportunity for the volunteer to learn about the organization and the benefits of being involved with it. In turn, it is an opportunity for the volunteer director to become acquainted with the applicant and to adapt the job, the necessary training, and the support and recognition to meet the volunteer's needs.

Training and Supervision

If training is required (and it usually is), it should be planned carefully. Training involves orientation to the organization, its people, the culture of the workplace, and the general expectations of volunteers as well as training for the specific job. You need to predetermine what the volunteer is expected to understand and be able to do as a result of the training. Depending on your purpose, training can include group presentations, case studies, role playing, tours, reading, and on-the-job training. A combination of these various approaches is usually most successful.

Support and supervision for the volunteer while on the job is very important. The worst message a volunteer can receive from an agency is to arrive ready to work only to find that no one expected her or him. The volunteer manager or director must assure that all volunteers have supervision and are constantly being supported. Volunteers must clearly understand who to go to with questions, problems, or to convey information.

Recognition and Evaluation

Recognition is essential for volunteer retention. Recognition must occur on an ongoing basis. This may be as simple as going to lunch, being included in staff meetings, or being introduced to other employees. Formal recognition through dinners, newsletter profiles, or volunteer awards are important too, but not sufficient in themselves. Don't neglect this fundamental part of human resource management.

Evaluation is another form of recognition. Evaluation reinforces the agency's belief that volunteers are important enough to give and receive feedback on their performance. The evaluation process should be an opportunity for both the volunteer and the supervisor to discuss how the work is going and how it can be improved, both from the standpoint of the volunteer and that of the organization. It can also be an invitation to explore other positions of greater responsibility within the organization.

The objective of a good evaluation process should be improved performance by both the volunteer and the organization. However, there are times when a volunteer's performance may be unsatisfactory. In these cases, if suggestions for additional training, improved supervision, or changes in the job responsibilities do not result in what is considered a satisfactory performance, it may be necessary to "fire" the volunteer. Of course, if the volunteer's performance has in any way been harmful to a consumer, the volunteer should be dismissed immediately. All evaluation and action should be documented in the volunteer's file. In short, the "hiring and firing" of volunteers should essentially replicate all of the procedural considerations given to the hiring and firing of paid staff.

In addition to individual evaluations, the organization should have a process whereby volunteers and staff can evaluate the volunteer program. This can be as simple as a questionnaire or may be done through group discussion or individual interviews. Suggestions should be acted on by the organization as soon as possible and taken into consideration in future planning.

Record Keeping

Careful records should be kept of all volunteer inquiries, interviews, and activities including training, hours of work, recognition, and evaluation. Depending on the nature of the job this may be as simple as an index card or as extensive as a volunteer file for future reference or job referrals. These records can be very useful in tabulating the dollar value of volunteer hours, planning for future marketing efforts, and for general volunteer program evaluation.

Paid Staff

Motivation

Needless to say, all of the activities and considerations outlined for the volunteer program should be undertaken for paid staff as well. Good planning, clear job descriptions, targeted recruitment efforts, screening, selection, training, support, supervision, recognition, and evaluation are elements of good human resource management of paid or unpaid staff. Clearly, a paycheck is not the only motivation for a good employee. In fact, it is well known that while pay may be a demotivator if it is insufficient, it is not a major motivator for good job performance or job satisfaction. Challenging work, opportunity for advancement, training, support, mutual evaluation, and recognition are the common motivators for all staff, paid or unpaid.

Relationship with Volunteers

Nonprofit organizations face a challenge with respect to paid staff that does not exist in for-profit corporations: the relationship between paid staff and volunteers and between paid staff and the volunteer board members. The relationship that will exist between paid staff and volunteers must be carefully considered in the planning phase of the volunteer program.

Sometimes paid staff members consider volunteers to be unreliable. (If that is the case, it is the problem of the agency, not the volunteers.) On the other hand, volunteers can be seen as a threat by some paid staff either because they are more qualified or because they are in a position to criticize how the paid staff member is performing. Volunteer supervision may be seen as an additional and unrewarding responsibility by an already overburdened staff. For all these reasons, it is very important that paid staff be involved in planning the volunteer program. They must be assured that volunteers will enhance the staff's ability to do its job and will contribute to the achievement of the organizational mission. In addition, paid staff members must be trained to work with volunteers and recognized for their efforts. The volunteer manager must be clear about his or her relationship with staff members who work with volunteers and where the lines of responsibility and authority lie.

Relationship with the Board and Director

The relationships between the board, the paid staff, and the executive director can also be a source of problems. This is particularly true if the organization has just hired a paid director to assume functions formerly done by volunteer board members. As noted earlier, the distinction between the board's role as policy maker and the director's role as implementor must be made as clear as possible.

In the simplest of terms, the board of directors hires and fires the executive director and the executive director hires and fires everyone else. This means that the board is responsible for reviewing the performance of the executive director and supporting the executive director in carrying out the mission and plans of the organization. In general, the board determines the budget and sets policy and the executive director implements it. This means that the board allows the executive director to run the daily operations of the organization and that individual board members do not give directions to the executive director or to staff members.

Communication from the staff to the board should go through the executive director and communication from board members to the executive director should go through the president of the board. Although there may be exceptions such as when paid staff provide support to board committees, in general, everything is cleared through the president and the executive director. Their relationship, therefore, is crucial for effective organizational functioning. When communication between individual board members and staff members circumvents the president and executive director, the results can be disastrous.

Summary

No matter how it is sometimes perceived, managers do not manage things, or projects, or events, or even agencies. The only thing they really manage is people. People are an agency's greatest resource. The special dynamics between individuals within an organization and between groups of people who make up the structure of an organization will clearly determine whether or not that organization is successful in meeting its stated mission.

Continuing Concerns

1. Explain how empowerment at all levels in an organization enhances organizational effectiveness.
2. Describe three similarities and three differences between volunteers and paid staff members.
3. Explain the statement, "While the mission drives the organization, the consumer drives the mission."
4. How might volunteers provide an early warning system regarding the clarity of an organization's mission?
5. Explain your most important recommendation to grassroots directors on how to prevent staff burnout.

Chapter

6

The Politics of Thriving as Well as Surviving

Richard Male

> The plain fact is that our political environment is so complex and interconnected and our knowledge base so limited that it is a testimony to human skill and ingenuity that social programs work as well as they do. We characterize this generally unsure, rapidly changing environment of public management as "life in the administrative swamp." Administrators frequently do not know the best path through the murky, unsafe surroundings. Danger abounds and there are few reliable clues to guide one to safety. They may well select the wrong path and sink into the marsh or be eaten by alligators. Sink or swim has a much too real meaning in these uncertain days.
>
> —N. Joseph Cayer and Louis E. Weschler
> *Public Administration: Social Change and Adaptive Management.*

Richard Male is the Executive Director for the Denver-based Community Resource Center. The Center provides leadership training and consultation to community-based nonprofit organizations nationwide.

Introduction

It is important to understand at the outset that the notion of "politics" as used in this chapter has very little to do with the more accepted use of that word. Every grassroots organization has to resolve conflicts, overcome obstacles, reach consensus, achieve objectives, and attempt to fulfill its mission. To be able to do these things successfully is what "politics" should be all about. Further, if you can achieve these goals and do so in ways that are fair and equitable, with the absence of force or violence and without violating the integrity of another person, you have evidenced the art and practice of "politics" in its highest order.

During the past three decades, we have seen the street politics of this country evolve from the activism of the 1960s to the seeming indifference of the 1990s. Times change, situations shift, people come and go, but the "politics" of being a director of a grassroots, nonprofit organization remains basically the same. The directors of these small, community-based entities still have to know how to read their unique, local "political maps" if they are not to "sink into the marsh or be eaten by alligators." And unlike the more commonly accepted world of politics, the "politics" of grassroots organizations should say as much about *thriving* as it does about simply *surviving*.

The Internal Politics of Your Organization

Lesson One: No One Can Do It Alone

The director of a major nonprofit resource support agency describes how he learned a very important lesson in cooperation and support:

> My first job after college was with the James Cash Penny Company in San Jose, California where I took part in their Executive Director's Program. One of my assignments was to manage foundations (bras and girdles). It became clear to me that to keep my job (for which I had very little "technical" knowledge) I needed the support and cooperation of other people in my department. I realized very early that no one really

succeeds in whatever they do without help. Sometimes this is mistakenly referred to as humility. I call it insightful, pragmatic leadership.

Lesson Two: Have Good People Around You

Closely related to the first lesson is to be sure you have competent, committed people around you. The best way to maximize your position as director is to hire people who offset your weaknesses rather than mirror your strengths. And just as it is important to have good, strong people around you, it is also important to *listen* to what they have to say. You want people who can find exceptions, look for creative options, and who feel comfortable in disagreeing with you.

From the Directors

When we first started, the staff was very demoralized. They saw themselves as tied to this job because they could not speak English and they felt their skills were not marketable. I didn't want people to say that this was the only place they could work, so we really concentrated on strengthening our in-service training.

Most of the staff have now been here for over eight years. Through our flex-time opportunity, many of them have obtained degrees and other academic credentials. Now, they come up with wonderful program ideas from their own experiences of working in the community. It's terrific to see each staff member taking this kind of initiative.

Politics is also a very important aspect of this job. Not traditional politics necessarily, but networking and communicating with people in the community, city officials, and especially in state government.

As Asians, long-term planning goals for us may mean thirty years. Even now we are planning for eventual alternatives to nursing homes and other health care needs for those refugees of the past 20 years or so—the Vietnamese, Laotian, Cambodian, and Thai populations who are already in their late 50's and early 60's.

—Sumiko Hennessy, Director
Asian Pacific Development Center (Denver)

Lesson Three: Let Them Know You Care

By definition, every grassroots organization has to improvise, hustle, and go the extra mile. Every director of a small nonprofit expects his or her staff to work harder for less pay and still be better than their counterparts in the public and the private sectors, not to mention the larger more bureaucratic nonprofits.

Okay, but as a director, you have a special obligation as well. You need to work overtime to ensure that *every member* of the staff feels involved and appreciated. It is important for your staff to see you as a caring person who needs others to accomplish what cannot be accomplished alone. There are lots of ways to show appreciation but it basically comes down to this: look for things people are doing that should be rewarded and then—reward them! In *The One Minute Manager*, author Kenneth Blanchard describes a number of ways to convey rewards that cost virtually nothing in both money and time. A simple personal note of appreciation and acknowledgment of something well done can accrue enormous benefits later on.

The Politics of Surviving Financially

Lesson Four: Everyone Is Responsible for Raising Money

Perhaps the biggest challenge for the director of a grassroots organization is to raise enough revenue that the organization will not only survive but (occasionally) thrive.

For the first ten years of my professional career with nonprofits, it seemed as though I was always the solo pilot on every fund-raising plane I flew. I researched the grants, drafted the proposals, made the necessary phone calls, wrote the letters, made the contacts, talked to the people and, of course, eventually burned myself out. (The worst part of burnout is that you no longer have enough time to spend on the things that very likely attracted you to the nonprofit sector in the first place.)

Then I made an important discovery. Fund-raising functions are much less painful and, interestingly, much more profitable when they become the shared responsibility of everyone associated with the organization. The director certainly has specific responsibilities in developing the initial fund-raising strategy and the broad overview of the actual implementation of that strategy. But the director's most important responsibility is to ensure involvement and ownership by everyone in the process.

Lesson Five: "Controllable Funding Source" is the Name of the Game

The bottom line of this lesson is that you cannot depend on any money that is not raised through *controllable funding sources*. Included in this definition are such funding sources as membership dues or fees, small donors, large donors (with at least a three-year history of contributing to your organization), special annual events (which have a track record of success), contributions from local and regional church bodies, and income derived from direct services you provide.

Significant government and foundation grants should be viewed as *opportunities* that enable you to buy time while you increase your controllable funding sources. If you have not already diversified your funding sources, you should establish a goal to have at least 70 percent of your total income to be derived from controllable funding sources.

Lesson Six: Don't Be Afraid to Ask for Support

The following story about a young, idealistic activist in the 1960s provides a personal insight as to the fundamental criteria in asking others for financial or other kinds of support:

> My first nonprofit experience was in the early 1960s directing the Missouri Delta Ministry, a social action/civil rights organization in the rural Mississippi Delta portion of Missouri. I was 22 years old and had just quit graduate school because I was offered this position.
>
> Here I was, a Jewish kid who had never been inside a Christian church and had never raised a dime in my life, now directing an ecumenical ministry with a staff of twelve and the expectation that I would somehow find the necessary monies to meet the projected budget of $250,000.
>
> Needless to say, I was scared. I finally turned to a major donor of the organization and asked for help. He gave me the name of a person in Cape Girardeau, Missouri who was also a very large contributor to one of the organization's participating churches.
>
> Meeting him at his home, he ushered me into his study and immediately asked me what I wanted. Taken back at his directness, I proceeded to stutter and stammer. He raised his voice, interrupting me, and said, "Sir, you must have come here for some reason. What is it?" Then, as I remember, in a somewhat meek and trembling tone, I asked him for $5,000.

He said, "I want you to relax and listen to me. I am going to give you more than $5,000 but not because of your eloquence and poise. I'm giving it to you because, number one, I believe in this cause and, number two, the Bishop has asked me to give it to you.

Then, he said something to me that has kept me a survivor and a "thriver" in this business ever since: "If you don't believe in what you are doing, you shouldn't be doing it. And if you do believe in what you are doing, you shouldn't be afraid to ask for support.

This is a lesson still being taught to training groups today. If you believe in your program, don't be afraid to ask for support. Never assume that people cannot or will not help or support your organization.

Lesson Seven: People Give Money to People They Know

The experience related above highlights another fundamental rule in the "politics" of surviving and thriving in this business. *People give money to people they know!* If a classmate or colleague asks you to buy Girl Scout cookies from her daughter, chances are you probably will. You may not especially like Girl Scout cookies or particularly care about the Girl Scouts as an organization. Nevertheless, in all likelihood, you will buy some cookies because a friend asked you to buy some. And whether it's the purchase of cookies or the contribution of significant dollars, the principle is still the same.

If the potential donor does not know the person making the request, then find someone who has a natural connection with the donor and have that person accompany the representative of the agency. For example, a depositor of the bank should make the request from the individual in charge of corporate giving; a member of a church or synagogue should act as your representative in talking to the social action committee.

Lesson Eight: Reslicing the Workplace Giving Pie

The assumption by most small nonprofits is that the only way to receive funds from traditional payroll deduction programs is to be selected as one of the relatively few small organizations to be included as part of the local United Way funding program.

If you can become a part of the United Way "chosen few," go for it! The problem is that even with a near monopoly on workplace giving, only a small fraction (estimated to be less than 10 percent) of the total nonprofit organizations receive *any funding* at all through United Way contributions.

There is now a growing movement across the country that is successfully challenging this monopoly on workplace giving. The lesson here is double-edged. With the various United Way programs raising over three billion dollars annually, this is certainly a David and Goliath type of competition. On the other hand, many corporate executives and their employees are extremely receptive to an alternate giving program, especially one where employees can designate their particular small, community-based organization as recipient.

Admittedly, this is no small undertaking and the "establishment" will fight hard against any such threat to their monopoly on workplace giving. On the other hand, such a battle can be in itself a "thriving" experience, particularly as you are joined in the fray by other small, nonprofit organizations. And besides—what have you got to lose?

Lesson Nine: The Art of Negotiation

Learn to negotiate for everything—service agreements for copiers, office supply contracts, client fees, foundation grants, how and when you receive large grants or contributions (if you receive it all up front, you can earn interest on the unspent balance), administrative overhead, and even the limits and guidelines of the RFP (request for proposal).

Negotiation is a tool that successful entrepreneurs use; and grassroots organizations are small businesses that have to negotiate (spelled h-u-s-t-l-e) to stay alive. There is nothing so directly satisfying than to have earned a savings, no matter how small, through your own hustle and negotiation.

Lesson Ten: Hire a Financial Accountability Person

Most directors of small, nonprofit organizations are not trained bookkeepers and can get into a lot of financial trouble if they try to handle this part of the operation. For less than 1 percent of your total income you can hire a professional to do the balance sheet, income and expense statements, cash-flow analysis, and 990 reports to the IRS. In most cases, such a person will more than pay for his or her services by avoiding lost interest, financial penalties, and other unexpected contingencies. Hire someone who you have confidence in and is skilled in this area. Then compound your savings by using the time normally spent on these activities to raise new monies.

Lesson Eleven: "Schmooze" Your Banker for a Line of Credit

What happens when you are awarded a grant but the money will not be available for another three months? Or, even though your annual awards dinner for the past four years has netted $7,000, you currently lack the $1,000 up front to put on the event?

These are not uncommon or isolated situations. A typical for-profit business would not even think about operating without a line of credit. Yet, most nonprofits never even consider it. You will be surprised at the number of financial institutions that are willing to establish such a credit line.

The president of a local bank was once asked why he was so willing to provide unsecured lines of credit to various nonprofit organizations in his community. He stated that he had never lost a dime with a nonprofit loan. He said his experience indicated that, whereas a for-profit enterprise might just "walk" during financial difficulties, a nonprofit will go the extra mile to pay back the credit line.

Talk with your banker about your banking credit as well as your investment needs and options. You may never need it, but if you do, it can be extremely helpful in the smooth operation of your organization.

The Politics of Leadership

Lesson Twelve: Playing It Safe Is Risky Business

By nature, good grassroots, nonprofit directors are effective entrepreneurs who have to hustle to survive. Part of the hustling game is taking risks. If you wait until all of the contingencies are planned for, all the resources are in hand, all of the questions answered—you will wait forever. Worse yet, you will lose tremendous opportunities for growing and thriving.

This is not to say you should jump off the rooftop to see if you can fly. We're talking about taking calculated risks—the risks based on your instincts that have evolved through your experiences and the experiences of others. If you have worked at becoming close to your community, if you know who your constituents are, if you're constantly hustling for everything, if you have taken care of your internal "politics," your instincts will tell you when to take risks. Playing it safe is for the government bureaucracies and the traditional nonprofits—it's not for entrepreneurial grassroots organizations.

Lesson Thirteen: Develop Your Power Base

Nonprofit organizations need a power base just like political organizations do. It is important to recognize the influential power groups or individuals in your community, particularly as they relate to your organization.

There are *establishment* power groups such as city governments, school boards, corporations, banks, chambers of commerce, and so on. There are also groups within these groups such as ministerial alliances, PTAs, unions, arts councils, nonprofit associations, media groups, and the like.

What is most important to know when analyzing your community, however, is the *informal* power structure. Who are the people on the foundation boards? In the urban areas, who eats breakfast at the "power" restaurants? Or in the rural areas, who drinks coffee at the local cafe each morning? What are the active service groups (Elks, Kiwanis, Lions, etc.) and who are the key people in those groups? Regardless of what the issues are—purchasing a computer, passing legislation, seeking a story in the newspaper, convincing a church to cosponsor a special event—it is important to conduct an analysis of the informal power structure in developing your strategic plans.

You develop your power base by knowing who or what the power entities are and who the "key players" are in those entities. Not only are these the people you should be calling on for support but, once they become involved, they become your constituents. They will acquire a sense of ownership in your organization and "owners" are naturally protective of their organization. Of course, you have a fundamental responsibility to be accountable and to be honest with them at all times.

Lesson Fourteen: Breaking the "Be Nice" Rule

Most of us are taught from infancy to "be nice." There is certainly nothing wrong with this admonition. It's just that when it is directed toward staff and directors of small, nonprofit organizations, it seems to suggest some type of subservient and obsequious type of behavior.

We need to remind ourselves that our political/economic system is based on the fundamental principle of competition. This principle seems to be easily adopted by the for-profit and even the governmental sectors of our society. For some reason, however, most of the people in the nonprofit community have been conditioned to believe that it shouldn't apply to them. For them, the rules (or warnings) for the nonprofits are: don't upset anyone, don't rock the boat, don't confront, "be nice" or you may not get the donation or whatever else it is you are requesting.

Well, in the process of trying so hard to be nice we are put at a competitive disadvantage with others who are not so concerned about being nice; bank officers, building managers, developers, corporate CEO's and a whole host of others whom we might encounter on behalf of our organization's effort to provide needed services in the community.

The services offered by most nonprofits meet very real and basic human needs that have not been met by the bureaucratic institutions of government or through the benevolence of the private sector. Surely, the stakes are as significant—the delivery of these services is as important as those concerns which the private and public sectors pursue so competitively.

Sometimes it is emotion, excitement, and yes, even anger, that helps gain a competitive advantage with those with whom we are negotiating. As the women's movement has learned in recent years, it is not a contradiction in behavior to "be nice" and, at the same time, to be aggressive and assertive.

Lesson Fifteen: Making Friends and Neutralizing Your Opposition

As much as we want everybody to like us, there are times when our interests will be at odds with the interests of others. It is at these times when the friends you have developed can be so important in neutralizing those who have lined up in opposition to you.

On any given project, potential allies or friends may not be obvious at first. Try to determine who else might benefit, even peripherally, by the success of your project or by achieving your organization's goals. At the same time, analyze those whose interests may appear to be in conflict with yours.

Political lobbyists know the importance of this lesson better than anyone. And whatever else you may think of this often maligned group, most of them are very decent and forthright individuals. Ask around your local political circles. It's not hard to find out which lobbyists are well respected as well as effective. Ask one of them to conduct an in-service for your organization on the topic of how to make friends and neutralize your opposition. They'll be honored and your organization will benefit immensely.

Lesson Sixteen: Outlasting Your Opposition

There will be times when, no matter how hard you try, you will alienate certain individuals or groups. You won't do this through any conscious strategy, but simply because you are representing your organization's self-interest (such as when your agency competes against another organization for the same grant, or when two groups respectively lobby for and against a specific piece of legislation.)

People, however, come and go rather rapidly. Politicians are in and out of office, foundation staff move from one funding source to another, and corporate directors for community affairs change regularly. On the other hand, your organization should be around for a long time. You may not only outlast your opponents, but you may also find yourself allied with them on a future project.

Lesson Seventeen: Mix up Your Approach

As someone who frequently will be negotiating with other community leaders and organizers, you may find it helpful to have the "good guy/bad guy strategy" in your repertoire of negotiating skills. That is, the more you can mix up your approach, the greater advantage you have in negotiations.

When negotiating with a funder on a potential grant, sometimes the warm and friendly approach works best. At other times, however, the situation may call for a much more assertive posture. The same flexibility is important whether you are working with your board, purchasing a computer, or dealing with your banker. This is not quixotic behavior; it is strategically determined behavior.

Lesson Eighteen: Learn How to Communicate with Your Community

Small, grassroots, nonprofits generally do a very good job of communicating with their memberships, but they are usually not nearly as effective in their communication with the community-at-large. It is very important to correct this because the larger the public awareness is of your organization and what it does, the greater the potential pool of volunteers, membership, and financial support.

For the most part, that awareness is best gained through the print media, although talk radio shows are also excellent vehicles for your message. Check the reporters who seem to cover the types of issues or concerns that relate to the operation of your organization. Establish personal contacts. Just as it was recommended that you enlist a good lobbyist to give advice to your staff, a good media person can also be extremely helpful—someone who knows the business and can give you excellent advice on how to tailor your communication and publicity needs through use of the print media.

The Politics of Board Relationships

Lesson Nineteen: The Care and Feeding of Your Boards

Every director should spend at least one hour each month with every member of his or her board. Some people call this "schmoozing," but there is no substitute for, and nothing is more important than, a personal relationship with each board member.

The importance of the governing board to a small, grassroots organization is much more critical than that relationship is for the larger, more traditional nonprofits. By definition, board members of small nonprofits are much more personally involved with the activities and the operation of the organization than are members of their larger counterparts. If the board and the staff are not in sync with each other, the negative ramifications can be devastating to the whole mission and purpose of the organization.

From time to time it is important for you to ask board members how they feel about their involvement with the organization. Find out what areas they are personally interested in. Don't assume that just because a board member is an accountant, he or she wants to be the resident expert on fiscal responsibility for the organization. That person may have many other talents to offer. We all have certain needs and desires that keep us excited and involved in the things that interest us. Board members are no exception. Look for ways your organization can help meet some of their needs for involvement and personal growth.

Lesson Twenty: The Board President Is the Key to Your Success

The relationship of the director to the board in general is obviously important. Of special importance, however, is the relationship between the director and the president of the board. Take great care in fostering that union. At least once a week, get together and talk about issues, problems, and opportunities. If at all possible, you need to position yourself, either directly or indirectly, so that you have a significant influence on the *type* of person to be selected for this position.

If the director and the president of the board share common values about the mission and operation of the organization, two complementary things take place. First, you compound the synergistic energy necessary to move the organization forward. Second, you avoid spending an enormous amount of energy trying to gain that required common sense of direction and purpose.

Summary

As pointed out at the outset of this chapter, politics is often considered at best as a necessary and usually undesirable activity. It is very true, of course, that the actions of many people lend credence to this view. But, politics is also the process necessary to achieve stated goals and objectives. It involves strategic planning and risk taking. It especially involves the art of effective communication. The people who are good at it learn how to avoid the alligators and successfully swim in "the administrative swamp." Good management practices teach you to pay attention to your board, to your staff, and to the community. Good politics is doing those things and doing them effectively. If you are good at it, then you know the difference between simply *surviving* and *thriving*.

Continuing Concerns

1. Describe three specific ways to show members of your organization you care about them and value their efforts.

2. What are the most easily overlooked controllable funding sources?

3. "People respond to people they know." Why is this basic observation so frequently overlooked in the sink-or-swim atmosphere of a grassroots organization?

4. How might you assess the informal power structure in a geographical location unfamiliar to you?

5. Explain the importance of investing time and energy in cultivating positive relationships among the "players" in an organization and the risks of not doing so.

Chapter

7

Selling Your Organization

Iris Fontera

> *Most businesses and public service institutions alike believe it possible to be a "leader" in every area. But strengths are always specific, always unique. . . . The question, therefore, is first: "What are our specific strengths?" and then: "Are they the right strengths? Are they the strengths that fit the opportunities of tomorrow, or are they the strengths that fitted those of yesterday? Are we deploying our strengths where the opportunities no longer are, or perhaps never were? And finally, what additional strengths do we have to acquire? What performance capacities do we have to add to exploit the changes, the opportunities, the turbulences of the environment—those created by demographics, by changes in knowledge and technology, and by the changes in the world economy?"*
> —Peter F. Drucker

Iris Fontera owns and manages a public relations and fund-raising firm. She has been active as a consultant to nonprofit organizations for more than 20 years.

Introduction

Whenever you answer a phone, provide a service to a client, speak publicly, write a letter, distribute materials, participate in a fund-raising activity, work with the media, or have a board meeting, you are manifesting the *image* of your organization. Image is what sells products regardless of whether the product is a manufactured one or a service being delivered. Everything you or anyone in your organization does or says is creating an image, either positive or negative. The way you provide your service, the attitude of your staff, the location of your facility, your activity in the community, the printed materials developed about your organization, all communicate a message about your organization to someone.

The image of your organization is basically the manifestation of two impressions. One is the impression outsiders have formed about your organization and the other is the impression members within the organization have developed about themselves. A positive image is the *sine qua non* (without which nothing) of any successful organization. With it, you can enhance the service to your clients, help keep your donors happy, recruit additional volunteers, and greatly improve your opportunities for attracting and keeping a good staff. A positive image will help carry your organization through the bad times as well as the good times. A negative image, however, can be your downfall at any time.

The Marketing Plan Is the Vehicle

If it can be said that image is the final product of your organization, then an effective marketing plan is the vehicle for achieving that image. The first step in developing a marketing plan is to know who your clients are and who needs your service. And of course it ultimately means getting your service to those special clients in the most caring, effective, and efficient manner possible.

For marketing purposes, your "clients" at any given moment can be a broad range of individuals and groups. Your clients can be the recipients of your services, the people who fund you, the media, your board members, your volunteers, your staff, legislators, or that amorphous body known as the general public. A major goal of your marketing plan is to determine if your clients (all of them) are satisfied and, if they are not, deciding what to do about it.

Internal Marketing (Communication)

Your external marketing plan actually begins with an internal marketing plan. To be effective outside of the organization, you must first have a positive and dynamic culture within your organization. In your marketing director (leadership) role, you need to help create a culture within your organization that will cause each person working there to communicate a positive message with everything they do or say. In order to be able to do this, everyone involved should have at least a "working" understanding of the mission of the organization and what his or her role is in helping to carry out that mission.

The key to developing this understanding is good communication. The result of a well developed internal communication system will be a staff that cares about itself and about others. Good internal communication helps staff members realize how important they are and reinforces the idea that each specific job is a vital part of the organization. Remember, the image that exists within your organization is very likely to be similar to the image the outside community has of it as well.

From the Directors

We're trying to help nonprofits figure out ways to survive in the 1990s. The past decade has seen dramatic increases in numbers of nonprofits. That means increased competition for funds. With the fall-off in government funding, foundations have responded by making many more, but smaller grants.

We need to learn to use our strengths by 1) applying sharpened management skills to be as efficient and effective as possible, 2) gaining a new understanding of leadership, and finally, 3) we must raise our sights to see the forest and to be courageous about where we need to go. We need to focus "back home" on our constituents, for to the extent we do that, they will support us with their time, energy, and money.

—Dick Cook, Partner
For a Change (Baltimore)

Finding Your "Niche" in a Changing Environment

Among other things, marketing also means anticipating and preparing for a constantly changing environment. Your organization must learn how to anticipate such changes and to adjust its marketing efforts accordingly. Rapidly changing attitudes and cultural values are reflective of new paradigms taking shape within our nation and our communities. More often than not, these new paradigms are presenting us with new problems for which old solutions are simply no longer appropriate.

Anticipating Changes.   In a way, these changes have given the nonprofit world and its myriad organizations a unique opportunity for leadership in finding more effective ways of addressing these new concerns. To do this, however, these same nonprofits must learn how to anticipate and prepare for future changes or, at the very least, be aware enough to recognize the changes that have already taken place. It is reasonable to expect, for example, that the administration under President Clinton will be different in its impact and relationship to the nonprofit community than was the administration of President Bush. The main point here is not whether one will be "better" than the other, but that they will certainly be different. Has your agency anticipated and prepared for this change?

Will the newly passed Americans with Disabilities Act (ADA) have a significant future impact on the nonprofit community? Will the subsequent implementation of the North American Free Trade Agreement (NAFTA) have any relevance to the nonprofit world? The answer to these questions is a resounding yes. The real question is whether there are nonprofits out there who have anticipated such changes and can offer new and creative ways in meeting the challenges brought about by such events.

For each example of an ADA or a NAFTA on the part of the national government, there are literally countless other types of service agreements, new tax laws, demographic changes, and so on taking place in virtually every community. With every change comes the opportunity for a small, creative nonprofit to offer an innovative response.

Assessing Opportunities.   Essentially, there are two ways for a small, nonprofit organization to meet the challenge of change and to rise above its competition. One is to add and improve its existing services so that whatever is being done will be done better than anyone else who is providing the same service. Unfortunately, however, when a small, nonprofit tries to compete head-on as it were, it usually leads to added responsibilities and work with the same limited staff and resources. It also means one more entity offering the same (albeit, perhaps better) service in an already overcrowded field.

A more successful way to compete is to find a creative and unique "niche." What can you do that no other organization is doing? How can you do it more effectively than anyone else? To answer these questions you must diligently research the existing competition. Who are they and what do they do well and why? What do they not do well or at all—and why?

Will your proposed niche overlap with that of another organization? Will an overlap be complementary to both organizations or simply result in a new level of competition? Will your niche provide service to new clients or will it compete for clients already being served by existing organizations? What are the funding options?

Competition Can Create Opportunities.   Even in discovering your niche, however, you are still likely to have to compete. That's okay. Competition forces us to "get our act together." It causes us to reflect on our past, assess our present, and anticipate the future. Competition pushes us to analyze our organization realistically *but* with imagination. It requires us to take a critical look at what we do well and what we do not do so well. In short, competition makes us become entrepreneurs in the most literal sense of that word— those who organize and manage any enterprise with considerable initiative and risk.

Finding your niche will also necessitate asking some hard questions. Does the existing staff have the expertise needed to successfully implement your new direction? Can you develop the necessary board and volunteer support? What are the real costs involved?

Rather than viewing competition as an added burden to the successful operation of your organization, look upon it as an opportunity to help you pinpoint your special area of expertise— where you belong in the nonprofit world and how you can fill that leadership role.

Developing the Strategic Marketing Plan

For the same reasons that it is important for your organization to develop an overall strategic plan based on the mission statement of the organization, there should also be a strategic *marketing* plan. To develop this you need to look closely at the key elements of your organization.

Identify Your Clients.   The first step in this process is to determine who your different clients are. Each identifiable group, from direct service recipients to financial donors, requires different communication approaches. You need to determine what form and method of communication are most effective with each targeted client group. To do this, ask yourself what you want each group to do, i.e., give money, write an article, refer a client, become a direct service client, speak on your behalf, and so on. The more you can target your marketing effort in this way, the more effective and less costly it will be in the long run.

Assess Your Resources.   Another critical part in developing your strategic marketing plan is to realistically assess your resources. Essentially, an organization's resources can be divided into three broad categories: human resources, financial resources, and what can be called "tools of the trade." Your human resources are staff, volunteers, board members, consultants, and a variety of other special groups including celebrities, former service recipients, legislators, and even individuals with other agencies. Financial resources, of course, include anything that can directly affect the financial picture of your organization.

"Tools of the trade" include tangible objects such as brochures, logos, press kits, videos, slides, and charts. But this category also includes your training program and the capacity of your board members, staff, and volunteers to represent your organization with the media or to other groups and individuals.

Remember, the image of your organization is always being conveyed in some form. For every project or activity engaged in, you must constantly assess whether you have the people who can write the required materials, make a successful presentation, facilitate a productive meeting, manage an event, provide necessary support services, organize and direct the always-needed volunteers, work with the media, and on and on. If you know that you cannot do a project well, it is better to not do it at all. Keep reminding yourself that the image of the organization is at stake.

Develop a Time Line.   Finally, you need to develop a time line for the various activities and programs identified in your strategic marketing plan. Be realistic in setting deadlines however. Tasks always seem to take longer than originally planned. Flexibility is also important. Leave room for periodic review and change if necessary.

Positive Public Relations Is the Goal

Many people use the words "public relations" and "marketing" as if they were interchangeable. Public relations is the result of what takes place through the writing, speaking, behavior, appearance, and service communicated by your agency and representatives of your agency. Public relations is much more than the telling of your story, it is the *result* of telling your story. It is the final image. Marketing, however, is the "tool" that determines whether that final image is positive or negative.

Making Personal Presentations

Various people within your organization will be asked to make formal presentations. As part of your strategic marketing plan, a training program should be developed for those most likely to be formally speaking on behalf of the organization.

Audience.   The most important thing to know in planning for a presentation is to know your audience. What do they want from you and *what do you want to receive from them*? Clearly state your objective. No one should have to guess why the person making the presentation is doing so. Be very honest about what you want your audience to do, i.e., contribute money, volunteer time, or use the service.

Delivery.   Think about the method of delivery. Are you going to try to reach them on an emotional level or a cognitive level or both? Should the presentation be a speech or more of an informal conversation? Will the presenter need charts, slides, historical information, specific data, etc,? How long should the presentation be? (A general rule is the shorter the better.)

Preparation.   Whether the presentation is considered formal or informal, *always be prepared.* Indeed, a casual telephone conversation to a potential donor can often be as important to the organization as a formal presentation. This means you need to know about the organization, but it also means believing in the organization— believing in the service it is providing, the quality of the staff, the commitment of the volunteers, and the organization's place in the community. Genuine sincerity and enthusiasm will carry anyone talking about the organization a long way.

Soliciting Money

Maybe the single most important personal presentation that is made on behalf of your agency is soliciting money. Thinking like a "marketer" can help.

Background Research. When you contact potential donors, be sure you know as much as you can about the person or the corporation or foundation they represent. Have they given before, how much, how long ago, what other projects do they support? What is their motivation? What do they want from you: publicity, credit, something else? What is your purpose in contacting a potential donor? Is it clearly to obtain financial support now or are you simply trying to cultivate possible support for the future?

Utilize Everyone. How can you best utilize everyone in the organization in your fund-raising program? The fact is, everyone must share some of the responsibility for raising money—from the volunteers to the director and the board. Fund-raising should be part of the job description of everyone associated with the organization. At the same time, much anxiety can be alleviated if each person knows precisely what is expected from him or her in this regard and each can prepare for this in advance.

If each person truly believes in the organization and what it provides to the community, the shared responsibility for fund-raising is not nearly as distasteful as we sometimes make it out to be. When you communicate the importance of your service and your need for money to accomplish your goals, there is no need to be ashamed. Ask with pride. If your image is that of a well managed, successful organization, other people, foundations and corporations will want to be a part of that success.

When you make these considerations while developing your fund-raising plan, you are thinking and acting like a "marketer."

Utilizing the Media

While the term "media" can mean a wide range of things, in the context of this chapter we are primarily referring to newspapers, radio, and television. Clearly, the commercial print and electronic media can be useful to your organization in the promotion of special events, influencing public opinion, and simply making people aware that you exist. Gaining access to these outlets, however, can sometimes seem to be beyond the capacity of a small, nonprofit agency. While accessing the media for a small, nonprofit can be difficult it is certainly not impossible. Like everything else we have discussed, effective utilization of the media, relative to your organization, requires assessment of your needs and your capacity to develop the media portion of your strategic marketing plan.

The Media Also Needs You.   Regardless of the size of your organization, keep in mind that while you may need the media, the reverse is also true. Remember, when it comes to your organization and what it does, *you are the expert in your community.* The media needs to know that. You need to continually remind them about who you are and what you do. Developing this awareness will not happen overnight and certainly not without a strategic plan in place. You might want to make the effective utilization of the media one of your long-range goals within your overall marketing plan.

   In any case, always keep yourself informed about what is going on in your community. If a news story appears about something that relates to the activities of your organization, immediately send off a press release that connects your organization with the story that you heard or saw. Even if it is no longer of current interest to them, you have established a contact and offered your services and expertise.

Be Available and Be Credible.   Make yourself available to the media. This is not a serendipitous process; it requires planning. Even before the media knows about your organization, they need to know you or someone in the organization on whom they can depend as their contact person. Continually position your people as *the experts* in your organization's area of activity.

   Needless to say, always be accurate and truthful in the information given. Credibility is essential. Over time and with a plan, you can develop a positive, working relationship. Your expertise and that of others within your organization can often help shape and develop stories and issues the media is covering. It is this kind of effort that will pave the way later on for timely public service announcements and other forms of awareness, i.e., what the trade sometimes calls "free press."

Satisfied Clients Are the Result

   Finally, this chapter ends where it began—with the image of your organization. The image of your organization is determined for the most part by the level of satisfaction felt by its many and diverse "clients."

   A financial donor is a client and a satisfied donor will give you more money. A volunteer is a client and a satisfied volunteer will offer more time. A satisfied user is a client and will recommend your organization to others. A satisfied staff member (a very important internal client) will work harder and with more enthusiasm. Satisfied clients (all of them) say to the community through their actions and their words that your organization is successful and it is needed. Satisfied clients are the real messengers of your marketing plan in shaping a positive public image.

Determining this satisfaction means that you must be continually evaluating your efforts (see chapter four). Sometimes this will be done through formal questionnaires and focus groups or studied analysis of users, donors, and others. Sometimes, the feedback process is simply anecdotal. Take advantage of every opportunity to evaluate how you are doing.

Summary

A positive image of your organization is the product you are seeking and the marketing plan is the vehicle. Your strategic marketing plan sets the tone for your organization. It is the link to understanding the needs of your many and diverse clients (all of them). It is through the implementation of the marketing plan that your organization can effectively respond to the changes taking place in its environment. Fund-raising, media relations, working with clients, managing the staff and volunteers, and presenting your organization to the community should all be a part of your strategic marketing plan. It's called "selling your organization" to the community.

Continuing Concerns

1. Explain why an effective internal marketing plan is necessary prior to an effective external marketing plan.
2. What new opportunities for the nonprofit community may flow from the Americans with Disabilities Act (ADA) and the North American Free Trade Agreement (NAFTA)?
3. Distinguish between marketing and public relations in terms of means and ends.
4. Explain how an organization's attempts to use the electronic and print media for marketing and public relations may represent a contribution to the welfare of its community.

Chapter

8

In Order to Get Additional Funding

Michael Tang
Len Meyer

> *You have a vision of how the world could be better, and you have a plan to make it happen. You have an organization to achieve the plan and it has members willing to do the work to win the victories. What else do you need? Money!*
>
> —Joan Flanagan, author of *The Grassroots Fundraising Book*

Michael Tang was Director of Grants and Research at Metropolitan State
College for several years before going into private business. He is now Senior
Partner in Tang Research, a fund-raising and information-brokering firm, as
well as an instructor at the University of Colorado-Denver. Len Meyer is the
Executive Director of the Metropolitan State College of Denver Foundation, Inc.

Introduction

The purpose of this chapter is not to provide a "how to" blueprint
for seeking additional major funding for your organization. Nor does
this section directly apply to that situation where there is no current
organization. Rather, its purpose is to highlight some of the
activities and steps that are of particular importance *in order to get
additional funding for an existing organization!*

We will primarily look at obtaining monies from government
sources (both federal and state) and from private foundations and
corporations. It should be made abundantly clear at the outset that
there is no magic formula for obtaining additional new funding for
your organization. In the final analysis you have to develop your
own personal expertise in this area just as you must gain
competencies in all the other areas necessary to ensure the success
of your organization.

Successful fund-raising, whether it is from public or private sector
grants, direct mail, walk-a-thons, or even bake sales, follows
successful organizational development and effective administrative
behavior. If you have not been working hard to master the art of
"juggling" all the activities discussed in the previous chapters, it
will be very difficult at this point to suddenly find major new funds
to carry out the mission of your organization.

Government Grants

The Federal Government

It may go without saying that the federal government is not in
the philanthropic business. Nevertheless, it is important to fully
appreciate that fact when seeking funds from this source. Federal
agencies give grants because they are *required by law to do so*.
When a government agency awards a grant they are, in effect,
buying a service which that agency has been mandated by Congress
to provide and oversee. Your proposal for those grant monies is your
response to the terms of the contract the government is offering to
you and other nonprofits for delivering those services.

For example, the Office of Human Development Services is a federal agency under the Department of Health and Human Services. The office administers a program called the Administration for Children, Youth and Families—Child Abuse and Neglect. The *Catalogue of Federal Domestic Assistance* (CFDA) states that the purpose of its discretionary grants program is:

> To improve the national, state, community and family activities in the prevention, identification, and treatment of child abuse and neglect through research, demonstration service improvement, information dissemination and assistance. A specific portion of funds each year is made available for projects in the area of sexual child abuse.

Reading on, this same publication also states:

> Grants or contracts are provided for (1) technical assistance to public and private nonprofit agencies; (2) demonstration, research and service projects to identify, prevent and treat child abuse and neglect; and (3) research into the incidence, cause, and prevention of child abuse and neglect.

Simply stated, the program for this particular grant source exists because Congress passed a law authorizing its existence. That also means it will most probably be around for some time. This is helpful to know because if this is an area of interest to your agency you can take the necessary time to research and more fully prepare yourself before actually making the application for funds.

More than 90 percent of the grant programs authorized by Congress in a given year will very likely be authorized again the following year. At the same time, however, very few (less than

From the Directors

It's like sailing. No matter how good the leadership and crew, no wind equals no progress. For nonprofits, funding is their wind and lack of funding is their Achilles Heel. It's essential that board members own their responsibility to cultivate stable funding sources, including individuals. Without a diverse and continuing financial support base, creative plans designed to meet critical needs will be sabotaged by "crisis-oriented" management.

—Peggy Mathews, Executive Director
Community Shares (Knoxville)

10 percent) of all the grant applications received by the federal government are funded the first time they are submitted. Fortunately, the essential requirements and guidelines of a particular program are usually very similar for each subsequent year the program is authorized. In other words, if you are not successful on your first try, you can profit by the experience and still have another opportunity.

As stated before, most government agencies authorize grants to organizations to deliver some specialized service that has been mandated by Congress. Before you frantically start to chase some arbitrary deadline, however, consider this: it is in the self-interest of the directors and administrative staff of those federal agencies to award their allotted grants to those organizations which they think *can best deliver* those services for which they are responsible. You need to decide whether it would be more prudent to hurry your application in order to make the deadline for this year's grant awards or to take the extra time to make a more thoughtful and complete application for the next round.

The Catalogue of Federal Domestic Assistance (CFDA)

No single document can give you a better understanding of the realities of federal funding than the Catalogue of Federal Domestic Assistance (CFDA). The 1991 edition, less appendices and quarterly updates, is more than 1,000 pages, and the print is very small. Still, it is the best resource on how to apply for federal grants and where to find them. The catalogue costs about $40.00 and is available from the Superintendent of Documents, Government Printing Office, Washington, D.C. 20402. New editions usually come out in July, and those who truly understand how to get government money eagerly snap up new editions as soon as they appear.

There are two principal reasons why this is the best "how to" manual on federal grants. First, it is written by the people who actually give out these federal monies. Second, it contains the most comprehensive directory of available federal grants in print.

The CFDA describes all of the federal government's domestic programs to assist Americans in furthering their social and economic progress. It has a comprehensive subject index that explains the nature and purpose of the programs listed. It identifies the application and award process, including deadlines. It also shows closely related programs and much, much more.

At first glance it appears to be a formidable document. If you learn to use it effectively, however, you can gain very important expertise in the whole federal government grant process. Most services that publish directories of available federal funds get their information from the CFDA. Why pay others for their expensive directories and services, when you can get the same information directly from the original source and probably at less cost?

Calling the "Feds"

One of the best features of the CFDA is that it gives names, addresses, and phone numbers of people who can help you get started on your grant application process. Once you have found a federal agency that appears to be requesting the kind of service your organization can provide, call the individual listed as the contact person. Indeed, the CFDA states that, "A telephone call or a letter to the federal agency contact person . . . can provide invaluable help in the beginning stages of proposal development. The potential applicant should consult the program's information person before submitting an application."

Your purpose in making such a call is to determine such things as:

1. whether it is appropriate to make an application in the first place;
2. if there's money available and how much;
3. the applicable deadlines; and
4. the process used by the agency in accepting applications.

Developing the Concept Paper

The first step in developing a proposal requesting funds is to prepare a succinct, but well worded, concept paper about your organization and the particular service or project for which you are requesting financial support. You should develop this concept paper regardless of whether you intend to solicit funds from a federal agency, the state, or a private foundation or corporation.

A concept paper is just what the name suggests. It should not be a lengthy document in its final form, but it should *clearly* respond to the *who, what, when, where, why, and how* of your organization and, in particular, the specific project for which you are requesting funds. Your concept paper is, in effect, the *alpha* and the *omega* narrative of your organization. It defines your organization's mission, long-range goals, and immediate objectives. If it is well done, it should become your principal marketing tool showing why a federal agency, a state, a foundation, a corporation, or even an individual making a small personal contribution should help fund your organization.

The Mission Statement.   The concept paper begins with the organization's mission statement. This statement, like a company logo, is your calling card to be presented to *any funding prospects*. It should be formulated with a great deal of care and with the widest possible involvement of people who have a vested interest in your organization, including board members, staff, program participants, and other supporters.

   The mission statement itself need not be lengthy, but it must be carefully developed and thought out. If you have not already done so, your organization should seek advice and direction on how to prepare this important "cornerstone" of your entire operational structure.

Goals, Objectives, and Activities.   Along with your mission statement, you should outline a long-range plan (3-5 years) with the broad goals considered necessary to effectively implement the organization's mission. Then, within each of the long-range goals, you should define specific short-term (6–18 months) objectives. As an aside, when you have completed the preparation for your concept paper, you will also have the necessary planning tool for the immediate, internal operation of your organization. Within each short-term objective, for example, specific activities or steps can be identified which are considered necessary to achieve that objective. From the mission statement, along with the goals, objectives, and activities or steps, individual responsibilities, organizational structure and the budget itself can then be rather easily determined.

Preliminary Reality Check.   A good way to know whether you have clearly answered the six questions (who, what, when, where, why, and how) is to circulate your concept paper to individuals or groups representing academic, political, professional, and lay organizations in the community. This is a relatively cheap and easy way to test market your ideas. It can also be a way of gaining important contacts and, later, valuable endorsements if they are needed. Letters of support from key people in the community can sometimes be very persuasive, particularly to private foundations and corporations.

Identifying State Funding Sources

A good concept paper provides you with the basis for securing funds from a wide array of potential sources. There are, for example, many state agencies whose guidelines may also meet the general criteria of your program concept. Since approximately 80 percent of federal funding for grant programs go initially to the states, this may be the first place you will want to look for additional new funds. *The state source of funding is particularly important for smaller nonprofit organizations.*

Usually, a state agency or department will have developed lists of potential sources to whom they can award grants for specially designated services. Obviously, one way to increase your chances for getting a state grant is to get on one or more of these various lists. To do this you need to research and identify those agencies for which your programs or services might apply and then let the appropriate people know that you want to be added to their list. What you are doing is similar to asking a potential employer to keep your résumé on file in case something comes up that might fit your job description. After you have made your interest for specific grants known to several state agencies you will then begin to receive RFPs (requests for proposal).

Writing a Federal or State Grant

Many books have been written on how to write a federal or state grant. The previously mentioned CFDA also contains an excellent section on this topic. The purpose of this chapter is to alert you to some of the more important steps in this process. It is important that you examine what the "experts" suggest. Reading and researching in this area is invaluable but only if combined with actual implementation.

Again, it is important at this point to emphasize how critical it is to develop valid and verifiable data and information to support the basic concept of your proposal. If you have done a thorough job in this area, the "skill" necessary to complete the application for funds should be relatively simple. Never lose sight of the fact that the actual writing is only one piece (albeit, a very important one) of the overall "art" of obtaining grants.

The application packet that you receive when you are writing for a particular government grant will generally have extensive instructions on how to fill out the forms and write the narrative— *follow those instructions to the letter*. If the instructions say no more than twenty double-spaced pages for the narrative, then do not submit more than twenty double-spaced pages. (And don't cheat by reducing the type so that you can get more on a page.)

Another rule to follow very closely when writing the narrative is to use the selection criteria outlined in the application packet to develop your format. The selection criteria is a description of the key elements of the proposal that readers will use to evaluate your grant application. These criteria usually include such items as:

- Documentation of need (20)
- Effectiveness of the operation plan (20)
- Quality of key personnel (15)
- Impact of project on targeted population (15)
- Budget effectiveness (5)
- Quality of evaluation plan (10)
- Dissemination plan (10)
- Institutional capability (5)

Most grant guidelines will indicate the points to be awarded for each of the criteria. For example, the number "20" following the criterion "documentation of need" indicates that 20 points are to be allotted for that section of the proposal. Points allocated to all the section criteria will total one hundred. While you should certainly pay special attention to criteria that have the most points allocated to them, do not slight the others. Unless you have a very good reason to do otherwise, always write your narrative to correspond exactly to the order given in the guidelines on selection criteria.

Remember For Whom You Are Writing

It is important to keep your audience in mind as you write the proposal. Whether it is a state or federal grant for which you are applying, there will likely be a panel of individuals with particular expertise who will read and evaluate your proposal along with many others.

Typically, the main instrument for rating these proposals will simply be a sheet of paper with a space for comments. This evaluation sheet will have headings exactly in the same order as the selection criteria identified in the grant application guidelines. Each member of the panel will read your narrative and evaluate it according to the selection criteria on the evaluation sheet.

Despite criticism, the members of these reviewing panels are *generally very fair and objective* nearly to a fault. Take advantage of this. The truly "creative" grant application is the one whose *responses are the most clear, concise, and factual.* To do this requires no small talent!

The Rejection

The chance of winning a government grant the first time around is probably no better than one out of ten *even after doing everything right*. If you receive a rejection in the mail, it should not be viewed as the end of your efforts but as the beginning of the next application round. Wait for a couple of weeks and then call the project director within the agency. Talk to him or her frankly about where you ranked, what the strengths and weaknesses of your proposal were, and ask for the written comments and copies of the winning proposals. When you receive these, you can then begin to prepare for the next round of competition.

Continue to keep in contact with the project director. Ask for advice and keep him or her informed on what you are doing. At least three months before the next new deadline, start the application process again. You should now have a much better sense of the granting agency's expectations, priorities, competition, and so on. Even if you are rejected a second time, you will have made a substantial gain in the "skill" of proposal writing and, most importantly, in the "art" of seeking grants. As a result, you will have narrowed your odds considerably for success in future applications for this or other grant opportunities.

Winning!

When you are awarded a grant, the nature of your relationship with the project officer will change significantly. The role of that person will shift from "gatekeeper" to advocate. A decision to award your organization a grant has been made because you have convinced the project officer and a panel of experts that your organization can best provide the described service according to the objectives of the grant program. In effect, your nonprofit organization, along with the state or federal government, will have launched a joint venture to serve some special need in your community. It is an exciting moment.

Private Foundations and Corporations

A Primer on Foundation and Corporate Funding

As in the case of pursing federal or state funds, a primer on pursuing foundation and corporate grants and gifts could easily require its own separate publication. While the *processes are similar*, the following section will highlight some of the unique aspects of this special form of fund-raising. Again, the purpose here is to simply key in on some specific steps and to point you in the right direction.

Frequently, applicants for corporate and foundation grants tend to acquire an almost servile attitude toward potential funders. Clearly, you are requesting money; but you are also offering something in return. It is very important to keep an overall perspective about the role and function of foundation and corporate funding programs and those agencies requesting financial support for their various programs.

For example, it should be noted that while foundations and corporate giving programs are set up for "philanthropic purposes," there are usually other reasons for their existence, as pointed out by Lundberg (1968):

> Among other things . . . foundations can become tax-free receptacles for individual or corporate capital gains. An individual or corporation may have an investment it wishes to liquidate but which stands to incur a huge capital gain or large long-term appreciation. Payment of a capital gains tax may be avoided by turning the investment over to a foundation (no gift tax) and having the foundation sell the investment (no capital gains tax). The foundation may now lend the entire liquid sum back to the donor at a nominal interest rate (no law requires that the foundation seek maximum earnings).

The fact is there are numerous tax savings associated with private philanthropy in the United States. This is not to denigrate the truly altruistic purposes of such entities, but to simply point out that there are also other incentives to "give away money" including that of basic tax benefits or to promote better public relations.

You also need to recognize that it is the business of foundation and corporate giving programs to give away money for those special causes which, *for whatever reasons, they have deemed worthy of financial support*. In requesting money for your program, therefore, you are helping foundations and corporations attain their own goals. A trustee of a national foundation gives this advice:

> Don't be hesitant about asking foundation officials to consider your request. After all, those of us who have the special opportunity to be paid for giving away someone else's money cannot justify our professional existence unless large numbers of fund raisers seek our assistance (Kauss and Kauss 1990).

Obviously, there are ways to ask that will increase your chances of receiving but always remember that *if you don't ask, you will not receive*.

Revisiting the Concept Paper

As was the case in requesting monies from governmental sources, a well developed concept paper is equally important in asking for money from a foundation, a corporation, or even individual donors. All funding sources want to give to organizations that are anticipating and planning for the future. The heart of your concept paper is what you, the staff, and supporters have determined to be the organization's priorities. These are easily identified by your stated goals and objectives. Your list of activities or steps considered necessary to achieve a specific objective then allows you to attach realistic dollar amounts to each long-range goal and to each short-term objective. A good concept paper should make it easy for someone to answer the following questions:

- What is the purpose of your organization?
- What are its priorities?
- How much will it cost to meet these priorities?
- Why should prospective funders give your organization money in order to meet those priorities?

Foundation and corporation officials who read proposals like to say that they are from Missouri. They need to be shown why they should part with their limited funds.

Earlier we noted how important it is to *clearly* respond to the *who, what, when, where, why, and how* of your project or organization. We will not dwell on the extensive research and preparation needed in order to clearly and succinctly answer these six questions except to say that it is rare indeed that one can have too much information at the completion of the concept paper.

You may use very little of your collected information in the actual concept statement. (This is sometimes referred to as "the case statement" in the foundation and corporation communities.) The point to be remembered, however, is not to make any statement that you cannot support with data. The key to your research in responding to these questions is the validation and verification of your information and data.

"Minimal" Research

A trustee of a large, local foundation was once asked the principal reason she would turn down a proposal other than simply having limited dollars. Most rejections, she answered, occur because an applicant asks for money for a project which the foundation has *no interest in funding.* In other words, the applicant did not do even the most minimal research necessary to find out the foundation's funding priorities. This is a waste of everyone's time including the applicant.

Your best general sources to obtain this kind of information are *The Foundation Directory* and the respective state directories of local foundations. The Foundation Center, which publishes *The Foundation Directory*, designates various public libraries as foundation centers. Find out which library in your area is designated as such and use that library as much as possible as your personal research center. If that is not convenient, most neighborhood libraries will have at least a section on foundation and corporate funding which may be sufficient for your needs.

Identify those foundations and corporate giving programs that have given grants to projects or organizations with a purpose similar to your own. Focus your attention first on local foundations and corporations. This is especially true if your organization or proposed project will primarily have local impact.

Once you have identified what you consider your prime sources for funding, contact them through a letter or a phone call to ask for their latest annual report, along with guidelines and deadlines for grant proposals. This information will confirm if you are really on the right track in seeking funds from a particular foundation. After you have done all of this, you will have completed the minimum research necessary in order *to begin* your formal proposal.

Initial Contact

Go through the guidelines and literature. Unless the foundation or corporation literature tells you explicitly not to call, contact the person identified as being in charge. Briefly tell that person about your project and try to make an appointment so that you can discuss your concept further in person. Before you make this appointment, however, make sure you can answer the following questions:

1. Do you have evidence that the foundation or corporation has a commitment to fund a project such as yours?
2. Is it likely that the prospect will make a grant in your geographic area?
3. Does the amount of money you are requesting fit within the foundation's normal grant range?

4. Does the prospect have specific application deadlines, guidelines, and procedures and how will these affect your application?

Some foundation guidelines state explicitly they do not want personal contacts. However, most will welcome your visit *if you've done your homework*. Here are a few suggestions to employ in your personal contact:

1. Listen closely for clues that you can incorporate into your proposal to make it more attractive to a particular funder.
2. Consider bringing along one of the project's key volunteers. A committed volunteer can sometimes catch the attention of foundation officials who often become a bit cynical when dealing with nonprofit CEOs.
3. Be prepared to deal with someone who will play the devil's advocate. You should try to anticipate every possible question. This is one more place where a carefully prepared case statement can really pay off.
4. Keep an open mind, accept suggestions, and be prepared to revise your proposal if it can be done without negating your mission and purpose (Kauss and Kauss 1990).

After the initial meeting, follow up with a thank-you note. Briefly indicate changes in the proposal you are planning to make as a result of your conversation. This will demonstrate that you were listening and it also conveys appreciation for the input given.

You do not have to overly ingratiate yourself. You simply need to convey sincere appreciation for suggestions and modifications to your project concept with which you agree. Once again, remember that foundations are in business to help those eligible for their particular grants. After all, you know your project is needed, you know that it will work, and you know that it will have a significant impact on the community. You should have the *attitude* that you are giving the foundation or corporation the opportunity to fund a good project. This is not arrogance, it is positive assertive thinking.

Persistence

Successful fund-raisers are a distinct group of people, if for no other reason than that they are undaunted by rejection. An unscientific guess is that for every proposal a typical foundation will award, at least fifteen quality applications will be rejected. This does not count those proposals rejected outright because they were incomplete, did not follow guidelines, or were inappropriate for the grant maker.

If your proposal to a foundation or a corporation has been rejected, what do you do? Remember the advice, "Ask and you shall receive"? Perhaps, that should be modified to say, "Ask again and again and you shall receive." Study the letter of declination. If it says that there were not enough funds to go around, then it is certainly appropriate to ask again. When a foundation says "no" it may, in fact, mean "not now" (Kauss and Kauss 1990).

If, after your proposal has been rejected, you are still convinced that your concept meets the priorities and philosophy of the grantor, then a telephone call is in order. Let the person you are talking to know that you understand the foundation cannot fund all qualified applicants. Nevertheless, it is appropriate to ask questions directly related to the foundation's decision to reject your proposal.

In most cases, your queries will be genuinely received. Assess your conversation. Reevaluate your proposal. Give it to other people for another "reality" test. Then, if you decide to reapply, let the foundation know that you have done additional research and assessment of your application since it was initially submitted and that you are reapplying (Kauss and Kauss 1990).

Summary

This chapter ends with the same advice offered at the beginning. Grant monies, at best, can only temporarily "solve" your problems if you do not already have a strong, dynamic and effective organization. *Grants should be seen as sources of support to help you do better the task you are already doing well.*

Private sources of money and even government grants are more likely to be given to those organizations and programs that have provided evidence of being effective, efficient, and of making a significant impact on the communities they serve. In short, the organizations most likely to obtain additional funding from new sources are those whose staff and CEOs have demonstrated they can effectively juggle all of the "balls" discussed in this book.

Continuing Concerns

1. Review a copy of *The Catalogue of Federal Domestic Assistance* (CFDA) and identify three potential grant sources for an agency of your choice.

2. In your opinion, why do panels that review funding proposals choose to adhere so precisely to published criteria in the rating process?

3. Describe the "skill" of proposal writing and the "art" of obtaining grants.

4. Discuss the importance of expressing gratitude to potential funders both for assistance during written and oral contacts during the application process and for their consideration after a decision has been made, whether or not your application was funded.

Chapter
9

Good Communication— The "Glue" of an Effective Organization
M. E. Low

> *The key to the success of any social unit, whether it be a family, a government agency, or a giant corporation, is informed participation. If individuals are to pull together in the same direction, they must understand their mutual goals and have a solid sense of how their efforts to achieve these goals relate to those of others. Thus, the responsibility of keeping oneself and others informed is a basic job of any manager.*
>
> —Thomas R. Horton
> President and CEO
> American Management Association, 1985

M. E. Low, Ph.D. is a professor of English at Metropolitan State College of Denver and a consultant on such topics as writing in the workplace and multicultural communication.

Introduction

The small, nonprofit, community-based human service agency is one such "social unit" that functions best through "informed participation." By its very nature and constituency, this definitive, interacting group of people must use effective communication if it is to maintain its own internal operations as well as succeed in reaching and helping its external audiences and clients. If we accept the analogy of communication as the "glue" of an effective organization, we may also recognize that the absence of a successful communication system and network often indicates that a major management and leadership skill is missing or misused, usually from the top administration on down.

This chapter focuses on the manager's responsibility to provide both the information and participation required for clear understanding, rational action, group teamwork and cooperation, and accurate accountability—all direct or indirect outcomes of his or her ability to communicate successfully. The effective manager possesses the skills and understanding to speak personally, personably, and clearly; to listen sensitively, carefully, and responsively; to write honestly, effectively, accurately, and intelligently; and to communicate directly and appropriately to whichever audience and for whatever purpose the job entails.

What Do You Want Others to Know or Do?

A quick way to view and understand the basic components and functions of communication is to ask and answer this question:

What do you want others to know or do?

Within the context of any organization or even the smallest social unit of two persons interacting, these nine short words provide the key to what most of us are pursuing through the communication act:

What (do)	=	**Content of communication**
You	=	**The communicator**
Want	=	**Intent of communication**
Others	=	**Audience**
To know	=	**Information/understanding**
Or do?	=	**Action/response**

Each communication component is an intrinsic, interrelated part of the total schema: someone (communicator) generates a message (content) to satisfy or meet a need (intent) and transfers (medium) it to someone else (audience), thus enabling the receiving person to know or to understand (information) or to do or to respond (action). When the targeted audience is able to restate to the communicator, "This is what I understand that you want me to know or to do" quickly and correctly, then such feedback may well indicate that this communication act has been successfully initiated, transferred, perceived, acknowledged, responded to, and completed.

From the Directors

In order to be successful in obtaining money for your organization, the first thing you must do is establish credibility with your funders whether it's through foundations, the government, or simply individual donors. Then, you have to learn how to match the prevailing needs with the sources for funds.

And you need to establish coalitions with other agencies. There are many organizations whose purpose it is to help women. We need to learn how to work together better—to help educate each other so that we can serve more people with less dollars. This is no place for super egos.

To be effective as a director, you have to be flexible—to be able to change as circumstances require it. At the same time, you need to know what is going on around you. This is particularly true with women's organizations. So much is happening and changing all of the time that if you are not constantly staying alert, you will be left behind. And perhaps the most important characteristic is to hear what others are saying. A great deal has been written about a leader being a good communicator, but a good director must also be a very good listener.

—Hazel Whitsett, Director
   North East Women's Center (Denver)

While much of our day-to-day communication is spontaneous, we should try to integrate some basic understandings and practices about what, why, how, and to whom we communicate. Applying these principles to our interactive roles and relationships—as well as to our leadership responsibilities and modeling—will make us even more aware of what does and does not work in achieving informed participation and productive communication.

You will note in the following six sections a number of questions—each of which serves to focus on a particular aspect of the communication process. Effective communicators often use such questions to prepare formal presentations or written communication; during more spontaneous exchanges or interaction, they seem to intuitively draw out much of the same information about the audience, intent, and so on from the immediate context and relationship. As with any other art or skill, good communication gets even better with consistent use and practice; and, much like glue, the better it's applied, the better it works.

Content

"Everybody knows (or should know) what we're talking about" is an often-used but dangerous assumption, particularly in small groups or organizations. It is far better to state up front what is the topic under discussion, whether in speaking or writing. The astute communicator asks such questions as:

- *What is the topic and its limits?*
- *What specific focus should I bring to this topic?*
- *To what extent and depth should I cover this topic?*

Knowing the answers (or at least being willing to take the time to ask these questions and discover these answers) before launching fully into the communication act, enables us to articulate clearly the content and to establish its focus and boundaries.

Communicator

"Who says so?" may not always be asked, but we can be sure this question frequently arises in communication that delivers new or unexpected information or mandates specific actions or responses. Recognizing this, the communicator must possess, generate, or represent the kinds of credentials that validate, corroborate, or substantiate the message or request. Questions such as these are helpful:

- *How am I identified by the audience in terms of my role, position, agency, authority, visibility, etc.?*
- *What does the audience perceive to be my viewpoint/ bias/orientation regarding this topic?*
- *Which perspective (first, second, or third person) should I assume in this communication?*

First Person

Use of first person denotes communication from the perspective of the speaker or writer: it reflects what the speaker thinks, believes, or feels. It is the most personal and subjective point of view. While "I" is a direct reference to the speaker, "we" is often used to project or represent the official voice of the agency, or at least the collective identity of a company, department, or committee. It is important to remember that the first person perspective is speaker or writer-oriented and more frequently than not reflects the communicator's own subjectivity, opinion, or attitude.

Second Person

The use of "you," especially in writing, directly addresses the audience/reader and immediately establishes a personal relationship with the speaker/writer, whether or not this is intended. "You" can be used individually or collectively, depending on the situation. The communicator should avoid the indiscriminate or so-called "anonymous" use of "you" in speaking or in writing. In such cases, it is better to use "one" or "a person." For example, change "When **you** make an incorrect calculation . . ." to "When a **person** makes an incorrect" calculation. . . ." However, since it is the legitimate term for direct address of an audience, it should be used—but used correctly and consistently.

Communication in second person is often persuasive or corrective since it focuses directly on the audience. Thus, the second person perspective is audience/reader-oriented. However, "you" language can easily become accusatory or abusive if not used carefully and sensitively.

Third Person

The use of third person provides the most objective and neutral point of view since it allows the communicator to talk *about* the subject, which may involve persons or things or events or a combination of these. In the third person perspective, "he," "she," or "they" are used to refer to people, and "it" and "they" are used for everything else. Subject-oriented communication provides a good way to avoid engaging the personal perspectives and personalities of "I"- and "You"-oriented communication. A word of caution is in order, however: the overuse of third person can turn the communication into an impersonal, unfeeling transfer of information rather than a warm, personal exchange of information and human interaction.

Another question communicators should ask themselves is: What "voice" should I use in communicating this message?

- *Personal or friendly voice?*
- *Impersonal or neutral voice?*
- *Corporate or agency voice?*
- *Natural versus "assumed" voice?*
- *A combination of appropriate voices?*

Clearly, the communicator has to be many persons, choose from several roles, speak with different yet appropriate voices, and at the same time be willing to change any of these to accommodate what is happening in a given communion event.

Intent

"Why are you telling this to us?" suggests that the audience may or may not fully appreciate or understand the reason for their receiving a particular message. In fact, many receivers of information seem to be at a loss, not knowing what to do with it or why they have received it. Others receiving the same information may be tacitly unreceptive or even openly resistant, reflecting their misunderstanding or misinterpretation of the communicator's intent. Consequently, there is still another essential question, "Why am I saying this to you at this time?", which the communicator must answer early in the communication process. Other questions serve as guidelines for formulating a sound rationale or intent:

- *What's the immediate purpose of this communication?*
- *What are the short- and long-range implications?*
- *What's the best way to make my intent known to the audience?*
- *What's the context/background for this need?*
- *What are some possible areas of misunderstanding?*
- *How can I address or preclude possible misconceptions?*

Audiences should not have to ask what any information is for or what to do with it; such queries are often the antithesis of or obstacles to informed participation and productive, interactive communication.

Audience

"Who is the targeted audience?" is one of the most significant questions any communicator needs to ask. Identifying accurately and concretely the person or persons who need the information or who are required to perform an action can often be the sole determiner of the ultimate effectiveness of your communication. While it is easy to take your audience for granted, it does take some time to generate a *current* profile of that audience, even though they may seem to be the "same old gang" or another familiar, cohesive group. Remember, attitudes and opinions change from day to day, and people have the propensity to shift loyalties or allegiances without much, if any, advance notice. Asking some quick questions may help identify the present constituency of an audience:

- *What is the general make-up/membership of my audience?*
- *What position may this audience have regarding the topic at hand?*
- *What relationship/roles do I have in regard to this audience?*
- *What other information/context about this audience should I keep in mind?*
- *What kind of reception can I expect from this audience? Openness? Bewilderment? Hostility? Excitement? Wholehearted acceptance? Indifference? A combination of responses?*

Once again, the receiver(s) of this information are significantly instrumental in determining the shape, substance, medium, and even length of the communication. Failure to consider the many variables of an audience can result in a sizeable loss of information or at least the reduction of comprehension.

Information/Understanding

"Just how much information and detail do I need to include?" Once the subject (content) has been clearly delineated, the effective communicator must address specific points and supporting details to provide the needed information. (Recall our original question: "What do you want others TO KNOW or do?") However, just knowing is not sufficient; information must also be understood, and the communicator must assume a large share of this responsibility.

Guiding questions to determine what and how much information is required include the following:

- *What does the audience already know (about my subject)?*
- *What is NOT known?*
- *What needs to be known?*
- *In what order or sequence?*
- *How much or how lengthy?*
- *How much contextual or supporting data is needed?*
- *What use(s) will this audience have for this information?*
- *How can I determine the extent of the audience's understanding?*

In the event that all of these questions cannot be answered, the communicator needs to exercise discrimination and sound judgment in deciding what and what not to say, how much to say, and with what tone and voice.

Another way to look at information is the degree of "newsworthiness" it may have for the targeted audience: essentially, what kind of NEWS is it? The communicator usually delivers five basic types of news:

Good news
Bad news
No news
Old news
New news

Interestingly enough, some people faithfully follow this exact sequence in presenting news or information to others. Yet, perhaps good news should almost always precede bad news, and no news and old news should be kept to the minimum. New news should not only receive the greatest attention but also the most extensive explanation or development.

Action/Response

The audience should not have to ask, "What is supposed to be done with this information?" Effective communicating of information should make it clear what action or response is appropriate or expected. Even so, certain contingencies need to be addressed:

- *What action(s) have already occurred?*
- *What action(s) need to take place?*
- *Who is responsible for doing what? how?*
- *What dates/deadlines/locations are relevant?*
- *What response(s) or feedback should be formulated and communicated?*
- *What conditions or circumstances may affect or determine any subsequent action or response?*

Explicit requests or directions for action help the audience make quick responses, perform appropriate tasks, assume designated roles, or follow specific regulations or policies. Good communication should result in responsive and responsible actions.

Good communication, however, is also predicated on the communicator's awareness of and sensitivity to how requests are made or directions are given. Here, it's useful to take a look at the "modal" auxiliary verbs (we called them "helping" verbs in grade school) used to indicate the type and degree of action being called for. Also it's helpful to note how much each modal verb connotes the limits and expectations placed on the actions requested of the audience. Requests or directions for specific actions take these forms (or modalities):

You may do
You could do
You should do
You must do
You must not do

These five modal verbs in the English language dictate these prescribed actions:

May	=	Optional action
Could	=	Suggested action
Should	=	Obligatory action
Must	=	Mandatory action
Must Not	=	Prohibited action

The selection and use of the right modal verb require the communicator to distinguish what freedom or choice of action the audience has; indiscriminate use of these modal verbs often creates uneasiness or resistance. Since most people do react to some degree when told to "do" something, the communicator needs to recognize the value of providing either options or valid reasons whenever possible.

Summary

Good communication *is* the glue of an effective organization. Is it possible to emphasize this too much? If the "glue" holds an agency together, shaping and supporting a cohesive yet working group, then the manager/communicator has to be the active, careful dispenser/spreader of that glue. Beyond that, the analogy may suffer from a gooey, gummy breakdown. Suffice it to say, whatever you want others to know and to do ultimately rests on you and your skill in communicating each of the six essential components needed for the successful transfer of meaning . . . and the resulting understanding and performance.

Because this chapter has not attempted to provide a "how-to" guide to communication or list pages of communication exercises or activities, you are encouraged to refer to the annotated list of additional reading at the end of the book. This list brings together a number of useful, practical, and relevant resources geared to communication needs, skills, and the problems of today's manager.

Continuing Concerns

1. In what way is communication the "glue" holding an effective organization together?
2. How can using second person (you) language easily become accusatory if used insensitively, particularly in multicultural settings?

3. Describe the importance of these six queries in shaping the written and oral communication of an agency.
   What do / you / want / others / to know / or do?

4. Identifying the target audience for media messages can be difficult. Discuss some preliminary steps useful in defining a specific audience for an agency's information.

Chapter

10

The New Meaning of Leadership for Grassroots Organizations

Ken Torp and Lisa Carlson

Whether it's the siting of a new international airport, the renovation of a downtown structure, or the elimination of funding for a safe house for battered women, the number of stakeholders wielding veto power has proliferated to the point where new leaders with new skills are essential if we, as a society, are to solve problems effectively and move forward in this increasingly complex and competitive world.

—Ken Torp and Lisa Carlson

Ken Torp is the Executive Director and Lisa Carlson the Associate Director
of The Center for Public-Private Sector Cooperation with the University of
Colorado at Denver.

Introduction

The concept of leadership in our society, whether in the public
sector, the private sector, or the nonprofit community, has undergone a major paradigm shift over the past two decades. A "leader"
in any of these areas can no longer simply issue commands,
determine directions, or pronounce answers to problems and then
charge forward expecting others to follow. Rather, the role of the
leader has increasingly moved to a more participative style
requiring the input and buy-in of others along the way. The
movement to this new form of leadership, however, has not been
easy either for those expected to "lead" or for others who are trying
to define the new leadership paradigm. The problem is that the
broad, public desire for "leadership," more often than not, seems
to reflect a nostalgic yearning for the "good old days." On the
surface there is a demand for participation and involvement but,
at the same time, there is a contradicting expectation for someone
to take charge and get things done.

The Leadership Paradigm Shift

Impact on Grassroots Organizations

This changing context of leadership has had a profound impact
on grassroots organizations. First, our society has undergone a rapid
and irreversible diffusion of power away from traditional elites and
toward previously disenfranchised groups. In the 1950s, when the
United States built the urban interstate highway system, for
example, road alignments were simply determined by state and
federal highway engineers. More often than not, this was done with
little regard about the possible negative impacts on a city or a town
or with minimal concern for adverse environmental consequences.

Those days are over. Today, African-Americans, Hispanics,
neighborhood associations, parent and school groups, urban
preservationists, and environmentalists are all demanding to be "at
the table." These groups, along with many others, are now
recognized as legitimate stakeholders with a *right* to participate in

the decision-making process that was previously viewed as the private prerogative of leadership elites.

This irreversible change in the decision-making process often translates into "going slow in order to go fast." The need is to ensure sufficient participation in the planning process in order to garner the support of *all* stakeholders during implementation.

Important Trends

The proliferation of newly empowered interests is a reflection of two very important trends that have dramatically influenced the kind of leadership that small, grassroots organizations now require. The result is a major paradigm shift that conspicuously alters the old leadership model. The first of these trends was an awakening of the American conscience demanding that civil and human rights be accorded to those who had been previously excluded from the full opportunities of our society. Racial groups, ethnic minorities, and women pressed their claims and society responded, sometimes grudgingly, by legitimating a historic transfer of power—social, political, and economic—to these newly enfranchised groups.

The second major trend was the withholding of power proxies by ordinary citizens representing every stratum of society. These were the votes of power which had previously been passively delegated to traditional institutions such as legislatures, churches, corporations, and even the major political parties. To some extent this withholding of the power proxies was, and still can be, a cynical reaction to events such as corporate or government corruption,

From the Directors

*Outsiders seem to have this stereotype, this false impression that nonprofits are a breed apart, that they are completely different from regular businesses. That's wrong! We are businesses with our hearts and souls out front perhaps, but businesses nevertheless. The never-ending juggling act with personnel, finances, board members, strategic planning and clients requires high order business skills. The caring hearts of our nonprofit organizations **do** make them very special enterprises indeed.*

—Jean Anderson, Executive Director
   Cooperating Fund Drive (St. Paul)

and tawdry scandals involving everyone from television evangelists to presidential candidates. But it is also a reflection of longer-term trends that are changing the way nations, cities, organizations, and even families make decisions. The nineteen percent of the voting electorate who cast their ballots for Ross Perot in the 1992 presidential race is an excellent example of newly discovered empowerment by those who believed their views were not being seriously considered.

The Demise of Information Elites

Another important aspect of this trend toward decentralized power is the demise of "information elites." In today's world *information is power!* The personal computer, the modem, and high-technology media have now made information available on a scale and in a manner previously unimaginable. Those small groups of information elites who previously claimed to "know what's good for the people" are being successfully challenged on a daily basis by ordinary citizens who are equipped with the information required to demand attention and/or refute the claims of the "experts." Clearly, this new grassroots empowerment does not mean that all policy or critical decisions are now being made at this level. It does mean, however, that such empowered groups and citizens can, and often do, withhold enough power to say "no" to major policies or decisions.

The Power to Say "No"

Indeed, the ability of small groups to say "no" and to back it up is one of the more salient features of the new leadership terrain. Many groups, whether highly organized or loosely affiliated and *ad hoc*, have discovered that they may not have enough power to get something done; but they almost always can generate enough power to block or force major revisions on unwanted decisions or projects. Whether it is the siting of a new international airport, the renovation of a downtown structure, or the elimination of funding for a safe house for battered women, the number of stakeholders wielding veto power has proliferated to the point where new leaders with new skills are essential if we are to solve problems effectively and move forward in this increasingly complex and competitive world.

Although the growing diffusion of power to previously disenfranchised groups makes grassroots leadership more demanding and complex, we should remember that it is also a reassuring indication that the *articulated values* of American democracy are being taken seriously. In short, the hope and promise of the U.S. Constitution and America's two-hundred-year-old experiment with democracy is on the edge of realizing its full potential.

Problems and Solutions—Three Basic Types

Despite a rather widespread awareness of the changed context in which leadership must occur, however, we still hear those nostalgic yearnings for the simpler leadership methods that *seemed to* work so effectively in the past. The problems associated with the changing expectations of leadership can be categorized into three basic types (Heifetz and Sinder 1988), each of which is discussed in this section.

Type One

In a Type One situation, both the problem and the solution are clear and determining how to respond is fairly easy. For example, a neighborhood association calls the public works director and complains about a pothole in their neighborhood; the director clearly understands the problem. He or she sends a crew to fill the pothole and the problem is resolved.

Type Two

In a Type Two situation, the problem may be clear but the solution is unclear. The responsibility for solving the problem in this situation lies with both the leader and the stakeholders. For instance, in a Type Two situation, the same neighborhood association calls the public works director complaining about the amount and the speed of traffic in their area. The problem is clear—there is too much traffic and it is going too fast—but the solution is not as obvious. For one thing, there is more than one way to solve the problem: close some streets, install speed bumps, lower the speed limit, put in stop signs, patrol the area, or employ various combinations of all these remedies. Further, any "solution" may, at the same time, create new and equally complex problems. In this instance, the public works department needs to work closely *with* the neighborhood to arrive at a "best" solution for all concerned.

Type Three

In the Type Three situation, both the problem and the solution are unclear. In this case, it is the responsibility of *all* of the stakeholders—the neighborhood association and the public works department—first to define and *agree on the problem* and then to *agree on any proposed solutions*. Typically, important community issues tend to fall into this very complex Type Three situation. For example, a community finds that its air quality often violates E.P.A. carbon monoxide standards and a "brown cloud" is visible over the area. The *problem* may be excessive auto use, uninspected vehicles, underdeveloped mass transit, industrial sources, atmospheric inversions, and on and on. The *solutions* can be equally unclear. They could involve carpooling, cleaner burning fuels, investments in public transit systems, more stringent regulation of smokestack emission, and so forth.

Unfortunately, however, society still seems to want leaders who can both define the problem and solve it in the simplistic fashion represented in Type One situations. Ironically, when our leaders do, in fact, respond quickly and unilaterally to very complex problems, the public retribution can amount to career extinction if those decisions later prove wrong.

A more rational and effective approach would be to admit that most major problems fall in the Type Two or Type Three categories and can only be solved if the stakeholders are intimately involved in the decision-making process. With such a straightforward approach to decision making, we might at least have a chance to move on to the next step. Further, we might also be able to attract and keep very capable people in leadership positions because the expectations regarding *who* is responsible for problem analysis and solution will be vested with the stakeholders, not just the leader.

The Limits of Win/Lose
Political and Judicial Systems

Nowhere is the emerging leadership paradigm more evident than in its response to the limited win/lose options offered by our traditional political and judicial systems. Whether it is in the courts or legislative bodies, adversarial proceedings encourage competitive positional warfare that often overlooks opportunities for more durable and higher quality *collaborative* solutions. Furthermore, the "solutions" that emerge from these processes are immediately subject to appeal to yet another win/lose level in those systems.

In the political arena, of course, the "losers" can regroup, launch petition drives, organize recall campaigns, or gather enough signatures to get the issue on the ballot as a referred item. Even if these efforts prove successful, however, the resulting dichotomy of winners and losers remains. In the judicial arena, the appellate possibilities often seem inexhaustible with the result that veterans of contentious litigation will do almost anything to avoid going to court where that final win/lose decision will be made. Thus, we have seen the appearance of a growing new industry in America under the broad rubric of "alternative dispute resolution."

A New Way

Few, if any, of the complex challenges facing nonprofit organizations today can be solved by traditional win/lose decision-making models. Whether the mission of the organization is to eradicate sexual abuse of children or to provide a forum to encourage the arts in the community, the solutions are dependent upon how the problems are framed—a task that in some instances has as many perspectives as there are people.

In the traditional decision-making model, the leader or director decides on the "right" answers, sells them to the board, and directs the staff to implement them. Not only is this strategy not very effective in today's environment but, in most cases, it simply will not work. Organizations that continue to use this Type One or linear process generally produce staffs and boards who feel unempowered and have high rates of burnout and turnover. Further, most accepted research indicates that groups—not individuals—tend to make better decisions, particularly when people *actively listen* to each other, confront conflict directly, and do not rely on competitive, win-lose conflict management strategies (Hall 1971). In other words, better decisions will be made by groups when they commit to specific process choices regarding participation.

The contemporary leader must know how to effectively address *process* issues as well as content issues. The leader's role primarily becomes one of convener, catalyst, and consensus-builder. He or she not only must keep track of *what* is being addressed but *how* issues are being addressed and who is addressing them. The key word is *empowerment*. People need to feel that they have, in fact, been part of the decision-making process. Warren Bennis describes empowerment as *the collective effect of leadership*. He goes on to say that empowerment is evident when four conditions are being manifested:

1. People feel significant about themselves and what they are doing. Everyone is made to feel that he or she makes a difference to the success of the organization.
2. Learning and competence matter. It is understood that there is no real failure, only mistakes which provide feedback and help determine what to do next.
3. People within an organization feel they are part of a community where there is a team, a family, a sense of unity along with leadership.
4. Work is stimulating, challenging, and fun and where the leaders articulate and embody the ideals toward which the organization strives (Bennis 1989).

For the typical nonprofit organization, the work of empowering others is made more complex by the diverse number and type of stakeholders. Nonprofit organizations must learn to contend successfully with boards, staffs, volunteers, funders, and the general community they are serving. Obviously, the interests of these groups may conflict and leaders or directors need to be prepared to resolve those differing interests.

Many nonprofit organizations are finding that stakeholders often need face-to-face communication in order to solve complex issues. Organizations are discovering that it saves a great many problems down the road if they include a representative mix of stakeholders in their strategic planning and goal-setting sessions at the very beginning. Doing this helps the organization set more realistic goals which, in turn, are more clearly understood (and accepted) by those who will have to implement them. To do this, however, requires that the roles of the participants be clearly articulated to avoid creating other problems, such as the board trying to run the day-to-day operations or the staff making policy decisions without board approval and knowledge.

Summary

The changing definition of leadership demands leaders in the nonprofit sector who are able to recognize and include empowered stakeholders in the decision-making process. The new leaders will be those individuals who also appreciate that leadership is not simply a function of one person but a whole *team of leaders* with each person building on the strengths of the others. The challenge for effective decision making is made all the more difficult since our traditional political and judicial systems are not designed to complement this new leadership and decision-making paradigm.

In spite of nonsupportive, traditional systems and a continuing yearning for "the good old days," the new leadership paradigm is clearly taking over. It is predicated on the empowerment of stakeholders in the decision-making process. Small, nonprofit organizations may understand this leadership paradigm shift better than any other sector in our society. It is, therefore, up to the leaders and staffs of these organizations to provide the models of excellence for the rest of the country.

Continuing Concerns

1. Discuss the twin impacts on grassroots organizations of newly empowered subgroups and more independent voter activism at all levels of society.

2. Explain the frustrations that result when society wants Type One solutions to Type Three problems.

3. In what way should the collective effect of the contemporary leader be empowerment for all participants in the organization?

4. What characteristics of small, nonprofit, grassroots organizations position them to lead the development of the new leadership paradigm?

Gaining Trust for Your Organization

Henry Cotton

> *The ultimate test of moral leadership is its capacity to transcend the claims of the multiplicity of everyday wants and needs and expectations, to respond to the higher levels of moral development, and to relate leadership behavior—its roles, choices, style, commitments—to a set of reasoned, relatively explicit, conscious values.*
> —James MacGregor Burns

> *What is honored in a country will be cultivated there.*
> —Thucydides

Henry Cotton, M.A. is a nationally noted public school educator. He currently is an adjunct faculty member teaching ethics for the Graduate School of Public Affairs, University of Colorado at Denver.

Introduction

We don't need a moral code or ethical perspective if we choose not to live or work with other people. Robinson Crusoe could do precisely what he wished as long as he was the sole inhabitant of his island. His encounter with another person on the island changed the nature of his daily existence. Questions about what is right and wrong, fair and unfair, just and unjust, reasonable and unreasonable in the treatment of one another become important considerations. These questions and others like them require consideration of ethical relationships. This chapter explores ethics, fairness, and trust as matters of personal choice and as key components in establishing the culture of a nonprofit organization.

The Nature of Ethical Relationships

Most of us would not choose to live totally alone even if it were possible. The positive experiences in our lives are almost always related to our relationships with others. In our personal and in our work lives, how we relate to others plays a significant role in the success or failure of our activities. Working out these relationships depends a great deal on the ethical considerations we choose to live by. Nowhere are these observations more true than in the very close and personal work environments of small, community-based, nonprofit organizations.

Personal Choice

Unlike scientific principles that direct our physical actions, the law of gravity for instance, ethical principles are matters of personal choice. Watergate, Irangate, insider trading, the savings and loan scandals, and the almost hourly news stories of other breaches of conduct by our elected and appointed officials could easily lead one to believe that ethical conduct in our nation is rare. Yet the very fact that these examples of unethical conduct are so instantly recognizable is evidence that the public does acknowledge the difference between right and wrong. To say this certainly does not compensate for the misbehavior of individuals or institutions. It simply affirms the proposition that, as a nation, we have not lost our sense of ethical direction, we just need to work harder to attain it.

The Notion of Fairness

From childhood to maturity, Americans identify with the concept of fair play. Children are very quick to respond with "It's not fair" when they sense that a rule is being broken or another child is being given an undeserved advantage. In some of our athletic contests we have gone as far as electronic review to assure that even those who are responsible for enforcing the rules are making accurate

From the Directors

The idea for Brothers Redevelopment came from some of us who were living in the community. Most of us knew firsthand the problems that needed to be addressed, particularly in housing for low-income families. We felt we could create an opportunity for ourselves and, at the same time, maybe we could also help others.

Of course, we didn't have any money. All we had were good intentions. But we started anyway. Initially, everything was done through volunteers and donations. At first, we recruited the volunteers within the community. Then, after we began to develop a little organizational structure, we began to look for volunteers outside of the community.

I remember our first "outside" volunteer was a Mennonite from Kansas. Thinking back, we were very fortunate. He was a classic example of an effective volunteer—a man with a generous heart, a strong commitment, and lots of skills. It didn't take long before we started tapping into other religious denominations. The response was terrific.

I suppose if I had to point to one thing which underlines our success it would be that we surrounded ourselves with good people. Over the years we have been able to hand pick our board members as well as our staff. Since we receive no tax monies, we're not saddled with a lot of governmental guidelines. I think most federal and local government guidelines are intended to do good, but my experience is that many times they just don't work.

—Joe Giron, Director
Brothers Redevelopment (Denver)

judgments. In our courts, the ability to determine right from wrong is a crucial aspect in establishing a person's responsibility for his or her actions. We expect from our judicial system that similar cases will receive similar treatment; that is, that circumstances being approximately equal, what is right or wrong for one person is right or wrong for another.

That the punishment should fit the crime is another aspect of fairness that we insist upon. We go to extraordinary lengths to see that accused persons in our society get a fair trial before guilt is established. Fairness, then, is a major ethical consideration in all our personal, professional, business, and legal interactions. We seem to know quickly and consistently when we are being treated unfairly. It would seem that we ought to know just as quickly and consistently when we are treating another unfairly.

The Test of Universality

One test we might use to determine fairness is what the German philosopher Immanuel Kant called the *test of universality*. Would we want a particular action applied by all persons in similar conditions at all times to all others including ourselves? If we can answer yes to that question, we would quite likely consider the action fair. If we were to lie to another, for instance, would we accept a similar situation in which it would be fair for another to lie to us?

When we apply the test of universality to situations consistently, we are quite likely to end up preferring that the truth be told more often than simple convenience might dictate. This would seem to suggest that ethics involves more than just a *situational application*. Indeed, ethics seems to require that it be applicable in *all situations*. If we just tell the truth when it serves our own interest or convenience, we are not going to be pleased when others choose to do the same. Of course, it is possible for reasonable people to disagree about a number of things. Personal preferences are often what distinguish one human from another. We can, more often than not, exercise our preferences without doing harm to anyone else. It is precisely when we meet the point where our preference or action interferes with another's preference or action that ethical considerations become important.

Determining a Code of Ethics For Your Agency

The question of what is the right thing to do becomes a matter of ethical concern. It is a question to be answered personally by each individual. It is also a question to be answered in establishing the culture and ethical code of each nonprofit organization.

Organizational and Personal Promises

Are the explicit or implicit promises your organization makes to its clients, its funders, its staff, its volunteers, and even to itself merely impersonal organizational promises? When you join an organization as a paid or volunteer member, do the organization's promises become yours? To what degree are you obliged to keep them? Are there any acceptable reasons for not keeping them? Is it situational and/or a matter of degree? Suppose, for example, that a person promises to pick you up at the airport but, at the last moment, decides to go to a movie instead. You are left waiting at the airport without the expected ride home. Would you be satisfied with an explanation that states, "I just changed my mind," or "I didn't know that particular movie was playing when I made the promise"? Would you feel differently about not being met if the person said, "I was on the way but had a serious accident and could not get there"? We expect the promises of the organization to be kept if they are made either explicitly by a person or implicitly by the statements which describe the agency. We can also expect people to understand and accept the unplanned conditions that prevent a promise from being fulfilled. Certainly there can always be an exception that would keep you or the organization from keeping a promise. The point, however, is that such an exception needs to be a compelling one in order to justify a promise not being kept.

Promises Are Voluntary

Remember, neither your organization nor anyone in your organization is compelled to make a promise. Whether it be part of a contract, a *quid pro quo* arrangement, or simply a one-way commitment, a promise by its very nature is a personal act. If it is made under some form of duress, it could not ethically qualify as a voluntary process. Once made, there should be the expectation on both sides of the act that a promise will be kept. Violating it, at minimum, requires an apology and explanation. When the consequences are of a more serious nature to the person, group, or organization promised, it could easily result in *a lack of credibility for the entire organization*. There is little that is more important in establishing the ethical character of a person than the legendary "my word is my bond." Similarly, when applied to an agency, it becomes "our word is our bond." There can be no higher complement of ethical behavior for either a person or an organization.

The "Trust Factor"

Persons in positions of public or nonprofit responsibilities are particularly judged both by others and by history on the basis of whether promises made were in fact kept. This judgment, particularly as it relates to the acts and behavior of our public officials and institutions, is constantly being measured by pollsters and is often called the "trust factor." How do we come to trust a person or an organization? More specifically, why should the public trust you and your organization? When you are ill and go to a doctor for diagnosis and prescription, do you trust that you will be well served? How much do you weigh credentials, past performance, someone else's recommendation? These are the same considerations being made by those individuals whose trust your organization seeks.

Trust or distrust are factors that exist in some manner in practically all human interaction. For the most part, trust is something we take for granted as we go about our daily activities. When we give our clothes to the cleaners and they say, "They will be back on Thursday," we trust that when we return on Thursday our clothes will not only be there, but that they will be cleaned to our satisfaction. In turn, the cleaner trusts that if the service was performed, payment will be made.

Many of us start our day with a cup of coffee. If we add a little cream and sugar, we are placing trust in the belief that the coffee is not contaminated, that the cream has been pasteurized, and that the sugar has been refined. If we needed to pretest all those assumptions, we would not get much further in our day than the morning cup of coffee.

Members of an organization should be able to automatically place their trust in the other members of the organization. We should neither expect our customers or the people of our community to have to "pretest" the trustworthiness of our organization nor should we demand any more from the members within the agency. Internal trust is just as important to an organization as the trust we hope to establish externally. Trust is fundamental to all human relations. We would have a very difficult time living in our complex society if we could not trust a myriad of complete strangers to perform in a trustworthy manner. Surely we should expect no less in our relationships with each other within the agency.

The Apotheosis of Ethical Behavior

Fairness, honesty, and trustworthiness are naturally accomplished if we live up to another of Immanuel Kant's principles: that each person be treated as an end and not as a means to some other's end. That is, we recognize and act on the knowledge that each person has an individual dignity worthy of respect on its own terms.

Respect for the Inherent Dignity

Of course, we know that not all individuals act fairly, honestly, or trustworthily. According to Kant, however, you can despise the unethical *behavior* of an individual while, at the same time, separating the *act* from the inherent worthiness of the person committing the act. The child, for example, who behaves badly is not a bad child and, despite the behavior, has within him or herself the possibility for goodness.

It is particularly difficult to separate the act from the ultimate nature of the actor if we are the one being acted upon. But this is the very essence of ethical behavior as it has been defined from its earliest consideration. Socrates, in Plato's dialogues, argues persistently that to receive harm is better and more virtuous than to do harm. He argues that good cannot come from evil but that only evil can come from evil. The Sermon on the Mount in the Bible makes the same argument when it advises that one struck on the cheek turn the other cheek. These arguments require considerable forbearance on the part of the harmed but represent the apotheosis of ethical behavior.

Our Personal Sense of Conscience

In colloquial terms, we hear people talk about "what goes around comes around" or in proverbial terms "time wounds all heels." Whether in sophisticated philosophical discussion or in more pedestrian language, the idea that we are held responsible for our actions in this world (or in another) is a significant factor in motivating us to behave ethically. Without attempting a complex discussion of conscience, observation of human behavior quickly leads us to believe in its existence. It is conscience, according to Shakespeare, that "doth make cowards of us all." We readily accept that there is such a phenomenon as a "guilty conscience" and we say we feel better about ourselves when our "conscience is clear."

From the classical writing of Aristotle to Thoreau, Ghandi, and, in modern times, Martin Luther King, they all make appeals to conscience when required to justify their actions. There is inherent in this appeal an assumption that there is something more that ultimately determines our action than simple advantage, opportunity, might, or success as defined by our own interests. It is that sense of conscience that defines for us what is right, what is good, what is just, and what is fair.

Using Your Conscience As a Guide in the Workplace

This same sense of conscience must also guide our behavior. In a very real sense, it is the person who represents the organization's collective behavior that determines the ethics—the trust—of the organization. That person must also support the organization's need to provide services that are expected, to respect people as individuals, to refrain from hurting others, to repair damages caused, to apologize for errors in judgment, and to support equality of opportunity and a level playing field for all.

Summary

Over the past decade we have seen a growing expression of cynicism by the public for governments and government employees (elected or otherwise) in what they do and why they do it. When nonprofits grow to such a size that they become indistinguishable from the large bureaucracies in the public sector, they tend to also get linked with the same negative perception in the minds of the people. Witness, for example, the public relations disaster that occurred in the recent aftermath of the financial improprieties of the former director of the national United Way program. State and local United Way chapters are still trying to recover from the drop in contributions brought about by that situation.

Of course, many small nonprofits have no doubt engaged in similar behavior which has brought about an equal or even greater lack of trust in their operations on the part of the public. Being small may make such behavior less noticeable, but it is no less important to the immediate community or clients being served.

Whether it is the federal government, a city or a state, a large nonprofit or a small one, to some degree, the public's perception of their trustworthiness continues to be eroded. Most scholars of public and nonprofit administration say the same thing about the public's perception of trustworthiness—it is essentially the product (either positive or negative) of ethical behavior manifested by those who work in these sectors.

It is important to note that such behavior is not limited by only those ethical norms found in a specific law, a personnel handbook, or some other written document. Indeed, the cornerstone for developing a position of trustworthiness is generally determined by that ethical behavior for which there are no defined, written rules. In a feature article on the ethical behavior of members of Congress, *TIME* magazine once noted that most of the acts being questioned were neither illegal nor in violation of that institution's self-imposed written rules of conduct. For the most part, the public angrily objected to the behavior manifested by these members that should have been based on a very simple understanding of right and wrong.

As we have seen in this chapter, ethics is basically that sense of good which we wish for ourselves as individuals and for all those we care about. It is that same sense of good that we must demand in our interpersonal, intrapersonal, and professional relationships. It is a set of self-determined guidelines that should direct our behavior under *all* conditions. It is virtually impossible to have one set of ethical norms for work and a completely different set off the job.

The culture of any organization is essentially determined by the collective and individual acts and behavior of each person within that organization. When the members of a family lose faith in each other, the family will not hold together very long. Similarly, when workers, customers, and the community can no longer place their trust in an organization, that organization will not hold together very long. Sometimes the conditions of the moment blur the case and render it difficult to make appropriate ethical decisions. But consider that without such ethical behavior, our lives would be without meaning and purpose. We grow and prosper *only through our relationships with others*. When we only care about ourselves, we end up with a very small self to care about.

Continuing Concerns

1. How might the *test of universality* be a justification for the existence of small, nonprofit, grassroots organizations?

2. Explain why organizational promises unkept are unethical.

3. How might grassroots organizations offer paid and unpaid employees unusual opportunities to integrate personal work-related ethical values?

Chapter

12

Thriving
Survival Skills for Jugglers
Alan M. Dahms

Life only demands from you the strength you possess. Only one feat is possible—not to have run away.
—Dag Hammarskjold, *Markings*

Your position never gives you the right to command. It only imposes on you the duty of living your life that others can receive your orders without being humiliated.
—Dag Hammarskjold, *Markings*

Introduction

Grassroots administration requires a special talent. Attempting to do the seemingly impossible with limited resources tests our creative abilities as well as our intellectual, physical, and emotional stamina. We tend to overlook our own needs. Yet, being an effective juggler requires that we pay attention to personal intellectual, physical, and emotional survival. What can we change? What must we accept without change? Who says so? What are the alternative solutions? Are the personal costs too high? In what ways do we act to challenge limitations? How do we strike a productive balance? Such questions have ever-changing answers. Asking such questions is a matter of survival.

Hammarskjold's reflections, appearing in his posthumously published *Markings* (1964, 1983), invite us to think about ourselves in terms of our behavior. At thirty-six, Chairman of the National Bank of Sweden, he went on to devote his life to public service, his own juggling act. He served as Secretary General of the United Nations from 1953 until his death September 18, 1961, in an air crash in Northern Rhodesia.

The ideas in this brief chapter are meant to influence your behavior. If you accept the invitation to focus more attention on your own needs, an important process will be set in motion. You will come to perceive your own choices, costs, risks, and life-style options in new ways. The need for action on your part will seem more immediate.

Whereas the preceding chapters in this book have dealt with various aspects of the "juggling act," this chapter will focus on your intellectual, physical, and emotional survival. In doing so, there are several questions we must consider:

- *Why do we postpone, through avoidance, necessary emotional business with each other?*
- *Why is avoidance so popular and primary or secondary control based on awareness so unpopular?*
- *Why do we think our agencies can* simultaneously *hurt staff members while being effective providers of help to others?*
- *Why do we sometimes give* things *a higher priority than* people?
- *Why do we ignore the emotional needs of ourselves and others?*
- *Why do we sometimes behave so ineffectively?*

- *Why do we sacrifice the precious present moment on the altars of past and future?*

When administrators and staff members in grassroots agencies are asked what they're doing to take care of themselves, many of them answer by saying, "I've never thought of that. After all, I'm here to help others. I've completed academic work in human services, social work, community services, and business, and no one ever invited me to put *myself* first. I was taught how to help *others*." As you work through this chapter, think about *your* needs. If you ignore those needs, you will pay an exorbitant personal and professional price.

If we ignore our own needs, those thousand points of light referred to in the first chapter will be very dim. They will be dim even with appealing financial incentives for participation available. Ignoring human needs within agencies will result in a human energy crisis.

Along with all of their other responsibilities, administrators of small, community-based, nonprofit agencies must also deal with conflicts between staff members and volunteers, self-serving board

From the Directors

We will be 17 years old in March. We started as a total volunteer effort. Now we have a paid staff of 12 and our operating budget is nearly $500,000. And we still do not receive any government support whatsoever.

It used to be that you had to have six degrees printed on your forehead in order to even discuss the problems families were having. Some of our volunteers do have degrees, but we don't focus on their formal education. We are more interested in whether a person is a good listener, whether he or she has the ability to be truly nonjudgmental and, most importantly, whether that person can be nurturing in his/her relationship to the family. We were pioneers in using lay people in this way. It works!

But just "doing good" isn't enough. We owe it to our consumers, our customers if you will, and to every person or entity that supports us to be financially accountable in everything we do.

—Sally Holloway, Executive Director
Family Focus (Denver)

members, part-time clerical help, piles of urgent phone messages, negative publicity, and on and on. How do they survive emotionally? What skills do they need? As a consultant to many grassroots organizations, I've asked administrators these questions to determine why some are victims of stress, whereas others seem to use stressful situations to further their own growth.

In the following section we will look at costs associated with avoiding rather than coping with emotionally meaningful issues. Then a later discussion of the four thriving skills offers us opportunities to reflect on survival for administrative jugglers.

Avoidance

Experts in addictive processes talk about avoidance. So do public figures who describe their own healing processes in the print and electronic media. One way to view avoidance is to draw on the following prayer as an illustration.

> God, give us grace to accept with serenity the things that cannot be changed, courage to change the things which should be changed, and the wisdom to distinguish the one from the other.

This serenity prayer was written by Reinhold Niebuhr in 1943 and reportedly was first used in a worship service at the Congregational Church in Heath, Massachusetts, where Professor Niebuhr spent his summers. It is possible that only the Lord's Prayer is more widely recognized among many people. The serenity prayer may reveal as much about current conditions of accelerated change as the table prayer discussed in the first chapter (with its focus on the categorical imperative) revealed about concerns in Victorian England. The Niebuhr prayer recognizes the universal role that *change* plays in human experience.

The serenity prayer is commonly used by all varieties of twelve-step, self-help programs patterned after the model pioneered by Alcoholics Anonymous. Twelve-step groups currently address issues of limitless variety from substance abuse to specific psychological disorders. A 1990 cover story entitled "The Twelve-Stepping of America" in a popular news magazine reflects this wave of interest.

Psychologists have written about control in ways that seem to be variations on the serenity prayer. Americans have generally focused on *primary control*; that is, active intervention in an attempt to change existing realities. The myth of the rugged individual who, through hard work and self-denial, conquers the hostile new frontier is a very familiar part of American folklore enshrined in scores of western movies. In *secondary control*, individuals adapt themselves to circumstances by accommodating themselves to events. In Japan (Weisz, Rothbaum, and Blackburn 1984), secondary control has a much more central and culturally defined role than in the United States. It is possible to argue (Ho 1985) that North America has overemphasized primary and Asia has overemphasized secondary control.

Avoidance or denial leads us to turn our awareness from what needs to be done and instead to pretend all is well. Avoidance as a posture almost always leads to difficulties, whether it be emotional problems such as depression (Burns 1989), physical illness (Holmes and Rahe 1967), or a lack of healthy pleasures in life (Ornstein and Sobel 1989).

Deciding whether to take action (primary control) or to adapt oneself to circumstances (secondary control) is comparatively easy in routine settings in which our feelings of worth are not centrally involved. For example, if a salesperson gives you incorrect change after a purchase, you probably decide between primary or secondary control based on how much money is involved. If the error involved a few pennies and the store is ten miles from you, you probably implement secondary control and say, "Oh well, it's just a few pennies . . .". You do not avoid deciding what to do.

In our jobs and especially in those relationships that matter to us at home or work, things become more difficult. When differences of opinion arise between a staff member and supervisor or between two colleagues working as peers, it is so tempting to ignore the disagreement, to avoid, to deny, to pretend the issue will go away. It will not. The conflict silently escalates until a blowup occurs. Why? Because an informed decision, a choice about primary and secondary control, was not made.

In our daily lives, it takes *courage* to cope openly with issues. Addictionologists call the unfaced, avoided issue the "elephant in the living room." It is as if the big issue, the source of pain, whether in the living room or the agency, is the unfaced issue. The elephant is a very emotionally costly end result of a game of "let's pretend" requiring at least two participants.

On the other hand, thriving demands that we minimize avoidance as we hone our skills in fashioning the appropriate blend of primary and secondary control. For example, when a parent dies, we cannot use primary control to restore life, so our main approach is secondary control. We must accommodate ourselves to new circumstances in that person's absence. Yet we can exercise some primary control by attending funeral services, extending ourselves to comfort others, and taking action in a variety of other ways.

Just as we need to balance primary and secondary control in our individual lives, so do agencies need to maintain a similar balance in the broader context in which they exist. What if an important external funding source dries up unexpectedly? What action, if any, can be taken by my agency? Is there a way to change circumstances? If not, how do we accommodate to the new situation? It is through the process of weighing primary and secondary control factors and diminishing avoidance that our thriving is enhanced.

Thriving Skills

An analysis of responses from individuals regarding their methods of surviving emotionally has elicited four thriving skills (Dahms 1980):

1. cultivating available choices;
2. weighing personal costs and benefits in situations;
3. challenging alleged limitations by taking risks; and
4. assuming responsibility for designing a life-style with an appropriate, delicate, ever-changing balance of primary and secondary control.

These skills are examined in the following sections. Each of us needs to practice these skills every day. What we know is of no help to us unless we apply it. Consider how important these skills are as you meet (or choose *not* to meet) your day-to-day responsibilities.

Cultivating Available Choices

Thrivers believe that it's better to choose actively than to avoid issues and, by default, let circumstances dictate outcomes. They realize that choosing involves taking risks and they assume responsibility for the consequences of their choices. They know that one excellent definition of *emotional illness* is "the inability to perceive available choices." They recognize the dangers inherent in waiting for others to initiate change; they initiate needed change on their own. For example, you can choose your occupation. If you feel trapped at present, you need to consider some alternatives. You *do* have a choice. It is estimated by futurists that 75 percent of the current American labor force will be producing services or goods that aren't currently available at a future point in their working careers. If it is true that the average person experiences five to seven major career changes in his or her lifetime, then effective "choosing skills" related to work have never been more important.

The process of choosing includes *selecting* certain beliefs that are personally valued and then *acting* in terms of those beliefs and values. Choosing skills are most effective when individuals have a clear understanding of their own belief/value systems.

Individuals who neglect to develop their choosing skills may become victims of their own version of the South Indian monkey trap. The trap consists of a hollowed-out coconut chained to a stake. The coconut contains rice that can be grabbed through a small hole. The hole is big enough to accommodate a monkey's hand but not a fist filled with rice. When a monkey reaches into the coconut, it becomes trapped by its own behavioral routine and doesn't "choose" to release the rice. We need to remember that we have choices, and need to learn how to develop our choosing skills.

Choosing Relationships.   The most critical choices individuals have to make are those that determine with whom they relate. Although these choices are important to everyone, they are particularly important to those individuals who provide human services. On what do people base these choices? Each of us learns at an early age that many people are different from ourselves; in fact, more people are different than are similar. We are made aware of the fact that others do not share our family name, economic status, skin color, ethnic tradition, sexual orientation, age, first language, or physical health.

To be effective, nonprofit, human-service administrators need to unlearn these categories and rediscover the needs shared by *all* members of the human family. Because we learn to categorize individuals so early in life, several groups—older persons, for instance—are accorded low status. It seems easy to forget that common needs are shared both inside and outside our agency.

The Multicultural Challenge.   Tragically, it seems easier for us to harm those who look and act differently from ourselves than to harm persons more similar to us. Children are often taught by parents, and later by society, that certain people are "different." They often learn to use words such as *gook, jap, commie, homo, burnout, druggie, beaner, egghead, retardo, queer, honky, spic, yuppie, gimp, nigger*, and so on. Unfortunately, little people who learn prejudice become big people who view African Americans, Anglos, Native Americans, Mexican Americans, senior citizens, gays, handicapped persons, and others as different—so different that inflicting intellectual, physical, or emotional injury on them is not considered wrong.

As children then, many people learn to base their actions on what

Slater (1970) called the *toilet assumption*; that is, the notion that unwanted matter (unwanted difficulties) will disappear if removed from our immediate field of vision. It is an avoidance posture. Those who base their attitudes and behavior on this assumption deal with social problems by decreasing their visibility. In what amounts to avoidance at a societal level, issues are not faced through either primary or secondary control and the elephant runs free. Examples of this approach abound in our society: the flight to the suburbs, the isolation of the ghettos, the institutionalization of the aged and the physically and emotionally handicapped, and so on. As a result, the underlying problems of our society are removed from daily experience and consciousness, and the knowledge, skills, and motivation needed to deal with them are lacking.

Weighing Personal Costs and Benefits

You cannot help others if you are not good to yourself. By becoming a victim of a choice-blind monkey trap, you engage in behaviors that exact enormous personal costs. For example, you might ignore messages from your internal "personal-cost accountant" that indicate you are overtired and overextended. When asked what pleasures you enjoy (Ornstein and Sobel 1989), you might respond, "What do you mean?" You might associate with people who drain your energies and cause you to feel depressed (the "death dealers"), and fail to relate to people who give you energy and extend growth invitations to you (the "life givers"). You might refuse to give yourself permission to be good to yourself.

Depression (the "common cold" of emotional problems), feelings of helplessness or hopelessness, insomnia, and loss of appetite (Burns 1989) signify that personal costs exceed personal benefits. When you adopt a stiff-upper-lip attitude and disregard your own well-being, you invite high blood pressure, heart attack, bleeding ulcers, ulcerative colitis, and emotional turmoil.

Life-Change Stress. Major changes and developments over which individuals have little control are sources of a great amount of stress. Research reported in some detail as early as 1967 (Holmes and Rahe) shows that a relationship exists between stress and illness and that, in many instances, reaction to stress precipitates physical as well as emotional illness.

Holmes and Rahe of the University of Washington, Seattle, devised a system to simplify the prediction and recognition of stress-related illnesses. Holmes and his colleagues at the University of Washington School of Medicine constructed a scale of stress values measured in "life-change units" (LCUs). Positive events such as marriage were found to be nearly as stressful as negative events such as divorce. They reported a relationship: more LCUs in a given time related to higher incidence rates for many types of physical illness.

Administrators of small, nonprofit agencies and programs should realize that, when life-change stress is high, special care should be taken to ensure adequate rest. They should postpone important decisions and avoid policy "shoot outs" with board members until stresses have subsided.

"The Last One in the Box" (Dahms 1972) is a little story that underscores both causes and effects of isolation. It does so by looking at various species of laboratory animals. Hamsters bite and are generally disagreeable. Mice bite also, and they fight among themselves. Guinea pigs, however, docilely accept their fate and seem to love their handlers. Occasionally, scientists have to kill a number of guinea pigs in order to obtain certain tissues or fluids for research purposes. As fifteen or twenty pigs are removed from a box one by one, you can imagine the remaining pigs saying, "Where is Agatha? She's been gone a long time. Herschel still isn't back. What are those frightening sounds coming from the other side of the room? What will become of us?" The guinea pigs crowd together in the box. They rub against one another to draw comfort and strength. The last two pigs huddle together as the group once did. When only one pig remains, it is shaking, frightened, nervous, and *biting*.

In this respect, humans are like guinea pigs. Isolation hurts. We are often afraid of change, failure, illness, and death. When these events occur, it sometimes seems as though we are the "last one in the box." Perhaps less wise than the guinea pigs, we can define ourselves as the last one in the box even when surrounded by others. (Guinea pigs don't do that.) No one understands us any more. No one cares about us. We end up sentencing ourselves to solitary confinement.

When administrators and agency staff members assume new responsibilities, they frequently report a feeling of isolation and estrangement. Excessive change, seemingly thrust upon us, can be especially debilitating during a period of isolation. Each of us can recall a time when we felt like the last one in the box—when we felt that, even if we tried to express our feelings, others wouldn't understand. Such feelings are often associated with geographical relocations, changes in relationships, and career changes. The five more serious life-change events, according to Holmes and Rahe (1967), involve the loss of relationships by one means or another.

Tentative results of continuing research show that emergence from isolation usually involves another person or persons (Dahms and Scully 1992). It is seldom the result of adopting a diet of brown rice, reading a popular self-help book, starting a program of lifting weights, or taking medication. It may have been a chance telephone call or unexpected contact with a stranger. The "hole in your box" was probably a person.

For most of us, "high-cost situations" exist when one (or more) basic need is unmet. Each of us needs 1) to feel good about ourselves—to feel worthy and able, 2) to feel connected with others, and 3) to be prized for our uniqueness without sacrificing that connection. If you find that these needs are being met in your daily activities, you probably are happy. If you feel that these needs aren't being met, costs may be high for you just now.

Challenging Alleged Limitations by Taking Risks

Most of us underestimate our abilities. The only way in which we can discover our real limitations—intellectual, physical, and emotional—is to test ourselves. We may have been taught to be passive, to be "nice," even though we may "pay the price" by bottling up anger, remaining unassertive, and experiencing depression. We continue to tolerate conflicts while we consume antacid tablets, use alcohol to excess, or desperately search for new employment.

We sometimes tolerate high-cost/low-benefit situations because we are waiting for others—superiors, peers, or employees—to give us permission to change our situation. But we can test our *own* limits simply by taking action. Your idea for a new project is unsound? Who says so? Try it! You aren't the person to prepare and deliver public-service announcements? Who says so? Prove them wrong by doing an excellent job in your own way. You haven't enough experience to lobby for increased funding for your agency? Who says so? Try it! You can't find the time to pursue further academic study? Really? Try it!

The work of Shoma Morita, a Japanese psychiatrist and contemporary of Freud, has formed the basis of the work of David Reynolds (1989, 1984). Morita's approach provides a very practical basis on which to approach thriving. The Moritist approach presents yet another conception of the primary and secondary control issues as discussed by psychologists and in the serenity prayer. In a view influenced by Zen Buddhism, the principles for effective behavior are made up of three basic directives:

1. *Know Your Purpose.* Although we often assume we know what we want to accomplish, if we are honest, very often we do not. (Do we wish to continue careers in grassroots agencies? Do we want to be a director? Do we want to quit? What career path is available to us?)

2. *Accept Your Feelings.* We are not responsible at a given moment for how we feel. (If that showdown with a staff member is a scary prospect for us, so what? Accept being scared. Or sad. Or angry. Or confused. Although we are not responsible for our feelings, we are responsible for our actions.)

3. *Do What Needs to be Done.* What needs to be done to assist us in our thriving process is to put more energy into primary and secondary control than into avoidance. (If an issue looms large, or even not so large, deal with it in your own best way. Active choosing is the key. Choosing the appropriate balance of primary control—intervention—and secondary control—accommodation—is the central task.)

The Pipe of Oughts and Shoulds. Many of us urgently need to reexamine the adjustment demands that control our lives. We often seem to move through what might be termed a ''pipe of oughts and shoulds.'' For example, administrators might feel they *ought* to work eighteen hours a day, be socially active, expand agency services, develop an independent consulting service, be the perfect role model for staff members, and always appear supremely capable. They might be caught in a ''pipe'' of impossibly demanding, narrowly defined oughts and shoulds.

People who find that their ''pipe'' is killing them, both emotionally and physically, often hesitate to change their schedules for fear of being labeled *lazy, irresponsible*, or *incapable*—they go on until a disaster occurs.

If we dare to admit that we would prefer a less stressful, more personally rewarding role, we probably wouldn't receive a very enthusiastic response. In fact, in our culture, there are only a few socially acceptable ways in which we can leave the ''pipe.'' Some of the more popular ways of gaining permission to leave are to suffer a nervous breakdown, a bleeding ulcer, or a heart attack. Following one of these unfortunate ''mishaps,'' those who are closest to us will give us permission to change our life-style.

We can leave our ''pipes'' if we decide that the costs are too high. We can choose other life-styles with different combinations of costs and benefits. We might have to give up a great deal in order to make the change, but, after all, physical and emotional survival is at stake.

Designing Lifestyles:
Balancing Primary and Secondary Control

Thrivers take pride in designing their own professional and personal life-styles. There are many alternative life-styles and value systems to choose from in our contemporary society. Marriage is no longer required as a condition of social acceptance. Great wealth does not grant an automatic title of honor. There is a growing feeling that status should be measured by the *quality* of one's life and that helping should be a valued unit of exchange.

This is not to suggest that we should be without constraints. You can dress as you wish, for example, except for those specific occasions—budget hearings and advisory board meetings—on which it is best that you wear a proper "uniform." A compromise? Yes, but an insignificant one when you realize that one of the richest rewards of administering human-service agencies is the fact that real human values and concerns are at issue.

"Letting the Crazies Out." You hear some interesting replies when people are asked what they would do if they were allowed to "lose control." What would *you* do if stresses were overwhelming and you no longer cared what people thought about your behavior? Would you bite people on their ankles, scream, paint graffiti on office buildings, have the worst temper tantrum in the history of civilization? What *would* you do?

Healthy people are usually able to find appropriate ways of letting their "crazies" out. Although a full-blown "crazy" might involve a permanent and abrupt move to Pago Pago, a "minicrazy" might involve a weekend at the beach or the nearest National Park. The point is, when people are unable to release their frustrations in appropriate ways, they eventually pay an exorbitant emotional price.

Summary

You are ultimately responsible for seeing that your survival needs are met. You cannot expect supervisors, boards of directors, or staff members to give you the help you need. *You need to assert yourself in productive ways!*

Careers in grassroots organizations take a lot out of you. So, you need to gather strength for yourself by applying principles of good mental health and encouraging colleagues to do the same. Although there are no quick fix solutions, there are some general guidelines.

1. Gathering information and then electing to use an appropriate balance of primary and secondary control is preferable to avoidance and denial. If you fail to practice choosing skills—if you refuse to explore your alternatives—you can be led to feel as though you are trapped in dead-end situations.

2. Active choosers live professional and personal lives characterized by forward momentum.

3. You are wise to monitor personal costs versus benefits on an ongoing basis. When personal emotional costs escalate, you need to adapt by reexamining your choices instead of grimly setting yourself up for physical and emotional illness.

4. Active limit testing is a vital part of personal growth. When you give yourself permission to test yourself—to try new ventures—both professionally and personally, you adopt a growth posture. Tasks you once felt were impossible are accomplished. People who inadvertently hurt you are taught to respect you in new ways.

5. The quest for an appropriate balance between primary and secondary control, as reflected in the serenity prayer, will result in a unique life-style. This emerging life-style is a work-in-progress reflecting the richness of jugglers' thriving processes. You become a reflection of your challenges, setbacks, and triumphs.

Continuing Concerns

1. From your personal point of view, list some categories of people, the source of your attitudes toward these people, and the ways in which your behavior toward them reveals your feelings about them.

2. Try to remember a period of isolation in your life. What did you do to help yourself? Because of the variety of feelings associated with isolation—hopelessness, depression, and hostility—you may have tried many things before you found a solution.

   A. Describe a last-one-in-the-box experience in your life. It may have been intensely painful or only mildly disturbing. How did you feel?

   B. What did you do to try to escape from your box? Be specific.

   C. What happened? What did you do to move past this painful experience? Be specific.

3. List the five most demanding oughts and shoulds in your life and the costs associated with them.

4. Indicate how you would like to change these oughts and shoulds by the exercise of some blend of primary and secondary control.

5. How do you cope with stress? In your opinion, what will be the result of your present coping style?

6. How would you like to be able to deal with stress? Why don't you do that?

Appendix

A

Finding the Right Computer System

E. Sam Overman

> *The value of a personal computer will depend upon the personal interests of the person using the computer. Personal computers play games—from chess to Missile Command—better than anything else around. But you must fancy games. They will chart your biorhythms with great accuracy. But you must care to know what your biorhythms are. Using a telephone to plug into a large computer, you can research any subject imaginable. But first, you must have something to research.*
>
> —Peter A. McWilliams
>   Author of *The Personal Computer Book*

E. Sam Overman, Ph.D. is a former director of the Doctoral Program in Public Administration for the University of Colorado at Denver. Dr. Overman has been specially cited for his work in developing computer systems for nonprofit organizations.

Introduction

The following story highlights the challenges inherent in finding the right computer system for your small, community-based, nonprofit agency:

> I recently completed a feasibility study for the local United Way in which we were trying to find out how a large number of small, nonprofit, human-service agencies, thirty-four to be exact, could computerize their information and referral activities. After months of meetings, detailed survey, and hours of technical research, we came up with a beautiful design for a computer system that was resoundingly rejected by the majority of nonprofit agencies. Why?
>
> A number of reasons were obvious, others not so obvious. Many of the agencies responded that to undertake such an endeavor would simply take away precious resources from what they considered to be their more "important" activities. Others said that the level of computer expertise in their agency was too low and it would be too expensive to obtain. Some were just unconvinced that a computer system could help them with the work they did, and still others could only see computers as a mechanism for greater administrative control of some form or another, by someone or another.
>
> Not so obvious were the problems that some people were threatened by computers and beset by a human-service/social work mentality that requires everything to be "people oriented." Others feared that computers would require them to change the way they worked, and simply resisted the idea of having to change. You know the line, "If it ain't broke, don't fix it."

We have all heard these excuses before in one context or another. Taken together, they spelled disaster for enhancing the computer capability among this particular set of nonprofit agencies. Very likely, they could spell disaster for your computer plans if you are also considering obtaining and implementing some kind of computerized support system in your organization.

The purpose of this appendix is to help you get beyond these "psychological" roadblocks in order to successfully find and develop a computer system that will work for your agency. There are no foolproof methods to do this, but there are certain guidelines that are recommended. Specifically, there is a systems development life cycle (SDLC) that has been used by many in the industry to help develop customized computer systems for organizations. This appendix will mix some of the general ideas of the SDLC with some basic, practical advice about *finding the right computer system*.

Computer Systems

What is meant by computer system? There are two components here: the computer and the system. When someone decides they need a computer, quite often the first thing they do is go out and buy a computer. This is obviously a necessary step, but the wrong way to start. You must first define the context and the use of the computer if it is to be valuable and effectively utilized, i.e., the system. Buying the computer without first coming to grips with the system is an invitation to disaster.

This distinction between "computer" and "system" is much more than semantics. Consider this analogy. Buying just a computer is like buying a horse, but with no purpose in mind. Subsequently the horse spends its days roaming around the field or hanging out in the barn and, most importantly, costing you a lot of money in upkeep. On the other hand, having a system without a computer is like having a carriage without any horse to pull it. You can still get around in the carriage but it is slow, hard work for you to pull it, clearly unproductive. Put them together and you have a highly productive working combination. The computer is the technology, the system is your pre-defined and intended use of this technology. The problem is many managers get one without the other, most frequently the computer without the system. When this happens, the computer has a high likelihood of turning out to be a very expensive paperweight simply sitting around your organizational "barn"—taking up space at the very least and gobbling up your resources at worst.

The notion of developing a *computer system* may seem new to many in the nonprofit community, particularly those very small, grassroots organizations. In the fast-paced, jargon-laden computer world, however, it is now an old idea in an increasingly information-intensive environment, in which expanded systems such as information technologies, telecommunications systems, system networks, and decision-support software are now being developed. Indeed, there is a near endless litany of new terms and features that can be added to enhance the basic computer system. To make the focus of this section more defined, let's assume that we are mostly talking about single database-type applications on microcomputer systems. For most grassroots organizations, such systems will more than meet their needs since, even at this basic level, they are now capable of handling very large and complex tasks. Computing is a complicated world in which you cannot expect to become an expert at everything, but finding the right computer system is still the basic starting point for every organization.

Follow the Systems Development Life Cycle

Much like Dorothy was told to "follow the yellow brick road" in the *Wizard of Oz*, following the systems development life cycle will help you get where you want to go. And like Dorothy, you will face adventures and perils on the way to developing a successful computer support system. Clearly, there are no guarantees of success. Keep in perspective, however, that the trip matters as much as the destination, and the life of your organization can be made significantly better if you are successful.

The systems development life cycle (SDLC) is a standard methodology for planning and controlling the development and implementation of a computer system. The SDLC is also a prescription of how the systems development process should occur. It consists of a set of phases and activities that take a computer system from concept to implementation. The basic idea behind the SDLC is that there exists a generic, structured, linear, and iterative process for computer systems development, regardless of the size of application. Generally, the phases include 1) planning, 2) development, and 3) implementation. The activities and products associated with each phase are outlined in Table A-1.

Planning Phase

Conception and Concept Paper

Often someone will have the idea that perhaps a computer system could help the organization. This person could be the executive director just returning from a conference, or a key employee who has just discovered some of the many supportive options a system could provide. The idea could originate from outside the organization as it did in the story that began this chapter. It could also come from several points at once. Wherever and however the idea begins, everyone in a small organization must, to some degree, initially buy

Table A-1 The Systems Development Life Cycle

Phase:	Activity:	Product:
Planning	Conception Technical Analysis Financial Analysis	Concept Paper Feasibility Study Cost/Benefit Study
Development	Systems Analysis Systems Design Programming	Systems Description Specifications Program Code
Implementation	Installation Training Evaluation	Software User Manuals Evaluation Study

into the notion that the organization should at least *consider* developing a computer system.

This is, in part, what the planning process is for—to make sure as many people as possible understand the what, where, when, and why of the computer system being considered. It is very helpful at this early stage to write up a short *concept paper* that describes what it is your organization hopes to accomplish with a new or upgraded computer system. Obviously, the concept paper will raise more questions than it answers, but that is its purpose.

Since a computer's intended use *must be systematically considered*, i.e., planned, the obvious place to start is with the people who are going to use the computer on a daily basis. One way to start is by asking some basic questions. How do the *users* see the computer helping them? What exactly is the information that will be stored on the computer (financial data, client data, documents)? What is expected out of the computer (monthly reports, daily access, mailing lists, large documents, internal communication, cross referencing)? Who will be responsible for inputting, managing, and retrieving this information and data? Do not get bogged down by all of the possible constraints—there are plenty (especially financial). Also, *avoid most of the so-called experts at this stage*. Nothing will misdirect or close down the process faster than bringing in "the computer expert," particularly a vendor, to tell you what you need.

There are usually three groups involved in finding a computer system: the managers, the users, and the experts. Initially, the dialogue should be between managers and users, i.e., counselors, secretaries, accountants, and so on. There will be plenty of time later on to *take advantage* of the experts. Remember this is just the planning and exploring stage of finding the right computer system.

Technical Analysis and Feasibility Study

Once there appears to be some consensus on the need for a computer system, there remain many different directions and alternatives that the system might take. It is the objective of the *technical analysis* to narrow the range of alternatives to three to five, and, most importantly, to define the specific objectives to be met by any computer system.

The *feasibility study* will consider three aspects: technical, economic, and organizational. For the technical aspect you may now need the assistance of an expert who will help you define the technical alternatives. There are many options and technologies available as well as a plethora of products and people to tell you about them. Just keep in mind that there is no need to consider an elephant gun if you don't plan to hunt elephants.

Each alternative in the feasibility study should have a cost attached to it. Be honest about the costs—include initial and operating costs, hardware and software costs, and any indirect cost that may occur. Paying for the system is, in fact, a separate issue to costing, but in practice everyone knows that they consider how to pay for the computer system at the same time they are considering different alternatives.

Finally, organizational and logistics questions are also necessary to consider at this time. Specifically, computers require someone to watch over them. Where will it go (whose desk)? Who will have access to what information?

The feasibility study need not be a long, elaborate document; in fact, it probably *should not* be for a small organization. More than once organizations have gotten mired down in a feasibility study when they should have simply taken a few risks and moved ahead with developing the computer system. The objective of the feasibility study is to decide on one alternative, one specific computer system.

Financial Analysis and Cost/Benefit Study

Most SDLC models now require some form of *financial analysis*. Though this can sometimes be a tortuous task, with little direct benefit, it may be a required component. The point is, that if you have already honestly considered the economic costs in the feasibility study then probably you have a pretty good idea how much the system will cost, although you most likely will have underestimated it! Matching these costs to the expected benefits is the purpose of the *cost/benefit* study. This requires an explicit outlining and estimation, in dollars or by other comparisons, of the benefits you expect to derive from having the new computer system.

Most organizations are, by this point, ready to invest in a system or ditch the whole idea. The cost/benefit study can become a timely game of justification for either position. If questions arise, you should primarily rely on the pluses and minuses of the feasibility study.

One very useful purpose of the cost/benefit study is in the search for external funding. It may be very important to a funding source to be able to show that you have conducted a thorough feasibility and cost/benefit analysis. Securing the funds for a computer system may take as long as the entire planning phase and may provide certain restrictions on both the design of the system and the outer cost limits. With the concept paper, the feasibility study, and the cost/benefit study in hand, however, you are well armed to seek external funding if it is required. Committing internal resources can always be considered if there are sufficient funds, but this is generally not the case with small, nonprofit organizations.

At the end of the planning phase the organization is on the verge of several very important decisions. The first, obviously, is whether or not to even pursue the idea of developing a computer system. Generally, the momentum for going ahead grows at this point as staff and others become involved and invested in the outcome. This is a good sign, but should not necessarily be taken as the final commitment to proceed. Carefully weigh all of the evidence gathered in the planning phase and make the decision that appears right for your organization.

If you decide to proceed, a second decision that can often take a great deal of time is whether to pursue the process within your organization or engage outside technical assistance. There are advantages and disadvantages to both options. Most organizations have faced this same dilemma in other areas and it is no different in this process. When making this decision it is important to keep in mind that the future success of the computer system depends on developing a high level of in-house expertise. If the system is not developed in-house, then any consultant or contractor must guarantee to train the users.

Lastly, if you decide to use outside technical assistance, then you must choose a vendor or consultant. Consider them all, but also investigate them all. Though there is no general prescription for choosing a vendor, the best question to ask is "Have you done this before? If so, show me!"

Development Phase

Systems Analysis and Systems Description

At this point, the decision will have been made to proceed with a computer system and the necessary financial resources will have been found. There is no turning back now, at least not without the loss of some direct and indirect costs. The first activity in the development phase is *systems analysis*. Systems analysis is the process of determining what specific work processes are to be computerized and determining how these work processes are best accomplished. Systems analysis considers the flow of these work processes and the information that accompanies them.

For example, a common application for many nonprofit human-service programs is a case management system. To develop such an application, it would be important for the systems analyst to put him or herself in the client's position within the agency and walk through the process from intake to discharge. Along the way, all the forms and information taken by various staff in working with the client will be gathered. Such "walk throughs" are very helpful and, indeed, may be mandatory in producing the system description.

The product of the systems analysis is called the *systems description*. Preferably, it is a picture in the form of a flowchart of how work is accomplished and information gathered and produced. The systems description sets the boundaries on what information is to be included and who will access and use it. The natural tendency is to include as much as possible in the computer system description. You may think you are getting more when you do this, but this can be risky. The ultimate success of your system will depend on how close you stick to the original ideas and designs developed during the planning stage. There will be opportunities to add other capabilities later, but only if your basic system is successful.

Systems Design and Specifications

The next activity is *systems design*—where everything becomes very specific. It is best to think of systems design in terms of inputs, processes, and outputs. Such questions to consider at this point are, "How many digits will be required for the client identification number," "How do you calculate overtime pay," and even such seemingly trivial concerns as whether the name should appear at the top of each report page. Essentially, whoever is designing the computer system must be *absolutely certain* as to what numbers and letters are going into the computer, what will happen to them while they are in the computer, and how they will look coming out. System design also incudes such concerns as deciding how long to store certain files, determining who will have access to the various databases, and whether each computer should have its own printer.

These are only a sample of the myriad of detailed questions that must be answered in the systems design activity. The answers to these questions are the *specifications*. Specifications are the detailed outlines that the programmer will follow in writing the computer code. For example, a data dictionary is a list of all specific data elements and how they are to be entered into the computer. If you get the specifications wrong, then the programmer and, ultimately, the computer, will also do it wrong.

Generally, there are two types of specifications. *Functional* specifications tell you what the computer system will do and how (e.g., input data from one source and produce annual reports). *System* specifications spell out the exact contents of each step in the process. Do not brush-off any of the specifications as being too trivial. Study and review them very carefully with the analysts as well as with the designers and programmers. *Many people consider the systems design activity to be the most critical step in the SDLC process.* It is very important that you begin to consider how the computer screens and menus will look, as well as understand how the system will operate (i.e., how many cases will the computer system store and how fast will they be processed?). Now more than ever, pay close attention to detail.

Programming and Program Code

At some point in the systems design activity the actual *programming* begins. Programming is translating your logical instructions and specifications into a language the computer will understand, known as the *program code*. A programmer will spend hours in front of a computer writing the program code. There are many new tools to aid programmers, including program generators that actually write code, screen-design tools, report writers, and so forth. Since most of us are non-programmers the best advice may be just to make yourself open and accessible to the programming experts who are working on the system. If they do not ask you any questions, then you should ask them some. As a nonexpert, this may be difficult, but do not allow a programmer to go off on his/her own and make a critical decision about how a system should operate without having all of the necessary information.

Implementation Phase

Installation and Software

After the system is developed, the organization is finally ready to get some return on its investment. Very likely, it will have been a few months since this whole process began. Some large companies and agencies have been known to literally take years to complete the SDLC process. The first activity that should happen in the implementation phase is the actual installation of the software. Installation simply means hooking up the computer, if it has not already been done, and installing the newly designed software (which should have been pre-tested and "de-bugged" by the programmer). This should be treated as a special event for the agency and everyone connected with the project should be present to welcome the new system into the office.

Everyone should also be reminded *why* the computer system is being installed. If there is one recurrent problem in a small agency it is that the computer system will be dominated by one activity— word processing. If that is what you have designed the system for, so be it, but if you are installing a new database or accounting system then be sure to ensure that those functions are not subsumed by the need for word processing. This is not to say that a computer should not serve multiple functions and users, but all the resources spent to plan and develop the system are wasted if the new computer system does not have the chance to fulfill *all* of its intended purposes.

When the system is installed, you need to get the actual *software* in your hands. Backup and system disks should be neatly and safely stored. If you have not already settled "ownership and propriety" issues (who does what, when, and for what reasons), do so now. Finally, insist on technical assistance when some little thing goes wrong. This post-installation assistance should have been part of your contractual agreement. Most reputable designers and programmers will encourage you to call them with problems. Play fair, however; fix or adjust what is needed but do not ask for a whole new routine or request a new report format.

Training and User Manuals

Next to systems design, *training* is perhaps the next most important activity in the systems development life cycle. You have found the right computer system; now you need to find the right people to work with it. Ideally, several key staff will have been involved all along in the SDLC process and are anxious to get their hands on this new "toy." *Redundancy* is the key to successful training and operation. Once learned, actual operations are, in fact, relatively simple. Repetition of steps is the most effective learning methodology. Training should not be restricted to just one person, but neither should it include the whole office staff. Both formal classes and individual hands-on tutoring are essential. System documentation and *user manuals* should accompany the training and installation. In general, the industry has done an outstanding job in developing easy-to-understand training manuals. Like any learning process, however, they should be used in combination with hands-on practice and instruction.

Evaluation and the Evaluation Study

Though they are rare, *evaluations* of the computer system can be important. The reason evaluations are rare is because once you begin the computerization process in your organization, you rarely have time to look back, at least formally. Instead, organizations are always moving ahead to another system application, to new technology, or to enhancing the current system to make it more efficient. You rarely get it perfect the first time, or even the second and third times. What you strive for is that the new computer system is doing what you initially planned and expected it to do. As time goes on, however, it will become wistfully obvious that there is so much more than could be done. Just like the development of a sound system in your home, once you get started you will always want something better. The fact is that the technological potential is still very far ahead of our ability to incorporate it into our work settings. In short, the end of the first SDLC process is really only the beginning of the next one.

Summary

The systems development life cycle may seem imposing. It should not. Basically it is simply incorporating the same planning and implementation process you would for any goal or project. The SDLC is nothing more than a step-by-step prescription for finding the right computer system. It does not, by itself, guarantee success. Following the basic phases and specific activities, however, will dramatically increase the chances of developing and implementing a successful computer system for *your* organization. Paradoxically, one of the greatest problems with the SDLC is that it is sometimes followed too rigidly, especially in the planning phase. Frequently, too much time is spent thinking about a specific problem or working on the feasibility study, when more would probably be gained by working directly on the problem in sort of a trial and error approach. For example, it may be very helpful in the initial phase to jump ahead and do a "short and dirty" systems analysis.

In addition, given the flexibility in computing and various off-the-shelf software, some experts suggest "prototyping" as an equally effective development strategy in place of the SDLC. The basic premise behind prototyping is to start with the actual programming and design and then let the system grow and modify from a simple prototype model. Clearly, the prototyping approach has as many dangers as it may have advantages. Nevertheless, it may be useful for organizations that already possess a fairly high level of technical competency.

One final thought. The SDLC is not meant to be a rigid lock-step process. Rather, it should be used as a guide broken down into phases, each with a *minimal* list of recommended activities. The key, however, is to START!

Appendix

B

Financial Management
Peter Konrad and Alys Novak

> *Few have heard of Fra Luca Pacioli, the inventor of double entry bookkeeping, but he has probably had much more influence on human life than has Dante or Michaelangelo.*
> —Herbert Muller

Peter Konrad, Ed.D., CPA, is the Vice President Administration and Chief Finance Officer for the Colorado Trust, a philanthropic foundation. Alys Novak, MBA, is President of Discovery Communication, Inc.

Introduction

A dictionary definition of accounting is "the theory or system of organizing, maintaining and auditing the books of an organization; the art of analyzing the financial position and operating results of an organization from a study of its revenues, expenses, overhead, etc.," The dictionary also notes that accounting is different from bookkeeping. Bookkeeping is defined as: "the work of keeping account books or systematic records of money transactions."

As a nonprofit manager, you need a general idea of how your organization's bookkeeping gets done, but ideally you are not the person keeping the account books. That should be the job of a bookkeeper who is on staff, a privately hired contractor, or as with most small nonprofits, a carefully selected volunteer. The managers should concentrate on the organization's overall financial concerns and needs.

Often, nonprofit entities are described as "nonbusinesses" whereas corporations or private sector companies are thought of as being "real businesses." In a broader sense "business," as in the phrase "businesslike," means operating in a serious, practical, efficient, and effective manner. Clearly, this applies as much to the nonprofit sector as it does to the private sector.

Perhaps the greatest difference, however, is not between the for-profit and the nonprofit sectors. Rather, it is found more dramatically between the larger, more institutionalized, nonprofit entities and their smaller, "grassroots" counterparts. As has already been pointed out in this publication, the typical small, community-based, nonprofit organization generally does not have the luxury of staff accounts, finance departments, or financial consultants.

The irony of this is that while the capacity for specialized fiscal management for grassroots organizations is almost always limited, the corresponding need for such management, in a comparative sense, is even greater. Sound fiscal operations are important regardless of the size of the organization; however, ineffective management of finances for the small nonprofit can spell the difference between survival or collapse of an agency.

Taking good care of financial matters makes good sense for all individuals, all organizations. Knowing where you stand with your financial resources is critical for the survival and success of any entity. However, as nonprofit managers—whether you are an executive director or a board member or a program manager—you have a special financial imperative. The financial resources you manage are entrusted to you by the public(s) you serve as a philanthropically and publicly supported organization. You are expected to be a wise steward of those resources.

Accountability thus has a double meaning for you. You generally must account for (keep track of) the monies entrusted to your organization. And you must be accountable (on the line) for the prudent use of the resources. Nonprofit financial management, therefore, is not simply a matter of good business; more important, it is a matter of ethics.

The work of nonprofits directly affects people's lives in ways that for-profits—whether McDonald's or United Airlines—cannot. Nonprofits are all about meeting the human, health, cultural, and educational needs that impact the very core of a community. If for-profits can demand good financial management, then nonprofits absolutely must guarantee it because they affect the lives of so many in such meaningful ways. It is vital, therefore, that you understand:

1. how nonprofits are unique "business" organizations—their special place in society;
2. how to handle the finances—measuring your organization's financial position through the use of balance statements and following its financial activities via income statements;
3. how to use the accounting process—to control the financial flow of income and expenses and safeguard against mismanagement and fraud;
4. how to follow the rules of accounting—Generally Accepted Accounting Practices (GAAP) and Internal Revenue Service regulations;
5. how to use accounting information—to make good financial decisions about costs, about cash, about investments; and
6. how to budget thoughtfully—a nonprofit's resources are so scarce, it is vital to spend them on priorities.

With nonprofits, the bottom line is not all-important. If a nonprofit program loses money, it does not necessarily mean that it is a bad program or that it was poorly managed. Many nonprofit programs are not designed to make money, or even to break even. Nonprofit financial managers often make decisions to subsidize a program that cannot be self-sustaining because the need for the program is so great and the clients cannot afford to pay enough—or anything—

to cover costs. Financial management allows you to know the costs of the program and to determine how much program support you will need to seek from other sources.

You can use simple accounting methods to identify units of cost minus units of recovery (income you get back) and then you will know the units of support necessary—the underwriting you must seek for the program or the subsidy amount you must expect from other programs. In sum, an accounting system helps nonprofit managers make value judgments and wise choices and it ensures ethical practices.

Who cares if a nonprofit is fiscally sound? All its stakeholders—its funders, its clients, its nonprofit colleagues, the government, the general public, the media. Each of these community players has a stake in a nonprofit organization's survival and success because of its special societal mission—to meet special community needs.

Key Components

The keys to an effective accounting system for nonprofits are the same as they are for any business organization, with just a few twists. This section will focus on these key components—budgeting, developing financial statements, basic accounting principles, the accounting process, cost accounting, cash flow management, reviewing and analyzing financial statements, and tax considerations.

Some upfront facts of life about nonprofits to keep in mind as you go through the chapter are:

1. *You must recognize the cycle of financial management.* There is a timing, a rhythm of daily, weekly, monthly, quarterly, and annual events to observe. For example, certain bookkeeping duties are carried out on a daily and weekly basis and then consolidated and reformatted into financial statements at month end. These statements are reviewed and analyzed with special attention each quarter in terms of how closely the actual financial condition compares with the budget forecast. At year end, an annual analysis is done, year-end adjustments are made, and final financial statements are developed for review or audit purposes.

It is important that you be aware of this cycle because each event triggers certain important information for you to use as you monitor and manage the business health of the agency. For example, you may need to keep track of its cash position on a day-to-day basis. You certainly will want to know if monthly expenses are under control. Projection-to-actual analysis is especially important at midyear, which is a critical time for making any necessary adjustments to your financial plan. At the end of the year, everyone involved with the agency's management—the board, executive director, program managers, etc.—will need to carefully analyze all the annual data so they can begin the new year with a solid understanding of the organization's financial position and of the factors they must consider in the next year's budget.

2. *You must recognize that the organization's financial system is an integral part of every aspect of the overall management of the agency.* It is directly related to the organization's strategic plan, its financial development/fund-raising, its marketing, its program of work, its personnel, its facilities/equipment, its governance. It is dangerous to treat accounting as a nuisance handled by a bookkeeper in isolation from the day-to-day life of the organization. Rather, it is a key indicator of that life and as such must merit full attention of every manager, and indeed, every employee.

3. *You must accept the fact that although it takes considerable time and effort to set up a financial system for recording and analyzing accounting data, the system will "free" you to concentrate on managing the rest of your resources more effectively.* So be sure to take the time with accounting/bookkeeping experts to establish either a manual or automated system and related procedures to capture and consolidate data. Fortunately, there are numerous accounting software packages available today for personal computers that greatly expedite accounting tasks.

4. *You must acknowledge that there are several pitfalls related to nonprofit fiscal management that can cause severe damage, if not avoided.* These involve the factors already mentioned as well as the fact that it is fairly common for small nonprofit managers not to be very knowledgeable—or worse yet, very interested—in financial management. Since the mission of a nonprofit is normally program focused rather than profit focused, its managers often "forget" the monetary aspects of the agency.

Decisions about which bills are paid can also be a pitfall. Sometimes nonprofit managers faced with limited cash in the bank make decisions about accounts payable with good intentions but bad results; e.g., paying employees but not sending in payroll taxes or buying major equipment but not factoring in insurance and maintenance expenses. As we'll discuss later, the IRS does not forgive such sins. Finally, nonprofit managers may focus so much on future financial expectations—"the grant is sure to come in any day"—that they neglect to notice a disastrous slip into a cash deficit position. Good financial management techniques and knowledge on your part about critical indicators will safeguard you from such pitfalls.

Tax-Exempt Status

The Importance of Nonprofit Organizations

Nonprofits have a significant impact on the nation in two ways. First, as already noted, they play a vital role in fulfilling community needs that are not met by commercial enterprises (private sector) or government entities (public sector). Because of their special role, which is implemented in large part by volunteers, they are granted tax-exempt status by the government. Second, they have an impressive economic role. According to the publication, *Giving and Volunteering in the United States,* 1990 Edition, as of 1987 there were 907,000 nonprofit (independent sector) organizations. This includes many large philanthropic and voluntary organizations such as schools, hospitals, and religious institutions, but it also includes the tens of thousands of small, community-based organizations.

In addition, the same publication notes that 7.4 million were employed in a paid capacity by the "independent" sector compared to 20.9 million in the government sector and 91.6 million in business. The total revenues generated by the independent sector were $413.7 billion (including volunteer time) and $327.2 billion (excluding volunteer time). Operating expenditures were $384 billion (including volunteer time) and $261.5 billion (excluding volunteer time).

Perhaps even more dramatic is the fact that approximately 50,000 new organizations apply for tax-exempt status each year, with about 40,000 receiving this designation. Thus, the independent or nonprofit sector is expected to continue its steady growth. One reason is the trend for nonprofits to deliver services that used to be provided by neighbors, family, or government. Today's mobile, complex personal life-styles and economic constraints on governmental social programs have put the community service ball squarely in the nonprofit court.

Nonprofits have become an integral part of the American value system. This is particularly apparent when you consider that Americans put their money where their mouth is. In 1989, according to *Giving USA*, Americans contributed $104.37 billion.

Individuals gave $96.43 billion; bequests were $6.57 billion; foundations gave $6.70 billion; and corporations gave $5 billion.

Similarities to Private Commercial Organizations

Contrary to popular thinking, nonprofits are similar to for-profit organizations in many ways. These include:

1. They both are *legal entities*. They can be sued just as individuals can be.

2. They both must have *operating instruments*. These include defining themselves as a corporation or association, writing bylaws that specify the rules of the operation, and establishing a legal structure by filing articles of incorporation or association.

3. Like their for-profit counterparts, the nonprofits *vary in size*. The Catholic Church, for example, is as large as General Motors. Certainly the number of small nonprofits exceeds the number of large ones, but that is also true in the for-profit sector.

4. They both have *common fields of endeavor*. Examples: health care, education, counseling. There are both proprietary hospitals and colleges as well as nonprofit hospitals and colleges.

5. They both can earn *profits* although there are differences as to how those profits can be used. Nonprofits not only can make a profit, they should maintain a surplus—more revenue than expense. While they both can reinvest that surplus back into the organization, only the for-profit organization may choose to give some or all of the profits to the stockholders.

6. They both can provide for *personal gain*. In fact, some individuals in large nonprofits receive the same kind of compensation package as those in corporations. Needless to say, however, this is rarely a problem for the typical small, community-based nonprofit organization.

7. They are both *businesses*. As noted before, entities in each sector need good management, effective communication, good leadership, a strategic plan and both must aim to be fiscally sound.

8. They each need *boards of directors*. Any organization needs a governing body with fiscal and legal responsibility for the entity. A nonprofit board is comprised of constituents and stakeholders. A for-profit board includes representatives of its stockholders and investors. In both cases, board members invest their time, money, and talents in the organization.

9. They both require *staff* and support personnel. Every organization needs people power to get the work done. In the case of nonprofits, some or all of that people power may come from volunteers . . . or unpaid staff.

10. Both are *engaged in competition*. Each must compete in a defined marketplace for its share of revenue and recognition. Among themselves, nonprofits compete for funds, clients, public awareness, volunteers, and media attention. In some cases, nonprofits and for-profits compete for the same disposable dollars of consumers.

11. They both have *similar economic values*. Each believes in a balanced budget, cost containment, and a healthy "return on investment."

12. They both have *similar financial stream*. Both can borrow, although small nonprofits often do not consider this option. Each has contributors, "investors." Each must have funders who will invest in the organization's mission. Each must give something of value in return. In the case of the for-profit, that return on investment is monetary. For the nonprofit, the payback may simply be the good feelings from giving to a good cause.

13. They each have *common tax responsibilities*. Corporations, of course, pay corporate income taxes. Nonprofits have a special tax-exempt status and do not have to pay corporate taxes unless they are involved in unrelated business activities. However, they may have to pay some local taxes such as sales taxes if they are selling products or services. Donors to nonprofits can deduct their donations on their income tax returns and the nonprofit does not have to pay taxes on these contributions. These are significant tax breaks . . . but corporations get breaks too.

14. Both must be able to *answer to their particular investors*. Nonprofits are on the line to their public "stakeholders" and the for-profits must satisfy their stockholders.

Differences between Nonprofits and Commercial Enterprises

Although nonprofits and for-profits are surprisingly similar, a few differences remain. These include:

1. They have different kinds of *owners*. A for-profit has stockholders who own the corporation and who receive profits for their ownership. They directly receive benefits for being shareholders. Nonprofits may, and should, make profits/surpluses but

these profits are always invested back into the organization. They are not distributed to individuals. They are "owned" by the entity. And importantly, if a nonprofit organization dissolves, any proceeds or remaining assets must go to another tax-exempt organization or to the government. They cannot be given to any individual or sold.

2. They have different *fiduciary responsibilities*. Commercial enterprises attempt to maximize profits for their owners, while nonprofits are primarily responsible for providing optimum services for the least amount of money. Nonprofits are judged not on bottom-line profit, but on their efficiency and effectiveness in providing services.

3. They have different *legal definitions* related to income. First, the IRS specifies that in nonprofits, "no part of the income or profit is to be distributed to its members or officers." (This constraint does not mean that staff and board members cannot receive reasonable compensation, which is considered a salary expense.) For-profits can and do distribute profits to their investors. Second, the American Institute of Certified Public Accountants (AICPA) Audit Guide specifies that for nonprofits, "more than half of their organization's revenue is normally from voluntary contributions of the general public and a substantial part of their mission includes the rendering of health, welfare, or community service." This is not necessarily true for colleges and hospitals, but is generally true of most other nonprofits.

4. They have different *governmental benefits*. Already mentioned is the fact that nonprofits have a federal income tax exemption. This is described in Section 501(c) of the IRS Code, which designates charitable nonprofits as 501(c)(3) organizations. And as mentioned, nonprofits can receive tax-deductible contributions. In addition, they get preferred postal rates. In some cases, services performed for 501(c)(3) organizations may be exempt from federal unemployment tax. Lastly, nonprofits may receive a variety of state and local tax exemptions and modifications that for-profits do not.

5. They have other *miscellaneous* differences. Some of these have already been discussed. For example, nonprofits receive significant amounts of resource from contributors who do not expect to receive economic benefit. Nonprofits have operating purposes that are primarily other than to provide goods or services at a profit. Nonprofit entities do not have ownership interests that can be sold.

In addition, there are two operational differences. First, nonprofits use *fund accounting*. Unlike businesses organized for profit, nonprofit organizations receive gifts, grants and legacies to support their activities. Often these contributions are for specific purposes, and the organization must assure the trustees, donors or other external parties that funds were spent, or preserved, according to the purposes for which they were given. Accordingly, nonprofit organizations have developed a method of accounting called fund accounting.

Fund accounting is a procedure by which, for accounting and reporting purposes, resources are classified into funds associated with specific activities or objectives. Each fund is a separate accounting entity with its own set of accounts to record assets, liabilities, fund balances. The fundamental principle of fund accounting is stewardship: accountability for the receipt and use of resources.

Second, nonprofits may receive donated capital assets (buildings, property, equipment, etc.), which is very unusual for commercial enterprises.

501(c)(3) Exemption

When a group of people determine that there is a community need that is not being met and then decide to start a nonprofit dedicated to that interest, they must go through a process to make the organization a legal entity before they can request a tax exemption. This involves developing articles of incorporation and filing them with the Secretary of State in the state where the nonprofit wants to be registered. The articles state the purpose of the organization, provide the names of at least three board members, and note the name and address of an "agent for service." The law requires that a real person with a real address be named so a specific individual is available to receive legal documents. Listing "President at Box 6" is not adequate. In addition, when filing, the articles must be accompanied by a set of bylaws. Bylaws state the operating procedures for the organization.

When this has been accomplished, the group can apply to the IRS for a 501(c)(3) tax exemption. This requires completing a variety of forms and providing certain evidence. Most important, it means verifying that the entity has a charitable purpose, which is more broadly defined as having an educational, religious, charitable, scientific, literary, or safety testing purpose.

In addition, the organization must acknowledge that it cannot engage in *excess* lobbying. Otherwise, it forfeits its nonprofit status.

It also should be noted that Section 501(c) of the IRS Code designates many different kinds of nonprofits, including professional associations, advocacy groups, chambers of commerce; homeowner associations, etc. Each of these receives some level of tax exemption; however, the 501(c)(3) group receives the most favorable.

Governance of Nonprofit Organizations

Most nonprofits choose the corporation form of governance. However, they can also choose to format themselves as trusts, associations, unions, public entities, or religious organizations. These require different legal documents, but basically they are similar in intent.

The *corporate model* involves: (a) shareholders who elect a board of directors to represent their interests; and (b) a board who sets direction/policy and hires administrative staff and provides oversight. For nonprofits, the same two elements are used, except the shareholders are constituents and the board represents the public interest.

As stated before, a key tool of governance is the nonprofit's *articles of incorporation*. This document states the organization's reason for existence, its name, its duration (perpetuity or until a conference of members designates its demise), its powers (what it can and cannot do to attain its purpose), and its board of directors structure. This document is imprinted with the corporate name and seal.

Bylaws also are critical for governance. They designate the rules of operation in terms of fixed policies. They state, for instance, how board members are selected and replaced. They also specify meeting rules, the quorum, the number and roles of officers, the responsibilities of the executive director, the types of committees, how the budgets, books and fiscal records will be handled, how to prevent conflicts of interest, and how to amend articles and bylaws.

Board of Directors

The board's duties are numerous in terms of accountability. First and foremost, the board members represent the shareholders' interests in terms of fulfilling the mission of the organization. Second, they are responsible for refining the "raison d'etre"—the reason for being—of the organization into goals and objectives via the strategic planning process. Third, it is their responsibility to develop policies to achieve the purpose, goals and objectives.

In addition, they must ensure that resources are available to accomplish the purpose of the organization. This primarily means financial resources; the board is fiscally responsible for the agency and thus is ultimately on the line for its fundraising as well as its financial management. In sum, it has to get the funds before it can manage them. Lastly, *board members may incur personal liability for their actions or inactions.*

This liability is limited somewhat by state statutes that limit board liability to more blatant acts of self-interest or gross misconduct. It also can be mitigated by having Directors' and Officers' insurance and by putting an indemnification clause in the articles and bylaws. Such a clause would state that the organization will cover the costs/damages of any liability suit. Of course, that assumes the organization is financially able to do this. An insurance policy provides further protection for the board, who are often perceived as having "deep pockets" when being sued.

An exception to the limit on liability is payment of payroll taxes. As noted before, the IRS can make claims against directors personally for nonpayment of payroll taxes. Thus, board members should inquire at each meeting if payroll and associated taxes are paid. In addition, the Treasurer occasionally should personally review bank statements to ensure the checks actually were sent. In fact, in some organizations, the Treasurer sends the taxes to the IRS, though this is usually not necessary. The point: late or nonpayment of payroll taxes results in an automatic 10 percent penalty—plus interest.

Staff and Administration

The purpose and function of the staff is to implement the decisions and policies of the board. Staff members are the ones who actually achieve the goals and objectives specified in the strategic plan. They carry out the functions of the organization, they report to the board about achievements, and they bring ideas about new directions to the board. In short, they have leadership responsibilities as well as operating responsibilities.

Budgets

Budgeting is a top priority for a nonprofit organization, just as it is with for-profit companies and individuals. None of us are very effective financial managers if we do not develop and maintain a budget. For a nonprofit, it is particularly important to have such a financial blueprint. A budget is used in several ways, as explained in the following sections.

Budget Definitions

A budget represents the anticipated future financial statement of the organization. That is, it outlines the anticipated expenses and income of the organization during a specific period, usually one year. (The annual 12-month period used for financial planning purposes is called a fiscal year, which need not correspond to the calendar year.) The budget, therefore, is an *educated guess* about the money you will need to run your agency (expenses) and about the expected funding (revenue). A budget is today's plan for tomorrow's operations.

Indeed, a budget is a plan of operation in financial terms. It represents the allocation of resources based on the planning process: more often than not this means the allocation of *scarce* resources. A fact of life for nonprofits is that the need will always be greater than what an agency can realistically fulfill. Thus, a prime challenge in planning and budgeting is to "bite off no more than you can chew." One agency cannot save the world, but it can make a difference.

Budget Elements

You will get more comfortable with the budgeting approach if you understand that it grows out of the *organization's purpose* or mission and its goals and objectives. The budgetary process actually begins when the annual strategic planning starts. After specifying the organization's mission and long-range goals, you develop a budget that identifies how you expect to pay for the cost of next year's objectives within the long-range goals. The budget becomes the tool for accomplishing the plan. It is a vital management weapon in the battle for survival and success. And, it is not all that exotic or difficult. It is mostly common sense. It aims to provide an estimate of what the future holds and to represent the strategic plan in terms of future dollars.

It is critical that you begin the budgeting process by *identifying expected revenues* as well as expenses. First you must figure out how much funding you can reasonably expect from a variety of sources. Then you match the costs of the programs you would like to offer with the income. Very frequently you will discover that expenses exceed revenue. In this case, you may need to adjust either the long-term program goals or the annual objectives and their related expenses.

The budget must necessarily be based on estimates. These estimates, however, must represent your best professional judgment, the history of revenues and expenditures of the agency, contract/grant information, and economic projections; e.g., cost of living, inflation, and recession.

The strategic plan and budget must be officially approved by the board but they should be developed by both the board and the staff. Otherwise, neither party will have ownership, and neither will strive to ensure the success of the plan and budget.

Fiscal controls must exist to ensure compliance to the budget. Each month a comparison of budget forecasts to actual results must be done and corrective actions taken. If the agency exceeds the amount budgeted for a line item expense, the executive director must report this and the reason for the variance to the board—unless the director has been given authority by the board to shift a certain percentage of expenses or has been told to focus just on bottom-line results rather than individual items.

At specified times, which may be quarterly, semiannually, or annually, it will be necessary to *review fiscal performance* and to develop new budgets based on experiences up to that point in the budget year. Budgeting is a *dynamic process* because the world is dynamic.

Phases of Budgeting

You start the budgeting process with a *preparation* phase. In this phase you begin with a statement of long-term goals and annual objectives. Objectives should be measurable and time-specific; e.g., to increase revenues by 25 percent by mid-year. Unless you take this step, you slide into incremental budgeting, which lacks real purpose or direction. That is, you simply use a "more of the same" approach . . . "let's add 10 percent to that item this year."

Also in this preparation stage you identify the *action steps* which are necessary to accomplish these goals and objectives. In addition, you need to show the *cost of the action steps* involved. For example, if the financial plan calls for the development of a brochure to help with fundraising efforts, this cost should be noted.

This type of narrative is very important for those reviewing the budget. It is especially important when you are sending your budget to your funders. They want to understand the thinking behind the forecasts.

After you have prepared the budget, you put it into *operation* and the focus is on *comparison*. During this phase you will want to compare actuals to estimates on at least a monthly basis. The treasurer and board particularly will want to check for any variances from policy related to *authorized* expenditures.

There are several ways in which to *react to variances*. First, it is important that the board and staff recognize that unplanned-for contingencies will happen. Second, they must determine how the organization will adapt to these variances. Will they accept them and adjust the budget accordingly or will they immediately activate revenue-generating and/or cost-cutting steps aimed to get back in balance? This decision often relates to whether or not you are operating with a *flexible or fixed budget*. A fixed budget is based on a specific amount that you expect; e.g., three grants of $25,000 each with related specific expenses of $20,000 each. This type of budget is not based on quantity but rather on known fixed revenues and expenses. In contrast, a flexible or variable budget changes with volume. Example: a health clinic gets funding based on the number of patients it serves, and in turn, its expenses will vary; e.g., $1 per patient for rubber gloves.

Types of Budgets

Revenue Budgets

There are several different kinds of budgets. You will want to be particularly concerned about *revenue-based budgets*. This type of budget provides a summary of anticipated receipts for a given time period (usually annually) expressed in quantitative terms, for example: Client Fees, $50,000.

Remember that the revenue budget is the starting point from which to base the expense budget—not the other way around. Some organizations reverse the process. They seek to raise funds to meet the expenses. That is not advised. Rather the focus should be on determining how much funding is reasonable to seek, and then to adjust program goals/expenses accordingly. When forecasting revenues, you can use previous revenue data and confirmed future contract/grant data as a basis for your "sales forecasts." This is similar to the approach a commercial enterprise takes when building a budget.

As you analyze past data, you will also want to review *basic revenue patterns.* Do you receive revenue in a regular pattern; e.g., United Way allocations, grant payments, patient billings, interest receipts? Or is your revenue flow seasonal—received on a regular but periodic basis; e.g., tuition receipts, seasonal rental of facilities, membership dues? Or is your income stream random—received on a helter-skelter basis; e.g., special bequests, short one-time grants? This type of information is critical as you think through the budget in terms of monthly peak and valleys and how they might affect your cash flow.

Other revenue considerations to keep in mind relate to adding new services, which can mean new revenues and new expenses. You also have to consider capacity constraints; i.e., how many more clients can you really serve with your present staff, facility, equipment, etc.? In addition, you must consider new competition. What if a "new kid on the block" comes along and captures some of your funding and clients? Also keep an eye on anticipated changes in economic conditions; e.g., a recession on the horizon does not bode well for funding. And what about a change in service pricing? In other words, is now the time to increase fees to cover rising costs? All of these factors need to be considered and built into the budget.

Expense Budgets

When you develop an expense budget, you are concerned with the use or consumption of economic resources. You want to estimate what items have costs attached, and how much these costs will be. These expenses will "behave" in different ways. This behavior depends on the extent to which expenses may vary according to the changes in the amount of services.

For example, you will have some *fixed costs* that will remain constant as the quantity of services increases. Examples include rent and salaries for your regular staff. These expenses are the easiest to budget and control since they are predictable, but they are the hardest to reduce. For instance, once you have signed a long-term lease, it is very difficult to get out of that lease.

In contrast, you will also have *variable costs*. These costs change in direct proportion to changes in volume of service. Examples include client treatment supplies, cost of goods sold, and electric utilities. These are harder to budget than fixed costs since they are unpredictable, but they are easier to control and to reduce.

In addition, there are *semivariable costs.* These involve both fixed and variable elements; for example, the phone bill with local (fixed) and long distance (variable) costs.

Another factor to consider is *traceability*. This refers to the degree to which costs can be traced to a specific segment or program area. Traceability involves *direct costs*, which are those incurred solely for the benefit of a particular segment; for instance, you hire a computer operator whose efforts are dedicated to one program. There are also *indirect costs*. These are expenses incurred for the benefit of many segments or program areas, such as the salary of the executive director.

Identifying and tracking direct and indirect costs requires you to use cost accounting methods. These are procedures for determining and recording how you allocate indirect costs. For instance, in the case of the executive director, you will need to identify how much time the director spends on each program and what percentage of the total each segment of time represents. This amount then is directly allocated as program costs. The rest becomes indirect or overhead administrative costs, and these also should be allocated to specific activities such as fund-raiding or general management.

Operating and Capital Budgets

Revenue and expense budgets together result in an *operating budget*, a budget that deals with ongoing programs. However, you also need to develop a capital budget for high-cost, long-term (more than one year), large-ticket items. Such items include a new building, leasehold improvements, or a computer system. It is very practical to keep these items separate and to plan these expenditures over time. Often the item can be amortized over several years. The board will be much more comfortable not having these items lumped in with the regular annual budget. Otherwise the expenditure would appear to be overwhelming.

Line Item or Program Budget

In terms of dealing with the information contained in the budget, you can present it in the form of a *line item budget* or as a *program budget*. Line item budgets are exactly what they sound like. Each item of revenue or expense is listed in the budget just as they are listed in the chart of accounts used in the financial accounting system. The chart of accounts is the fundamental structure through which financial data is collected. It will contain assets (a resource of value), liabilities (debts or obligations), and fund balances (the difference between assets and liabilities) as well as revenue and expenditure accounts. For example, the chart of accounts would have an account for rent, for salaries, for fees, for grants. The budget in turn would show the revenues and expenses for each of these accounts.

In contrast, you can present budget information as a *program budget*. In this case, program or departmental revenues and costs are pulled out from the various line item financial accounts and consolidated into totals. The line item budget is most often used, but is not necessarily the best. Either can be appropriate and each has pros and cons. The line item approach has the advantage of providing lots of information about each revenue and expense category. However, it does not allow you to see each program's financial impact and vice versa.

Other Kinds of Budgets

Other kinds of budgets that you may have to develop are the *zero-based budget* and the *cash flow budget*. Doing zero-based budgeting means building a budget with a totally fresh perspective. You do not consider historic data. Rather you pretend you have never had a previous budget and start at ground zero and justify every dollar. This approach ensures that you challenge assumptions and consider new possibilities.

The cash-flow budget ensures that cash is available to pay the bills. It is one thing to say that you will raise $50,000 in a year to cover anticipated expenses of $50,000. It is another to have cash in the bank when you have to pay your bills. To avoid a money crunch, it is helpful to develop a "cash flow chart" that outlines your anticipated expenses and income on a monthly basis.

The budget worksheet you use while developing your budget can also serve as a basis for outlining your cash flow. Although most organizations have fairly steady monthly expenses, they can fluctuate due to several factors. You must try to anticipate how your expenses will be distributed monthly during the fiscal year.

You must also estimate when you will receive anticipated income from each of your identified funding sources; e.g., fees, grants, contracts, etc. Remember that fund-raising takes time and that it may be months between an initial contact date and the actual receipt of money.

Financial Statements

Financial statements are reports that summarize your financial transactions in a variety of ways so that you can analyze how you are doing fiscally. Such statements have several purposes. The information they provide is particularly useful to compare with budget information.

Purpose of Nonprofit Financial Statements

A major purpose of financial statements is to report the nature and amount of available resources, the uses of these resources, and the net change in the organization's resources for a specific time period. In addition, the statements identify the organization's principal programs and their costs. They disclose the degree of control exercised by donors over the use of resources; e.g., through accounts restricted for specific purposes. They also help reviewers evaluate the organization's ability to carry out its objectives.

The statements disclose how the resources have been acquired and used to accomplish the nonprofit's objectives. They also disclose the nature of any restrictions and the degree to which these restrictions have been satisfied.

Comparison of Financial Statements to Budgets

Financial statements are used to compare actual operations with the budgets that were the result of the planning process. Indeed, financial statements provide a mirror image of budgets. They look backwards to what really happened and hopefully this mirrors the forecast that the budget represents. Remember, a budget is a projected financial statement. If you have been successful with your forecasts, your financial statements will reflect that your operations are right on target.

Basic Financial Statements

A major type of statement to consider is the *balance sheet*. This statement outlines the financial net worth of an organization *at a given point in time*, usually as of the ending date of a reporting period. The balance shows the total amounts of assets and liabilities and the balances in various funds that the organization has. These balances are generally compared to those at the end of the previous reporting period.

This snapshot of the organization's finances consists of statements about *assets*. Assets refer to what you own—materials in substantial amounts and items with a life greater than one year or the accounting period (cash, buildings, cars, computers, investments, inventory, and so on). It also includes statements about your *liabilities*; that is, what you owe creditors. Examples include accounts payable (bills you need to pay), mortgage payments due, and loans to be repaid.

In addition, the balance statement shows the *fund balance*, or owners' equity. This represents the net worth of the organization; i.e., assets less liabilities equals fund balance.

Another major type of financial statement is the *income statement*. It is a statement of activity over time, such as one month. These reports generally include a comparison to budgeted amounts. Such information allows directors, managers, and board members to make future spending decisions and helps them plan the budget for future periods.

Financial statements also include information about *revenue*. This includes cash received or promised for goods or services rendered; e.g., fees for service, sales fees, and contributions. Actually this statement contains information about both revenue and *support*. Revenue is defined as the receiving of resources in exchange for delivering goods or services. Support is defined as the receiving of resources without consideration; e.g., grants, donations, gifts.

Expenses are also reflected in the balance sheet. Expenses are those costs incurred by the organization while pursuing its purpose; e.g., salaries, rent, and program supplies. Most important, the balance statement shows *net income*. This is calculated by subtracting expenses from revenues. The result is profit or surplus. The net income is posted to the balance sheet as the fund balance.

Income statements are generally prepared more often than balance sheets. One common practice is to prepare income reports monthly and balance statements quarterly.

Basic Accounting Principles

Since an organization and its activities are ongoing, there is always unfinished use of resources. Because most accounting data are subject to interpretation in both their compilation and review, accounting standards have been developed by the accounting profession to resolve questions about objectivity and relevance in evaluating resource utilization. Known as GAAP (generally accepted accounting principles), these standards comprise a uniform system for both measurement and accounting.

They are controlled by the American Institute of Certified Public Accountant (AICPA) and by the Financial Accounting Standards Board (FASB). You should be aware that the Audit Guide for Nonprofits was last revised in 1974. It is expected to be changed in the next few years. You will want to work with a CPA to help you develop and analyze financial statements. Such an individual could be a staff member, a board member, or a consultant.

Fund Accounting

Some of the key principles relate to *fund accounting*. As noted previously, separate funds are often established in the fund balance to reflect different restrictions; e.g., grants awarded for a specific purpose. If, for example, your organization has received a grant earmarked for making loans to other nonprofits, your fund balance should reflect the status of those monies as a separate category from your unrestricted fund balance.

Fund accounting systems were devised to help the trustees of a nonprofit fulfill their legal obligation to use each of an organization's various funds according to the appropriate guidelines. Since nonprofits receive resources restricted for particular purposes, accounts (funds) are maintained for each. And each fund is a separate accounting entity with a self-balancing set of accounts for recording assets, liabilities, fund balance, revenues, and expenses.

Basic fund types include *current funds*, which are funds to be expended for current operating purposes; *plant funds* for fixed assets and the liabilities related to these assets; *endowment funds* from which the principal cannot be consumed, but the income can be used; and *custodian funds* that are held by the organization for someone else; e.g., a guardianship fund for developmentally disabled individuals.

Capitalization

Another set of accounting principles relates to *capitalization*. All assets with a life of greater than one year that are of material (significant) cost to the organization must be capitalized; e.g., a building, major computer equipment. You can do this in a couple of ways. One way is to use an historic cost basis. In this method the asset is put on the balance sheet at the historic cost, even if the asset appreciates in value. Example: Your organization owns mountain property that grows in development value over time.

Another method is *depreciation*. In this case the cost of the asset is charged to each period in which the asset is utilized. Example: A $10,000 car is charged off each year it is used over its five-year life or at $2,000 per year. You should know that there are a variety of depreciation methods that accelerate depreciation in the early years of its use. You also should know that there are conflicting rules for various nonprofits for depreciation. Some nonprofits do not take depreciation on collections, works of art, buildings of workship, etc. Be sure to check out the rules with your CPA. The rule of conservatism demands that assets be written down, not up. There is also a rule stating that donated fixed assets are placed on the books at fair market value at the date of the gift. This is also true for *investments*.

There are rules related to *consistency*, which basically demand that the same accounting principles and procedures be used in each accounting period. This ensures that you are not using an apples to oranges approach to accounting.

Many GAAP rules relate to the recording of *donations, pledges and grants*. These are presently under review and you can expect them to be changed in the near future. In the meantime, keep in mind that there are specific guidelines related to donated services; e.g., the services would be performed by a paid staff member if they had not been donated by a volunteer.

Accrual Versus Cash Accounting

One decision every organization must make is whether to keep its financial records on a cash-basis or accrual-basis bookkeeping system. In a cash-basis system, financial transactions are recorded at the time they occur. Income is recorded when it is received, and expenses are recorded when they are paid. A cash-basis system accounts for the flow of actual cash through your organization.

In an accrual system, however, income is recorded when it is earned, which may be several months before it is actually received. And expenses are recorded when they are incurred, which may be before they are actually paid.

In general, information provided by an accrual bookkeeping system is more useful to an organization because it provides a total financial picture for a given period. Seeing both the amounts due to the organization and the amounts it owes to others provides more information on which to base a financial assessment and to use in making financial projections.

However, accrual bookkeeping is more complicated and involves more time-consuming procedures than cash accounting. An alternative for small nonprofits is to keep their books on a cash basis and make accrual adjustments on their financial reports. You should be aware, however, that accrual accounting is required for all GAAP financial statements.

Managing the Accounting Process

To repeat the constant theme of this appendix, nonprofit managers should be less involved in the nitty-gritty of accounting but very much involved in the management of the process. There are many financial management responsibilities and these are divided among all the management players.

Board of Directors

The board is responsible for developing and approving sound fiscal policies. It also must select qualified corporate officers to manage the financial system (executive director, chief financial officer). In addition, it must provide adequate resources to accomplish this, whether an automated system or sufficient personnel. It must discuss and approve the budget. All, or at least the major, contracts should be signed by a board officer. Expenditures over a certain limit must be authorized by the board. A board member should approve all payments for expenses incurred by the executive director. Most important, it must conduct oversight of the process by reviewing the financial statements, spotchecking various financial transactions, and retaining an independent firm to audit the books.

The administrative staff is responsible for effectively implementing the agency's financial policies. Most important, the administration must participate in the development of strategic goals and objectives and their relative financial impacts. And they must help to build, monitor and maintain the budget. In addition, it is the task of the administration to ensure that the accounting process is carried out and that internal controls are in place.

Internal Control

The *objectives* of internal control are to provide reliable data, safeguard the assets, promote operational efficiency, and encourage adherence to policy.

Internal controls are particularly relevant to cash receipts, cash disbursement, fixed assets, and petty cash. In the case of cash receipts, it is best to avoid cash transactions—accept only checks. The moment a check is received, it should be endorsed in a restrictive manner; e.g., for deposit only to the agency bank account. Cash/check receiving, processing, recording, and reconciliation functions must be clearly segregated. Cash/checks must be deposited in a timely manner. Be sure to use prenumbered receipts and issue them to payors so that it will be easy to find any "holes" in the receipt process.

Often, small nonprofits will say "We don't have enough people for internal controls, and we don't need them because people who work in nonprofits are inherently honest." The fact is that you may need more safeguards in small nonprofits because there is more opportunity to misappropriate money. For-profits almost always have a system of billing/invoicing that ensures there is a paper trail for cash coming in. In nonprofits, cash donations can come in when you don't expect it and don't bill for it. When you get receipts that you are not expecting, you must have internal controls which will clearly account for such revenues.

If the agency is so small that you cannot assign two people, for example, to handle incoming receipts (one to open the mail and the other to list dollars coming in), then you need to assign someone who is not the bookkeeper, executive director, or fund-raiser to open and list the receipts. A secretary or receptionist can handle this task. The list then goes to the executive director and the bookkeeper (a double check) and the checks go to the bookkeeper for processing.

In terms of cash disbursement, again make sure that authorization, processing, check signing, recording and bank reconciliation functions are clearly segregated. Expenditures must be approved in advance by authorized persons and supported by appropriate documents. Checks should be prenumbered. Check-signing authority must be vested in individuals with a high level of responsibility in the organization. The check signer must review the documentation prior to signing; e.g., review the vendor's invoice. You also must make sure that signed checks are mailed—and mailed promptly.

Again, in small agencies, you can use such safeguards as having one person write checks and another sign and send them out. By the way, dual signatures are not always effective safeguards. Someone could forge the signature of the executive director. Thus, the executive director should be the one to reconcile the bank statements and examine each check at that time.

In terms of petty cash, disbursements should be handled by a single custodian. Those receiving petty cash must sign their requests or receipts. There must be a periodic count of the cash by a person other than the custodian.

Professional Review

There are different levels of professional review of a nonprofit's accounting/financial records. These include audits, reviews, and compilation. Typically, the smaller the agency in terms of budget size, the less formal professional review is required.

Audits

An audit is usually conducted for nonprofits with an annual budget of more than $500,000. However, agencies with a budget size of $250,000 to $500,000 also may be required to have an audit by its funders. The audit is an examination of financial statements by an independent CPA for the purpose of expressing an opinion on the fairness with which the nonprofit presents its operations (income statement). The auditor verifies that the agency's financial reports and supporting documentation are accurate and complete (a fair presentation) via the audit process, which is an in-depth testing of transactions and controls.

Reviews

A review is also undertaken by a CPA, but not in such depth as an audit. Nonprofits with budgets in the $100,000–$500,000 range often choose to have a financial review by an outside expert. The reviewer performs inquiry and analytical procedures that provide limited assurance that a fair presentation of the agency's financial condition has occurred; i.e., that the financial statements are accurate and are in conformity with GAAP. This less comprehensive procedure is still useful to the board and funders since it is an independent review.

Compilation

This approach is most often used by agencies with small budgets; usually less than $100,000 annually. This is a presentation of the organization's financial information in a generally accepted form, such as a year-end income statement and balance statement. Such a compilation does not provide any assurance of fairness or material errors since it does not involve in-depth analysis or an independent review.

Analyzing Financial Statements

There are several tools that can be used to analyze financial statements. Each provides a different perspective of the financial condition. Questions answered by an analysis of your financial statements include:

1. How financially secure is the organization? Can it meet its current obligations? Can it weather tough times? Is it making good use of opportunities to become self-sufficient? Does it have cash or can it raise cash to meet cash-flow demands?

2. How efficient is the organization in terms of the cost per unit and how does it compare to other organizations? Are the support services too high? Are the cash reserves properly invested?

3. How well does the organization perform financial planning in terms of comparing budget to actual? How is it preparing for future planning?

4. Generally what does the auditors' report say, and what do the notes to the financial statements say?

In addition to the standard analytical ratios that can be used in any organization (which we won't go into here), there are some specific ratio analyses used with nonprofits. One of these is *unit costs* (costs of output in financial terms). This involves looking at the cost of care (service) per client by comparing total cost of care/number of client days (or other units). You also compare your agency with other agencies or with previous years.

You also look at *personnel cost* per client served in terms of total personnel expenditures/clients served (per period of time). And you again compare your agency with other organizations or with previous years.

Adequacy of finances is also considered. In this case a financial condition ratio is used, which is expendable fund balance/total expenses (expendable fund balance equals assets less liabilities). This indicates the organization's ability to fund program and other expenses. This ratio should increase at least in proportion to the rate of growth of operating size.

Net operating ratio is another useful analysis. This is fee revenue/total support (grants) and revenues (fees). It is an indicator of how self-supporting an organization is. Again, compare this year's figure with other organizations or previous years.

Contribution ratios look at items of support or revenue/total expenses to assess the importance of various sources of support and revenue to the total program. Compare year to year and check to see if the agency depends too highly on a single source. This is dangerous.

Program demand ratios check program expense/total support and revenue to determine whether a particular program or administrative category is receiving a growing or dwindling share of resources. Compare between programs and between years.

Taxes

Nonprofits are subject to some local and state taxes, such as sales tax. A separate 501(c)(3) exemption is required by the state. Be sure to check the regulations in your area.

In terms of federal income tax, remember that as a 501(c)(3) you must adhere to the exemption regulations stated in the IRS tax code. Be very familiar with these.

Charitable contributions also require special attention in terms of taxes. Gifts to a 501(c)(3) organization are deductible for individual and corporate tax returns, but there are limits on deductibility. Individuals may deduct up to 50 percent of their contributions to public charities, but these cannot exceed 30 percent of their adjusted gross income. Corporations may deduct up to 10 percent of their taxable income for charitable contributions.

What is a "gift"? The IRS says that it is a transfer of something of value and that fair market value at the date of the gift must be used. The gift must be irrevocable and complete with no strings attached; that is, it cannot be lent to the nonprofit. There must be no meaningful contingencies—it is not a meaningful gift until the contingency has been met. It cannot be service, unless fee for service is taken into income. The gift occurs when it is actually paid; for example, the check is written and mailed or charge made on a credit card. Pledges do not count as a gift even with accrual accounting. The payment must be voluntary.

There are various reporting requirements for 501(c)(3) organizations at the local, state, and national levels. For federal reporting the IRS form 990 is of prime importance. It is required of organizations with over $25,000 in gross receipts or if the organization has paid employees. It is important to do this since there is a fine of $10/day up to $5,000 for noncompliance. It is an informational return—no tax is required.

When you have personnel, you will, of course, also have to file federal payroll reports, including a W-4 for each employee to claim exemptions for federal withholding and a W-2 for each employee at year end to report income and deductions.

One other tax matter to keep in mind is unrelated business income tax. The basic principle is this: An exempt organization should pay the basic corporate income tax on income generated from activities outside its charitable purpose. This tax is paid at the regular corporate rate, with the same corporate income tax rules. The tax is on income. The first $1,000 of unrelated business income is not taxed.

How do you know if you are involved in unrelated business? There are three conditions: 1) the activity must be a trade or business carried out for production of income by selling goods or services; 2) it must be regularly carried out; e.g., operation of a parking lot every weekend; and 3) it must not be substantially related to the exempt purpose of the organization.

Unrelated business has become quite a sensitive issue in recent years as more nonprofits become involved with entrepreneurial ventures that fringe into the commercial enterprise arena. It is not "wrong" for a nonprofit to have unrelated business income and to pay taxes on it. However, if this activity is substantial, it can jeopardize the agency's nonprofit exemption status. An alternative is to consider establishing a for-profit subsidiary.

Lobbying

Another area of sensitivity is lobbying. This is the expenditure of resources by an organization for the purpose of attempting to influence legislation. *Grassroots lobbying* is any attempt to influence legislation through an effort to affect the opinions of the general public. *Direct lobbying* is any attempt to influence legislation through communication with any member or employee of a legislative body or government official who may participate in the formulation of the legislation.

Congress has recognized nonprofits' rights and responsibilities to be part of the legislative process. However, no participation in the political election of candidates is allowed. In addition, the nonprofit must choose between two sets of limitation rules. Under the old law, nonprofits are permitted to lobby as long as no ''substantial'' part of the program is dedicated to lobbying; e.g., less than 5 percent. Under the new law, lobbying is permitted to definable limits (safe harbors); e.g., 20 percent of an organization's total annual expenditures of $500,000 or under.

Summary

Financial management helps nonprofits by providing sophisticated management tools for planning, budgeting, organizing, controlling, and evaluating the financial condition of the organization. The result is an effective system that will help your agency achieve financial health and stability so that it can fulfill its mission.

Throughout this publication, the metaphor of the juggler has been used. Any serious juggler will tell you that in order to maintain the delicate rhythm and symmetry necessary to keep all the objects in the air at the same time, you have to start from a central point of balance. In many ways, that central balance for nonprofits is the effective financial management of the organization.

Annotated Bibliography

> An education isn't how much you have committed to memory, or even how much you know. It's being able to differentiate between what you do know and what you don't. It's knowing where to go to find out what you need to know; and it's knowing how to use the information you get.
> —William Feather

The uncertainties inherent in the coming decade of nonprofit management have been referred to in several of the preceding chapters. Preparing yourself and your organization to better anticipate and manage those uncertainties is a challenging task for each nonprofit manager. It is a demanding mandate that requires the constant juggling of such activities as reviewing policies and procedures, surveying the needs of those being served, examining current operations and achievements, assessing mandates established by governing bodies, analyzing trends and predictions, reflecting on the organization's mission, determining goals and objectives, and evaluating your organization's success or lack thereof.

Hopefully, the content of this book has increased your awareness and furthered your interest in the organizational development and administrative practices of grassroots organizations. Let the various chapters serve as road maps and catalysts as you now begin your learning process in earnest. Indeed, the references that follow will help you further your insights, your knowledge, and your perspectives on what it takes to be an effective manager and leader of a small, nonprofit organization.

Argyris, C., and D. Schön. 1974. *Theory in practice: Increasing professional effectiveness.* San Francisco: Jossey-Bass.

Bennis, W. 1989. *Why leaders can't lead.* San Francisco: Jossey-Bass. This book investigates the obstacles leaders face when trying to effect change in any organization and suggests strategies for effectively taking charge and overcoming the forces working against them.

Blanchard, K., and S. Johnson. 1981. *The one minute manager.* New York: Berkeley Publishing Group. This widely read book offers three easy-to-master management techniques that will change your life! The book will help you save time and increase productivity in your business and in your home.

Block, S. R. 1990. "A history of the discipline." In *The nonprofit organization: Essential readings,* ed. D. L. Gies, J. S. Ott, and J. M. Shafritz, 46–63. Pacific Grove, CA: Brooks/Cole. Beginning with ancient societies, the author traces the history of the volunteer, nonprofit sector.

Bolman, L., and T. Deal. 1991. *Reframing organizations.* San Francisco: Jossey-Bass.

Buckley, W. F. 1990. *Gratitude: Reflections on what we owe to our country.* New York: Random House. A considered call-to-arms arguing for a required period of national service for 18-year-old men and women.

Burns, D. D. 1989. *The feeling good handbook: Using the new mood therapy in everyday life.* New York: William Morrow. In this sequel to *Feeling good: The new mood therapy* (1981), psychiatrist Burns applies cognitive therapy to a wide range of self-defeating behavior. A how-to-do-it, common sense approach for coping with rather than avoiding life's challenges.

Celente, G., with T. Milton. 1990. *Trend tracking: The system to profit from today's trends.* New York: John Wiley and Sons. Most of this book is devoted to assessing major trends that are currently developing. Of particular note are chapters 1–3, where the authors outline a simple, effective system for anticipating and keeping track of developing trends.

Cetron, M., and O. Davies. 1989. *American renaissance: Our life at the turn of the 21st century.* New York: St. Martin's Press. Marvin Cetron is the president of Forecasting International, Inc. and Owen Davies is a former Senior Editor of *Omni* magazine. In describing what our lives will be like in the next century, the two authors provide invaluable insights into how we should respond to the coming changes.

Covey, S. R. 1989. *The 7 habits of highly effective people.* New York: Simon and Schuster. For some, Covey's religious background will get in the way of what is really a very practical book about taking control of your own destiny. The book emphasizes the importance of understanding the paradigms of our lives and how to become "proactive" in meeting change.

Curti, M. 1973. "Philanthropy." In *The dictionary of the history of ideas,* ed. P. P. Wiener. New York: Charles Scribner's Sons. Drawing on ancient pre-Greek, Judaic, Eastern, and Christian traditions, Curti brings the historical development of the concept of philanthropy to life for the reader.

Dahms, A. M. 1972. *Emotional intimacy: Overlooked requirement for survival.* Boulder: Pruett. A philosophical and practical call to action organized around the need for intimacy. The dimensions of intimacy—intellectual, physical, and emotional—are discussed in a format tied to social issues.

Dahms, A. M. 1980. *Thriving: Beyond adjustment.* Monterey, CA: Brooks/Cole. An exploration of four central thriving skills cast against a background of the human age span. Discussions of Eastern thought and futurists' predictions are included.

Dahms, A. M., and J. H. Scully. 1992. *Patients as educators: Videocases in abnormal psychology.* Englewood Cliffs, NJ: Prentice Hall.

Deal, T. E., and A. A. Kennedy. 1982. *Corporate cultures: The rites and rituals of corporate life.* Reading, MA: Addison Wesley. This well-written book focuses primarily on the private sector and large organizations. Its presentation, however, offers insight into organizational culture regardless of the size or type of organization. It is particularly recommended for those who are considering making changes in their organizational culture.

Drucker, P. F. 1985. *Innovation and entrepreneurship: Practice and principles.* New York: Harper and Row. Drucker describes the "new entrepreneurial economy" and its challenges and opportunities for the future. He analyzes what businesses, the nonprofits, and the public sector "have to know, have to learn, and, above all, have to do" if they are to survive.

Gies, D. L., J. S. Ott, and J. M. Shafritz, eds. 1990. *The nonprofit organization: Essential readings.* Pacific Grove, CA: Brooks/Cole. A collection of significant articles, chapters, and papers written about nonprofit organizations. Its 31 selections cover historical trends as well as contemporary issues.

Hall, J. 1971. Lost on the moon. *Psychology Today*, Nov:151.

Hammarskjold, D. 1964, 1983. *Markings.* New York: Ballantine. Published after his death, this collection of Hammarskjold's personal notes is a spiritual classic by the intensely private and highly successful Secretary General of the United Nations.

Heifetz, R. A., and R. M. Sinder. 1988. "Political leadership: Managing the public's problem solving." In *The power of public ideas*, ed. R. Reich. Ballinger.

Ho, D. Y. F. 1985. Cultural values and professional issues in clinical psychology. *American Psychologist* 40:1212–18. Ho, of the University of Hong Kong, points out that the American cult of the rugged individual can encourage isolation-causing competition; whereas the Eastern, particularly Confucianist, focus on merging oneself into society can lead to a lack of individuality.

Holmes, T. H., and R. H. Rahe. 1967. The social readjustment rating scale. *Journal of Psychosomatic Research* 11:213–18. In this first appearance of the scale in the professional literature, the authors describe how life-change events were ranked. The scale included forty-three common events.

Kauss, T. R., and R. J. Kauss. 1990. "How to qualify for a foundation grant: A sophisticated primer." TAC seminar paper, Denver.

Kennedy, E. M. 1991. National service and education for citizenship. *Phi Delta Kappan* 72:771–73. A call to harness the energy of sixty million students by offering them opportunities in community service.

Kidder, R. M. 1987. *An agenda for the 21st century.* Cambridge: MIT Press. The author interviews twenty-two leading thinkers—artists, scientists, political leaders, and philosophers—asking each one this fundamental question: What are the major issues that will face humanity in the twenty-first century? Their responses make for some interesting reading!

Kilman, R. H., M. J. Saxton, R. Serpa, and Associates, eds. 1985. *Gaining control of the corporate culture.* San Francisco: Jossey-Bass.

Kuhn, T. 1970. *The structure of scientific revolutions.* 2nd ed. Chicago: University of Chicago Press. The second edition of the classic work in which Kuhn argues that progress among competing points of view in science is not gradual. Old approaches fight for survival as new views emerge.

Lamm, R. D. 1985. *Megatraumas: America at the year 2000.* Boston: Houghton Mifflin. A hypothetical projection into the future suggesting possible calamities *if* we do not deal more directly with major issues such as health care, education, and the federal budget deficit.

Lundberg, F. 1968. *The rich and the super-rich: A study of the power of money today.* New York: L. Stewart.

McGovern, T. V., L. Furumoto, D. F. Halpern, G. A. Kimble, and W. J. McKeachie. 1991. Liberal education, study in depth, and the arts and sciences major-psychology. *American Psychologist* 46:598–605. Report of the task force named by the APA Committee on Undergraduate Education. Eight common goals and four curricular models for the psychology major are discussed.

Naisbitt, J., and P. Aburdene. 1990. *Megatrends 2000: Ten new directions for the 1990's.* New York: Avon Books. Along with Tofler, Naisbitt is credited for popularizing the study of the future. At the very least, these two authors have sparked interest among the general population in a way that the highly esoteric mumblings of economists and political analysts never has.

Ornstein, R., and D. Sobel. 1989. *Healthy pleasures.* Reading, MA: Addison Wesley. A discussion of the life-enhancing value of pleasures. Positive attitudes and helping behaviors may extend both the quality and quantity of life. Chapter 14, "Selfless Pleasures," defends serving others as ultimately serving one's own best interests.

Reynolds, D. K. 1984. *Playing ball on running water.* New York: Quill. An approach to psychological health based on the work of Shoma Morita. A very practical, action-oriented call for attention to reality and the beauties of everyday living.

———. 1989. *Pools of lodging for the moon: A strategy for a positive lifestyle.* New York: William Morrow. A practical synthesis of the Morita lifeway and the Naikan principle of recognizing our debts to the world around us. Everyday experiences are seen as vehicles for growth.

Schein, E. 1987. "Defining organizational culture." In *Classics of organization theory*, ed. J. Shafritz and J. S. Ott, 390. Chicago: Dorsey Press. The editors provide a good introduction to organization theory and show how the concepts of organizational culture have added to the broader understanding of organizations. Several early contributions to the organizational culture perspective are included; however, the human resources perspective is missing.

Shafritz, J. M., and J. S. Ott. 1987. *Classics of organization theory.* 2nd ed. Chicago: Dorsey Press.

Slater, P. 1970. *The pursuit of loneliness.* Boston: Beacon Press. Slater identifies pressures in society that lead to the lack of personal fulfillment. He includes a disturbing analysis of our tendency to "throw away" citizens who do not meet arbitrary standards.

Spicer, J. 1980. *Outcome evaluation: How to do it.* Center City, MN: Hazelden Foundation.

Tocqueville, A. de. 1969. *Democracy in America.* Vol. 1 and 2. Ed. J. P. Mayer, Trans. G. Lawrence. Garden City, NY: Doubleday. This classic work, originally published in two volumes (1835, 1840) is based on Tocqueville's visit to the United States during 1831–1832.

Tocqueville, A. de. 1969. "On the use which the Americans make of associations in civil life." In *Democracy in America*, 513–17. Garden City, NY: Doubleday. Tocqueville contrasts the American volunteer associations with alternative approaches used in Europe.

_____. 1981. *Journey to America.* Ed. J. P. Mayer, Trans. G. Lawrence. Westport, CT: Greenwood Press. Tocqueville's fourteen notebooks kept during his journey through the United States in 1831–1832. These notes grew into his classic, two-volume *Democracy in America.*

Tofler, A. 1971. *Future shock.* New York: Bantam Books. The first book in what became a trilogy on the subject of *change.* In *Future shock* Tofler tries to prepare people for the inevitable changes of the future.

_____. 1980. *The third wave.* New York: Bantam Books. Although more than a decade has passed since the first publication of this book, the intervening years have only enhanced its value. Through the metaphor of his three waves, Tofler offers the reader insight into the development of broad, global paradigms. His prognostications are even more interesting with the benefit of more than ten years of hindsight.

_____. 1990. *Powershift: Knowledge, wealth, and violence at the edge of the 21st century.* New York: Bantam Books. In the preface to this book Tofler writes, "*Powershift* is the culmination of a 25-year effort to make sense of the astonishing changes propelling us into the 21st century." The clear theme of the book is that knowledge is power and those who have it and effectively use it will be the leaders of future changes.

Weisz, J. R., F. M. Rothbaum, and T. C. Blackburn. 1984. Standing out and standing in: The psychology of control in America and Japan. *American Psychologist* 39:955–69. The authors distinguish between action-oriented primary control and passive secondary control. Both types of control require coping with rather than avoiding important issues and are central to mental health.

Additional Recommended Reading

Communication
Management/Leadership

Callanan, Joseph A. 1984. *Communicating: How to organize meetings and presentations*. Franklin Watts. Communication consultant Callanan designs every page of this book with one purpose in mind: to improve a manager's skills as a business communicator. The book includes checklists for meeting preparation, and post-meeting evaluations; tips on giving and getting feedback and improving listening skills; and suggestions for running better meetings and handling dissent and dissidents.

Emanuel, Myron, and Arthur M. York. 1988. *Handbook of human resources communications*. New York: Panel Publishers. Both Emanuel and York have extensive experience in developing and improving employer/employee communication. Key sections include plain talk, human resources practices, employee publications, media alternatives, special programs and events, major upheavals, communication audits, and communicating with retirees.

Flesch, Rudolph. 1951. *The art of clear thinking.* Barnes and Noble. A classic of communication in its own right, Flesch's book is must reading for those who desire to enhance their skills in thinking and problem solving. For more than forty years this text has entertained, cajoled, provoked, and stimulated people who are responsible for demonstrating and modeling clear thinking and sound action.

Frank, Milo O. 1989. *How to run a successful meeting in half the time*. New York: Simon and Schuster. Nearly everyone has suffered through boring, time-consuming, unproductive meetings. Some of us have even run such meetings! But Frank—a consultant and lecturer in communication skills, strategies, and media training—shows managers how to save time, find alternatives, and define and focus on meeting goals.

Fisher, Roger, and William Ury. 1981. *Getting to yes: Negotiating agreement without giving in*. New York: Penguin. Based on studies and conferences by the Harvard Negotiation Project, a group that deals continually with all levels of conflict resolution from domestic to business to international disputes, this book shows how to separate people from problems; focus on interests, not positions; establish

217

pre-negotiation goals; create options to satisfy all parties, and negotiate
successfully with tough or unpredictable opponents.

Maddalena, Lucille A. 1981. *A communications manual for nonprofit
organizations*. AMACON (a division of American Management
Associations). This manual assists managers in communicating the
organization's goals, encouraging the organization's development, and
demonstrating the organization's significance as an integral part of
society. It looks at the total picture of a nonprofit organization,
examining idea/information exchange, public relations, speakers
bureaus, orientation and training, media relations, advertising, publications, and organization accountability. Especially valuable for a better
understanding and more effective development of external
communication.

Timm, Paul R., Brent D. Peterson, and Jackson C. Stevens. 1990. *People
at work: Human relations in organizations*, 3rd ed. St. Paul: West
Publishing. Chapters cover such topics as human perception and
human relations; understanding managerial communication; interpersonal communication; communicating in small groups; special pressures on minorities at work; and special pressures on women at work.

Weiss, W. H. 1990. *Manager's script book*. Englewood Cliffs, NJ: Prentice-
Hall. Finding the right words to communicate in difficult situations is
a challenge for even the most accomplished manager. This book makes
the job easier by providing scripts of the most appropriate and effective
words managers can use regarding work performance, productivity and
costs, regulations, discipline, motivation, personal qualities, assignments, problems, grievances, pay and promotion, training, responsibility, and change. Each section develops specific problems, showing
the situations, what one should say (followed by possible responses),
and ends with the reasoning and principle involved.

Interpersonal

Berlo, David K. 1960. *The process of communication: An introduction to
theory and practice*. Orlando: Holt, Rinehart and Winston. One of the
nation's acclaimed experts on communication, Berlo clearly presents
the way people communicate with each other. Well-written chapters
cover models, fidelity, interaction, social systems, meaning, perception,
inferences, and "good" definitions.

Cushman, Donald P., and Dudley D. Cahn, Jr. 1985. *Communication in
interpersonal relationships*. Albany: State University of New York
Press. Professors Cushman and Cahn team up to address the critical
problems and roles of communication in interpersonal relationships.
They look at individual self-concepts and how they are developed,
presented, and validated. They analyze the formation, maintenance,
and validation of relationships and show how to reassess such relationships. Other key topics include organizational communications,
cultural communications, cross-cultural communications, telecommunications, and interpersonal relationships.

DeVito, Joseph A. 1982. *Communicology: An introduction to the study of communication.* 2nd ed. New York: Harper & Row. DeVito's book is considered one of the best basic texts for studying and using communication. He does a thorough and pragmatic job in covering message reception, verbal and nonverbal messages, small group and public communication, and mass communication. The text is well-designed, easily accessible, and filled with interesting examples, extensive sources, and clearly written "units" for learning and doing.

Hargle, Owen, ed. 1986. *A handbook of communication skills.* New York: University Press. Hargle has assembled an astute group of communicators/writers to provide a diverse, yet focused handbook. Major sections cover core social skills such as questioning, reflecting, explaining, self-disclosure, and listening; group skills including interacting in groups, chairmanship, negotiating and bargaining, and case conference presentation; and dimensions of communication (humor and laughter, handling strong emotions, asserting and confronting, and showing warmth and empathy).

Cross-cultural and Intercultural

Sarbaugh, L. E. 1979. *Intercultural communication.* Hayden Book. Sarbaugh calls "the concept of participant homogeneity-heterogeneity" the discriminating factor and focal point of this book. He treats both intracultural (homogeneous) communication and intercultural (heterogeneous) communication as a continuum, while considering taxonomy, structure, environments, language, and specific cases and examples. The book ends with some guidelines for intercultural communication.

Thiederman, Sondra. 1991. *Bridging cultural barriers for corporate success: How to manage the multicultural work force.* New York: Lexington Books. Thiederman is president of Cross-Cultural Communications, a San Diego-based training firm specializing in programs that address the issue of cultural diversity in the work place. Her book provides a better understanding of key issues such as recruitment and retention of minorities; better communication despite language barriers; minimizing costly turnover and discrimination suits; culturally aware motivation strategies; cross-cultural management training; and establishing and maintaining harmony in the multicultural work place.

Taylor, Charles A. 1985. *Cultural retreat handbook.* NMCC Inc. Publications. Taylor says that "culture is the glue that holds all communities together." According to this handbook, "The cultural retreat is a weekend experience that can be sponsored inexpensively by just about anyone. It is designed to offer an innovative approach to understanding cultural differences" by exposure to the lifestyles and experiences of other cultural groups. The book provides schedules, calendars, menus, activities, media ideas, and sources—just about everything you'd need to set up your own culturally diverse weekend.

Listening and Speaking

Brownell, Judi. 1986. *Building active listening skills.* Englewood Cliffs, NJ: Prentice-Hall. Brownell identifies six separate listening skills—hearing, understanding, remembering, interpreting, evaluating, and responding—and emphasizes skill development through individual and group activities. She stresses management applications but also provides independent activities. Specific sections cover listening to superiors, listening in conflict situations, and listening in an interview. A pre-program needs assessment is included; theories are separated from skill building sections; and the bibliographies are most extensive.

Frank, Milo O. 1986. *How to get your point across in 30 seconds—or less.* New York: Simon and Schuster. "Thirty seconds can change the direction of your career and your life," maintains Frank. He shows you how to communicate effectively, persuasively, and concisely, and why thirty seconds is enough time to get your listener's attention, maintain his or her interest, and ask for and get what you want.

Hamlin, Sonya. 1988. *How to talk so people will listen: The real key to job success.* New York: Harper & Row. One of the nation's foremost communication experts, Hamlin has readers focus on themselves before telling them how to talk to others. She investigates why and how people listen; new techniques of telling; developing strategies, structuring and organizing business encounters; and designing presentations. Distinctive sections cover the art of being questioned, answering techniques, handling hostility, and creating and leading effective meetings.

Montgomery, Robert L. 1981. *Listening made easy.* AMACON. Montgomery—who has personally trained more than 150,000 people in listening, speaking, and interpersonal communication—begins with the biggest problem in listening, then quickly moves to total listening, stumbling blocks to active listening, listening between the lines, and applying total listening techniques. A brief but invaluable book for anyone who wants to become a better, more productive listener.

Roesch, Roberta. 1989. *Smart talk: The art of savvy business conversation.* AMACON. Managers, supervisors, CEOs, corporation presidents, management, consultants, training directors, educators, communication specialists, and industrial psychologists were all interviewed by Roesch. The results provide a compilation of the nuts-and-bolts tips on what to say, how to say it, and when and where to say it. The primary thesis? "Good verbal communication is based on good human relationships." It is a sound "how-to" and "why-to" book.

Stone, Janet, and Jane Bachner. 1977. *Speaking up: A book for every woman who wants to speak effectively.* New York: McGraw-Hill. This book is designed to deal with problems in speaking that may be unique to women. It shows ways to project self-confidence; how to eliminate unconscious apologies; coping with put-downs or interruptions; answering hostile questions; avoiding the need to qualify each statement; inappropriate joking or giggling, and saying what is meant and sounding like it. Stone and Bachner conduct communication work-shops throughout the United States—especially for women who need to learn how to "speak up!"

Writing

Brusaw, Charles T., Gerald J. Alred, and Walter E. Olin. 1987. *The business writer's handbook*, 3rd ed. New York: St. Martin's Press. This is it: the definitive writing handbook for every office or agency! Beginning with the five steps to successful writing (preparation, research, organization, writing the draft, and revision), it covers literally everything else you need to know about writing—from telling the difference between *a* and *an* to defining *zeugma* (which most communicators will never use, let alone need to know). The topical index lets readers find the informa-tion they need quickly and efficiently.

Jones, Helen Hayward. 1983. *Programming better writing: How to develop effective writing skills for a computerized age*. Englewood Cliffs, NJ: Prentice-Hall. Jones discusses basic writing problems specifically related to management writing and covers specific vocational com-munication, from computer manual writing to the writing of policy. The book shows how to improve writing ability by using the same thought processes as a computer programmer and by providing three basic writing patterns.

Parks, A. Franklin, and Richard M. Trask. 1985. *The complete writer's guide: Questions of language*. Philosophical Library. Parks and Trask of Frostberg State College run a nationally known "Grammarphone" service, answering dozens of questions daily about writing and language. Their experiences have led to this "how-to" book; they also call it a "mind-book" since it takes time to explain the history or rationale behind a given usage or convention. Thus, it makes for not only an accurate handbook but also a highly informative and readable book.

Miller, Casey, and Kate Swift. 1988. *The handbook of nonsexist writing*, 2nd ed. New York: Harper & Row. Miller and Casey's book has become the standard on nonsexist writing for publishers, educators, business people, and private and public agency personnel. It is both sensible and sensitive in presenting examples, reasons, historic perspectives, and suggestions for achieving clear, gender-free language and meanings. A valuable reference book.

Silverman, Jay, Elaine Hughes, and Diana Roberts Wienbroer. 1990. *Rules of thumb: A guide for writers*. New York: McGraw-Hill. This book is organized into four parts: Correctness, Meeting Specific Assignments, Putting a Paper Together, and Writing with Elegance. It's a short book intended only as a quick guide. As such, it saves time and probably reduces stress.

Tebeaux, Elizabeth. 1990. *Design of business communications: The process and the product*. New York: Macmillan. A comprehensive guide to the process and product of writing in a variety of settings, this book addresses nearly every conceivable type of writing found in the private, public, and nonprofit sectors. It offers a wealth of examples, writing paradigms, and step-by-step procedures for moving from process to product.

Fund-raising Information Sources

This list of references provides the grant seeker with a basic guide to fund-raising information sources. Most of the publications listed here are updated annually. Always ask for the most recent edition. Asterisks (*) indicate the *must* tools for people who are responsible for raising major funds for their organizations.

Foundation/Nonprofit

Annual Register of Grant Support. Marquis Academic Media, 200 East Ohio Street, Chicago, IL 60611. Annual. Details the grant support programs of government agencies, public and private foundations, business and industrial firms, unions, educational and professional associations, and special interest groups. It covers a broad spectrum of interest from academic and scientific research to travel and exchange programs. Four indexes facilitate the potential applicant's search for appropriate grant programs; 1) Subject, 2) Organization and Program, 3) Geographic, and 4) Personnel.

Encyclopedia of Associations. Volume 1: National organizations of the United States. Gale Research Co., Book Tower, Detroit, MI 48226. Good source of information on American nonprofit organizations of national scope. Particularly valuable for information on grant-making organizations not actually classified by the IRS as private foundations. Entries include location, phone number, principle officer, staff size, objectives, and publications.

Foundation Center National Data Book. Foundation Center, 888 Seventh Avenue, New York, NY 10019. This two-volume work provides brief information about 21,000 nonprofit organizations which have been classified as private foundations by the Internal Revenue Service. This publication was produced from computer records containing information taken from Forms 990-AR and 990-PF which are filed annually by private foundations with the IRS. The *Data Book* organizes information on foundations according to name, amount of grants awarded annually, city, state, and zip code location. Thus, it is possible to make a list of all the foundations in a particular geographic region by examining the zip codes of the various foundations.

*Foundation Directory. Foundation Center, 888 Seventh Avenue, New York, NY 10019. Annual. The most important reference work available on foundations that make grant awards, it contains information on 2,800 of the country's larger foundations. This directory contains such useful information as assets, names of trustees, foundation telephone numbers, grants made in year of record, statements of purpose and

activities, grant application procedures, frequency of board meetings, and so on. This work is arranged geographically and contains subject and personal name indexes. The *Foundation Directory* lists 90 percent of all the major foundations that account for 80 percent of all grants awarded annually.

Foundation Grants Index. Foundation Center, 888 Seventh Avenue, New York, NY 10019. Annual. Provides a cumulated record of grants (of 5,000 or more) awarded for the year. Lists grants by state, subject category, and recipient. Each listing includes geographic location, recipient name, amount and date of grant, and grant purpose.

Foundation Grants Index Bimonthly. Foundation Center, 888 Seventh Avenue, New York, NY 10019. This index is intended to provide current grant information on private, company-sponsored, and community foundations. Included in each issue is recipient and subject index, updates on grant makers and lists of publications that are available from the granting institution.

Corporate

Corporate 500, The Directory of Corporate Philanthropy. Public Management Institute, 333 Hayes, San Francisco, CA 94102. An excellent source of information on corporate contribution programs. Entries include the corporation's legal name (and the name of the associated foundation, if applicable), address, telephone number, areas of interest (including an analysis of their giving pattern), name of contact person, and sample grants awarded.

Corporate Foundation Profiles. 6th Edition. 1990. Foundation Center, 888 Seventh Avenue, New York, NY 10019. Published and reproduced from the Foundation Center's *Source Book Profiles* every two years. Gives name, address, telephone number, contact person, purpose, limitations, personnel, and financial data of most corporate foundations. Has indexes of subjects, types of support, and most important, geography. This index is arranged alphabetically by the state and city location of each foundation. At the end of each state's listing are the names of those foundations located elsewhere which give a substantial percentage of their grants to recipients in that state.

Corporate Fundraising Directory. Public Service Materials, 415 Lexington Avenue, New York, NY 10017. This directory provides information on the policies of over 350 of America's top corporations. Information includes name, address, current phone number, contact person, primary and secondary areas of corporate giving, best time to apply for a grant, and so on. A special section in the back of the book is devoted to oil company giving programs.

Corporate Giving Directory, 12th ed. 1991. Rockville, MD: The Taft Group. The Taft Group has been in the business of providing information on corporate giving longer than anyone else. It is based on responses to questionnaires and telephone inquiries, IRS 990's, and guidelines and annual reports provided by the companies profiled. Entries as detailed as permitted by the information available. Includes such items as officers, donors, trustees, geographic index, types of support index, subject index, and types of business index.

United States Government

Catalog of Federal Domestic Assistance. U.S. Government Printing Office, Washington, D.C. 20402 (Includes update). This valuable resource contains detailed information on federal programs that provide assistance or benefits to programs that provide assistance or benefits to the American public. It includes 975 programs administered by 52 different federal departments, independent agencies, commissions, and councils. The *Catalog* contains information on grants available, eligibility factors, application procedures, local contacts, etc. A must for organizations seeking federal support.

Commerce Business Daily. U.S. Government Printing Office, Washington, D.C. 20402. A daily listing of all potential contracts federal agencies plan to initiate. It is divided into sections dealing with various types of service agencies, titles of proposed contracts, RFP numbers, and when the proposal is due. Organizations can request copies of RFPs to determine interest in bidding. The *CBD* also lists all contracts awarded in excess of $25,000. Each listing in the *CBD* appears only once. Suggested only for the pros in government contracts and procurement.

Congressional Quarterly. Congressional Quarterly, Inc., 1735 K St., N.W., Washington, D.C. 20006. This weekly publication dealing with the legislative branch of government includes articles and information on bills, hearings, and activities on the floor and in congressional committees. An annual almanac highlights activities of the year.

Federal Register. U.S. Government Printing Office, Washington, D.C. 20402. A daily publication which lists regulations and legal notices issued by federal agencies. Also included are presidential proclamations, executive orders, and federal agency documents having general applicability and legal effect. Though not too useful for the small, nonprofit organization, fund-raisers for colleges and universities subscribe to it to watch for deadlines and notices of available grants. The latter contains much useful information if you know how to find what you want and how to use the information. When you receive a specific grant application to request for federal assistance, you will receive a copy of specific portions of the *Federal Register*.

United States Government Manual. U.S. Government Printing Office, Washington, D.C. 20402. The official handbook of the federal government, it describes the purpose and programs of most governmental agencies and lists top personnel.

Periodicals

The Chronicle of Philanthropy: The Newspaper of the Non-Profit World. Washington, D.C. Published biweekly except for the last two weeks in August and December. Recommended above other periodicals in this bibliography. Comes in tabloid form, reasonably priced for what you get. Contains feature articles, fund-raising news in brief, and a section featuring people and grants.

Foundation News. This publication no longer lists information on grants; however, it is an excellent source for background information and trends in the world of foundation giving.

Grantsmanship News. A monthly magazine which includes information on federal regulations; deadlines for federal grants (including name and address of granting agency), and funding news. An excellent source of information for nonprofits.

The Journal: Contemporary Issues in Fund Raising. National Society of Fund Raising Executives, Alexandria, VA. The National Society of Fund Raising Executives is the premier national association for professional fund-raisers. This magazine reflects their philosophy. All states have one or more local chapters. Contact them for membership and how to qualify for the CFRE.

Monthly Catalog of U.S. Government Publications. A convenient, single source of information on the publications of funding agencies. In Subject Index use the term "grants" or use Name Index under issuing agency.

On-line Databases

On-line electronic databases require a computer, a modem, and communications software. They are very useful in generating lists and abstracts of funding sources for specific projects. All of the following databases are accessible through DIALOG Information Services, Inc., A Knight Ridder Company, 3460 Hillview Ave., Palo Alto, CA 94304, 1-800-334-2564.

Federal Index. Corresponds to the printed *Federal Index,* which covers the *Congressional Record, Federal Register, Commerce Business Daily, Weekly Compilation of Presidential Documents,* and the *Washington Post,* as well as citations to the Code of Federal Regulations, U.S. Code, House and Senate bills, and Public Laws. Abstracts are available.

*Foundation Directory. Provides descriptions of foundations that have assets of $1 million or more, or that make grants of $500,000 or more annually. The file can be searched by subject, foundation name, city, state or zip code, or by amount of assets, contributions or gifts received, expenditures, and amounts of grants awarded.

*Foundation Grants Index. Contains all records from the *Foundation Grants Index* section of the *Foundation News* on grants awarded by major American philanthropic foundations. Can be searched by subject, foundation name, recipient type, name, city or state, and amount of grant. More information on foundations is contained in the *Foundation Directory.*

GPO Monthly Catalog. Produced by the U.S. Government Printing Office, it corresponds to the printed *Monthly Catalog of United States Government Publications*, covering congressional reports and hearings on bills and laws, as well as publications from the executive office, and all other federal departments and agencies. Abstracts not available.

*Grants. Corresponds to the printed *Grant Information System GIS* and *Faculty Alert Bulletin*, covering grants offered by federal, state and local governments, commercial organizations, associations, and private foundations.

National Foundations. Provides information on U.S. private, nongovernmental, nonprofit organizations that award grants for charitable purposes, covering grants given in the fields of education, health, welfare, sciences, international activities, and religion. Supplements the *Foundation Directory* file, which contains more complete data on the larger foundations.

SSIE Current Research. Produced by the Smithsonian Science Information Exchange, it covers research programs or projects either in progress or completed in the past 2 years in the physical, social, engineering, and life sciences. Research projects funded by federal, state and local government agencies, nonprofit associations and foundations, colleges and universities, and selected private industry and foreign research organizations are covered. Abstracts are available.

Fund-raising Guides

Bauer, David G. 1989. *Administering grants, contracts, and funds: Evaluating and improving your grants system.* With contributions from Mary L. Otto. New York: Macmillan. Bauer is an expert on federal grants and contracts. Useful guide to making improvements in your grant-writing process.

**Hall, Mary S. 1988. *Getting funded: A complete guide to proposal writing.* 3rd ed. Portland: Continuing Education Publications, Portland State University. Formerly published as *Developing Skills in Proposal Writing*, this is an excellent "how-to" manual for the novice grant writer. Includes bibliography. Geared toward writing private and foundation proposals.

Hillman, Howard, and Marjorie Chamberlain. *The art of winning corporate grants.* New York: Vanguard Press. A guide to finding grants in aid, charitable contributions, endowments, and research grants.

Lant, Jeffrey. 1990. *Development today: A fund raising guide for nonprofit organizations.* 4th ed. Cambridge: JLA Publications. Includes bibliographical references. Lant is a national "guru" of fund-raising. This is a practical and useful book.

Margolin, Judith, ed. 1990. *The Foundation Center's user-friendly guide: Grant seeker's guide to resources.* Compiled by the Public Service staff of the Foundation Center. New York: The Foundation Center. Any publication from the Foundation Center is useful and this one is highly recommended.

Ethics

Aristotle. *Nichomachean Ethics*. 1962. Library of Liberal Arts. Indianapolis: Bobbs-Merrill Educational Publishing.

Blanchard, Kenneth, and Norman Vincent Peale. 1988. *The power of ethical management*. New York: William Morrow. An excellent book written in a style that makes for quick reading. Blanchard is known for his book, *The one minute manager*.

Donaldson, John. 1989. *Key issues in business ethics*. San Diego: Academic Press. Business ethics for nonspecialists—covers business, industry, and unions but is applicable to nonprofits as well.

Frankena, William K. 1972. *Ethics*. Englewood Cliffs, NJ: Prentice-Hall.

MacIntyre, Alasdair. 1966. *A short history of ethics*. New York: Collier Books.

Spaemann, Robert. 1989. *Basic moral concepts*. New York: Routledge Publishing. Excellent introduction to basic ethical problems. Written clearly and without confusing jargon.

Wright, N. Dale, ed. 1988. *Papers on the ethics of administration*. Provo, UT: Brigham Young University Press.

Computer Systems

Herzlinger, Regina. 1977. Why data systems in nonprofit organizations fail. *Harvard Business Review*. Jan.-Feb.:81–86. This is an early classic in nonprofit management; best described as a brutally honest look at why computers and nonprofit organizations are like oil and water. Most of the blame for the failure is put on managers who do not adequately define the uses of information technology in nonprofit organizations. This is a very prescriptive piece that reads quickly and provides a number of lessons for nonprofit managers first considering computers in their organizations.

Horton, Forest W. 1985. *Information resources management*. Englewood Cliffs, NJ: Prentice-Hall. In the mid-1980s information resources management (IRM) became the vogue in many organizations—public, private, and to a lesser extent nonprofit. The basic concept is simple, that information technology is embedded within all organization functions (planning, organizing, evaluation, etc.) and that like people and money, information is a basic resource which requires managing. This is a textbook that provides many easily accessible models and ideas for managing information in the organization.

Lucas, Henry C. 1990. *Information systems concepts for management*. New York: McGraw-Hill. This author has been publishing on management information systems for the last two decades. Some of his work is highly technical, such as chapters on systems analysis and design, but other parts are very introductory and provide good overviews of technology and organizational issues. The strength of this book is how it helps managers see the link between organizational activities and computer technology.

Overman, E. Samuel. 1989. "Computing in nonprofit organizations." In
Nonprofit organizations: Essential readings, D. L. Gies, J. S. Ott, and
J. M. Shafritz, eds. Pacific Grove, CA: Brooks/Cole. This is a study of
nonprofit organizations as they have developed computing resources
in their organizations. It may help provide benchmarks for managers
trying to assess where their organizations are within the evolution of
nonprofit computing, as well as provide helpful hints and indicators
of future performance. The entire book is devoted to nonprofit
organizations and contains numerous other helpful articles.

———. 1988. Using the systems development life cycle for computer
applications in human services. *Computers in Human Services*. Vol.
3, No. 3/4:55–69. This is a step-by-step case study of the development
of a computer system in a large human services organization. It
demonstrates how the systems development life cycle was used from
initial idea to the implementation and operation of a case management
system.

Financial Management

Accounting and Financial Reporting. 1989. United Way of America, 801
N. Fairfax St., Alexandria, VA 23314. This guide for United Way and
nonprofit human-service organizations provides an overview of
accounting principles, accounting processes, investments, charts of
accounts, and financial statements as well as the elements of an
accounting system and its operation. Though specifically designed for
United Way agencies, it also provides examples from other types of
nonprofits.

Audits of Certain Nonprofit Organizations. 1987. American Institute of
Certified Public Accountants, 1121 Avenue of the Americas, New York,
NY 10036. Prepared by the subcommittee on nonprofit organizations,
this audit guide presents recommendations of the AICPA Nonprofit
Organizations Subcommittee regarding the application of generally
accepted accounting standards to audits of financial statements of
entities in the nonprofit industry.

*Financial Reporting by Not-for-Profit Organizations: Form and Content
of the Financial Statements*. 1989. Financial Accounting Standards
Board of the Financial Accounting Foundation. P.O. Box 5116,
Norwalk, CT 06856-5116. This document presents a draft of
revised/new accounting standards for nonprofits.

Financial Reporting for Voluntary Health and Welfare Organizations.
1988. National Health Council, Inc., 622 Third Avenue, New York, NY
10017. This third edition continues the mission of the previous
editions—to attain uniform accounting and external financial reporting
in compliance with generally accepted accounting principles by all
voluntary health and welfare organizations.

Haller, Leon. 1982. *Financial resource management for nonprofit
organizations*. Englewood Cliffs, NJ: Prentice-Hall. This guide presents
planning and decision-making actions related to projecting costs of

activities, purchasing goods and services, controlling expenses, organizing records and reports, and managing team members.

Konrad, Peter A., and Alys Novak. 1992. *Nonprofit financial management.* Denver: Discovery Communications, Inc. This executive overview for nonprofit board members, executive directors, and program managers highlights the keys to successful financial management in an agency. It emphasizes the elements of nonprofit finance that are essential for understanding how to ensure sound fiscal conditions. Every aspect of financial management is covered from a nonprofit perspective—from the economic role of nonprofits in society to the fiduciary role of the executive director.

Letters to a Foundation Trustee. 1986. The Center for Effective Philanthropy, 51 Brattle St., Cambridge, MA 02138. Subtitled, "What we need to know about foundations and their management," this brief text concentrates on providing guidance to private foundations, which are a special class of nonprofits.

Oleck, Howard L. 1980. *Nonprofit corporations, organizations, and associations.* Englewood Cliffs, NJ: Prentice-Hall. Of special interest in this book is its focus on state statutes related to nonprofits, the many kinds of nonprofits, the procedures involved with starting a nonprofit, such as articles and bylaws and the powers, duties and liabilities of directors and trustees.

Tax Economics of Charitable Giving. 1986. Arthur Andersen & Co., New York. The focus of this text is on charitable deductions, including deferred giving, the charitable remainder trust, and their tax considerations.

Truk, Frederick J., and Robert P. Gallo. 1984. *Financial management strategies for arts organizations.* New York: American Council for the Arts Books. This is a book of concepts and processes designed for practical application. It contains chapters on strategic planning, budgeting, organization, financial management systems, fund accounting, ratio analysis and asset management.

Vinter, Robert D., and Rhea K. Kish. 1984. *Budgeting for not-for-profit organizations.* New York: The Free Press. In addition to presenting a rational view of budgeting, this text looks at budgeting processes, budget development, cost analysis, expense/revenue management and other aspects of this critical element of financial management.

General References

Albrecht, Karl, and Ron Zemke. 1985. *Service America.* New York: Warner Books. The grassroots organization's product is service—this book suggests how you can make your agency customer-driven and service-oriented.

Bellah, Robert et al. 1985. *Habits of the heart.* University of California. A study of individualism and community in the United States. Highlights the value commitments and implications of two language systems;

namely, that of individual achievement and self sufficiency versus the collective and community well-being.

Dychtwald, Ken, and Joe Flower. 1990. *Age wave*. Los Angeles: Jeremy P. Tarcher. Perhaps no other demographic statistic will be as important to the future of America as the fact that we are in the first stages of what some are calling a "senior boom." Already, the 65-or-older crowd has become the most politically and financially influential group America has ever seen. You cannot possibly anticipate the future of this nation without understanding the potential impact this growing special interest group will have.

Harris, Philip R., and Robert Moran. 1990. *Managing cultural differences*. 3rd ed. Houston: Gulf Publishers. Contains valuable information on leadership and change, analyzing the organizational culture, making organizational diagnoses, and managing for synergy.

Hoffer, D. 1955. *The passionate state of mind*. New York: Perennial/Harper & Row. The longshoreman/philosopher offers wide-ranging thoughts on twentieth-century problems.

Kershner, F. 1983. *Tocqueville's America: The great quotations*. Athens: Ohio University Press. These quotations, drawn mostly from *Democracy in America*, are a pleasant introduction to Toqueville.

Kopp, S., and C. Flanders. 1979. *What took you so long?* Palo Alto, CA: Science and Behavior Books. Words by Kopp and photographs by Flanders explore the paradoxes of life.

Kouzes, James M., and Barry Z. Posner. 1990. *The leadership challenge: How to get extraordinary things done in organizations*. San Francisco: Jossey Bass. Discovering the ways we can become outstanding leaders—a step beyond being a good manager. Includes an excellent "personal best" exercise for personnel to identify their own leadership standard of excellence.

Primozic, Kenneth, Edward Primozic, and Joe Leben. 1991. *Strategic choices: Supremacy, survival, or sayonara*. New York: McGraw-Hill. Kenneth and Edward Primozic are management consultants with IBM. The authors have developed a simple and easily implemented strategic planning process to convert innovative ideas into reality. Their message is designed for today's highly charged, competitive climate in both the public and private sectors where organizations must show results.

Reich, Robert B., ed. 1988. *The power of public ideas*. Massachusetts: Ballinger. This book is about the philosophy of policymaking in America. The contributors to this book investigate such questions as: Is there really a public interest beyond the sum of our own individual goals? In this modern era of fierce competition between powerful special-interest lobbies, are ideas about what's good for all of us politically powerful? And, if public ideas do have power, how are they formed and communicated?

Shafritz, Jay M., ed. 1985. *The facts on file dictionary of public administration*. New York: Facts on File Publications. Shafritz provides an indispensable index covering the theory, concepts, practices, laws, institutions, literature, and people of the academic discipline and professional practice of public administration.

Tichy, Noel M., and Mary Anne Devanna. 1986. *Transformational leader*. New York: Wiley. Deals with organizational change and leadership qualities that can bring about a healthier organization. Includes sections on creating a motivating vision, the leader as a social architect, and leadership and paradox.

Index